Llewellyn's 2009

Witches'
Spell-A-Day
Almanac

Holidays & Lore • Spells & Recipes
Rituals & Meditations

Copyright 2008 Llewellyn Worldwide.
Editing: Nicole Edman; Design: Michael Fallon
Cover Design: Lisa Novak; Background Photo: © PhotoDisc
Monthly Introductions by James Kambos; Interior Art: © 2005, Terry Miura
(illustrations: pp. 9, 29, 49, 71, 91, 111, 131, 151, 171, 191, 211, 231);
© 2005 Eris Klein (holiday and day icons)

You can order Llewellyn books and annuals from *New Worlds*,
Llewellyn's catalog. To request a free copy of the catalog, call toll-free
1-877-NEW WRLD, or visit our website at http://subscriptions.llewellyn.com

ISBN: 978-0-7387-0727-3
Llewellyn is a registered trademark of Llewellyn Worldwide, Ltd.
2143 Wooddale Drive, Dept. 978-0-7387-0727-3
Woodbury, MN 55125

Table of Contents

About the Authors

Elizabeth Barrette has been involved with the Pagan community for more than twenty years. She serves as the Managing Editor of *PanGaia* and the Dean of Studies at the Grey School of Wizardry. She lives in central Illinois and enjoys gardening for wildlife and stone magic. Visit her LiveJournal "The Wordsmith's Forge" at http://ysabetwordsmith.livejournal.com/

Nancy Bennett is a writer of more than 300 articles, essays, and poems. Her work has also been featured in *We'Moon*, *Silver Wheel*, and other Llewellyn publications. She can be reached at nvbennett@shaw.ca. She is now writing a collection of essays, spells, and poems from a Canadian Witch perspective.

Calantirniel has practiced many forms of natural spirituality since the early 1990s. She lives in western Montana with her husband and teenage daughter, while her older son is in college. She is a professional astrologer, tarot card reader, dowser, and became a certified Master Herbalist in 2007. She has an organic garden, crochets professionally, and is co-creating Tië eldaliéva, the Elven Spiritual Path. http://www.myspace.com/aartiana

Raven Digitalis is a Neopagan Priest of the "disciplined eclectic" shadow magick tradition Opus Aima Obscuræ, and is a radio and club DJ. He is the author of *Goth Craft: The Magickal Side of Dark Culture*. With his Priestess Estha, Raven holds community gatherings, tarot readings, and a variety of ritual services. The two also operate the metaphysical business Twigs and Brews.

Ellen Dugan, a.k.a. "The Garden Witch" is an award-winning author and a psychic-clairvoyant. She has been a practicing Witch for more than twenty-four years. Ellen has written many books, including *Garden Witchery*, *Cottage Witchery*, and *How to Enchant a Man*. www.geocities.com/edugan_gardenwitch

Ember is a freelance writer, poet, and regular contributor to Llewellyn's annuals. She lives in Missouri with her husband of thirteen years and their two feline companions.

Lily Gardner has been studying and collecting bits of folklore and myth since childhood. In addition to writing for Llewellyn, she has written several short stories, a murder mystery, and is completing work on saint folklore. Lily has been practicing witchcraft in Portland, Oregon, for fifteen years.

Magenta Griffith has been a Witch more than thirty years, a High Priestess for nearly twenty years, and is a founding member of the coven Prodea, which has been celebrating rituals since 1980. She presents classes and workshops at events around the Midwest and shares her home with a black cat.

James Kambos wrote the monthly introductions as well as many spells. His interest in spellcrafting began in childhood as he watched his grandmother create spells based on Greek folk magic. He is a regular contributor to Llewellyn annuals. When not writing, James paints in the American primitive style. He calls the beautiful Appalachian hill country of southern Ohio home.

Estha McNevin is a Neopagan Priestess and is the head of the Opus Aima Obscuræ tradition. She is passionate about fine art and ancient history, is an avid bookworm, and is co-owner of the metaphysical business Twigs and Brews. In addition to public sabbat rituals, Estha hosts personal women's divination rituals each Dark Moon and holds private spiritual consultations and tarot readings for the community. www.myspace.com/twigsandbrews

Mickie Mueller is an award-winning Pagan Spiritual artist. She is the illustrator of *The Well Worn Path* and *The Hidden Path* decks. Her magically infused art has been seen on magazine covers internationally and on the Web. Mickie is an ordained Pagan minister and a Reiki Master/Teacher. www.mickiemuellerart.com

Gwinevere Rain is the author of three non-fiction books for teens. In 2002, Gwinevere was featured in *Seventeen Magazine*. Currently, she runs an online magazine for young adult Wiccans/Pagans at www.Copper-Moon.com

Cerridwen Iris Shea longs for a garden. She writes, teaches tarot, cooks, is owned by several cats, and is a fan of ice hockey and thoroughbred racing. Visit her tarot blog Kemmyrk (http://kemmyrk.wordpress.com) and her Web site Cerridwen's Cottage (http://www.cerridwenscottage.com).

Gail Wood has been a Witch and Wiccan priestess for more than twenty years, practicing a shamanic path celebrating the Dark Moon. She is clergy, teacher, ritual leader, tarot reader, and Reiki Master. She eagerly anticipates the publication of her book *The Ecstatic Witch* on shamanic Wicca. Gail is High Priestess of the Coven of the Heron of the RavenMyst Circle.

Winter Wren is the founding priestess of the Temple of the Sacred Lady of Avalon. She resides in southeastern Michigan with her partner, Phoenix, and a kindle of Maine coon cats. She spends her days priestessing through tarot, writing, and art.

A Note on Magic and Spells

The spells in the *Witches' Spell-A-Day Almanac* evoke everyday magic designed to improve our lives and homes. You needn't be an expert on magic to follow these simple rites and spells; as you will see if you use these spells through the year, magic, once mastered, is easy to perform. The only advanced technique required of you is the art of visualization.

Visualization is an act of controlled imagination. If you can call up in your mind a picture of your best friend's face or a flag flapping in the breeze, you can visualize. In magic, visualizations are used to direct and control magical energies. Basically, the spellcaster creates a visual image of the spell's desired goal, whether it be perfect health, a safe house, or a protected pet.

Visualization is the basis of all good spells, and as such it is a tool that should be properly used. Visualization must be real in the mind of the spellcaster so that it allows him or her to raise, concentrate, and send forth energy to accomplish the spell.

Perhaps when visualizing you'll find that you're doing everything right, but you don't feel anything. This is common, for we haven't been trained to acknowledge—let alone utilize—our magical abilities. Keep practicing, however, for your spells can "take" even if you're not the most experienced natural magician.

You will notice also that many spells in this collection have a somewhat "light" tone. They are seemingly fun and frivolous, filled with rhyme and colloquial speech. This is not to diminish the seriousness of the purpose, but rather to create a relaxed atmosphere for the practitioner. Lightness of spirit helps focus energy; rhyme and common language help the spellcaster remember the words and train the mind where it is needed. The intent of this magic is indeed very serious at times; and magic is never to be trifled with.

Even when your spells are effective, magic won't usually sparkle before your very eyes. The test of magic's success is time, not immediate eye-popping results. But you can feel magic's energy for yourself by rubbing your palms together briskly for ten seconds, then holding them a few inches apart. Sense the energy passing through them, the warm tingle

in your palms. This is the power raised and used in magic. It comes from within and is perfectly natural.

Among the features of the *Witches' Spell-A-Day Almanac* are an easy-to-use "book of days" format; new spells specifically tailored for each day of the year (and its particular magical, astrological, and historical energies); and additional tips and lore for various days throughout the year—including color correspondences based on planetary influences, obscure and forgotten holidays and festivals, and an incense-of-the-day to help you waft magical energies from the ether into your space.

In creating this product, we were inspired by the ancient almanac traditions and the layout of the classic nineteenth-century almanac *Chamber's Book of Days*, which is subtitled *A Miscellany of Popular Antiquities in Connection with the Calendar*. As you will see, our fifteen authors this year made history a theme of their spells, and we hope that by knowing something of the magic of past years we may make our current year all the better.

Enjoy your days, and have a magical year!

2009
Year of Spells

January is the first month of the Gregorian calendar. Its name comes from the two-faced Roman god Janus, ruler of gates and doorways. Its astrological sign Capricorn, the goat (December 21–January 19), is a cardinal earth sign ruled by Saturn. Once again our Earth begins its journey around Father Sun. From the ashes of the past January appears as a steady flame, lighting our way toward the future. For the ancients, New Year's Day was a time of gift-giving; for Christians, January 6 is Epiphany, the last night of the Christmas season. In northern Europe, January 7 was observed as a day to honor the return of the strengthening Sun—and as the old saying goes, "As the daylight lengthens, the cold strengthens." In many areas, a layer of snow softens the barren landscape, and the light of both the Sun and January's Full Moon, the Wolf Moon, shimmers on snow-covered rooftops. The night air is crisp—almost brittle—and the evening sky shimmers with starlight. For a January ceremony, follow Pagan tradition and place two pine branches in the form of a solar cross upon a ritual fire. As they burn, they will release their magical power of everlasting life. To bring a wish into your life, charge an ice cube or a bowl of fresh snow with your intent. Place the ice or snow outdoors; as it melts, your wish will be absorbed by Mother Earth.

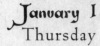

January 1
Thursday

New Year's Day – Kwanzaa ends

 1st ♓

Color of the day: Purple
Incense of the day: Jasmine

Prosperity and health

Happy New Year! As the new calendar year begins on a day that aligns with Jupiter, let's start this year off right with a spell to promote prosperity and good health. Light a green spell candle for Jupiter's energies of prosperity and health and a light-gold spell candle to symbolize the new year of 2009. Set these candles in their holders on a safe, flat work surface. Carefully arrange a photo of yourself and your loved ones around the spell candles— just be sure to protect your photos from the wax. Now repeat the charm:

> Today the New Year has
> begun, and quite merrily,
> Bring prosperity and health
> to me and my family.
> Ring out the old and ring in
> the new, on this happy day,
> May this year hold many
> blessings, and happiness
> I pray.

Let the candles burn out in a safe place.

Ellen Dugan

Notes:

Holiday lore: New Year's Day calls for safeguards, augurs, charms, and proclamations. All over the world on this day, people kiss strangers, shoot guns into the air, toll bells, and exchange gifts. Preferred gifts are herring, bread, and fuel for the fire.

January 2
Friday

1st ♓

Color of the day: Coral
Incense of the day: Vanilla

Resolution Meditation

With the revelries in the past and the New Year now officially underway, it's a good time for reflection. Resolutions are often easily forgotten a few days into the year, but meditation can focus the energy of your intentions to produce your goals. Settle yourself in a meditative manner with a piece of parchment, a pen, and a white seven-day candle. Write your goals in a positive, active manner, being exact about what you are working toward. Once all your goals are listed, fold the paper once and place it under the seven-day candle in a safe location. Light the candle, sending positive intent toward your goals and asking for the universe's energy to aid you. Each time you walk past the candle, send thoughts to the goals again. Each morning as you pass the candle for the first time, reaffirm your goals and fold the paper once more. By the time the candle burns out, the paper should be folded seven times. Put the paper in a place of honor on your altar and continue sending your energies toward your goals at each ritual throughout the year.

Winter Wren

Notes:

(spirit). Light the candle and say: "Saint Genevieve, be our beacon and our light in darkness." Focus on the flame and repeat this chant until you feel the mundane world slip from your consciousness. When you feel ready, braid the three lengths of wool together as you say:

> I am safe. I am protected.
> I am free from fear and danger.

Continue this chant until your braid is finished. Thank Saint Genevieve and let the candle burn itself out. Keep the braid with you whenever you need a dose of courage.

Lily Gardner

Notes:

January 3
Saturday

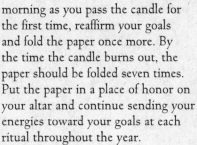

1st ♓
☽ → ♈ 4:50 am

Color of the day: Indigo
Incense of the day: Sage

Spell for Courage

Saint Genevieve used her faith in a higher power to rally Paris when Attila the Hun marched against the city back in AD 451. Who among us doesn't fear something, or many things? To help find the safety within your heart to face your fears, you will need a red candle and three 9-inch lengths of wool yarn, one red (love), one green (security), and one white

January 4
Sunday

1st ♈
2nd Quarter 6:56 am

Color of the day: Orange
Incense of the day: Hyacinth

A Spell to help Make a Decision

When faced with a difficult decision, write your options out on paper and go to an open space. Use a hiking compass to place

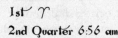

these choices or paths directionally around you; in other words, align each option with a direction: north, south, east, and west. Keep in mind elemental alignments and their common occult associations. If there are more than four options, place them between the cardinal directions. Once everything is laid before you, spin around in a circle with increasing speed and chant the following:

> Circle round, quarterly bound
> I travel now lost; obscure is
>   this ground
> Circle round, quarterly bound
> Awaken my magic, stir all
>   around
> Circle round, quarterly bound
> Let me be found
> Let me be found
> Let me be found

Repeat once for each option you have before you. On the last line of the final round, fall to the ground and toss the compass into the air. Where it lands will provide you with answers. If you have fewer than four options and the compass lands in an unassociated direction, keep in mind that you might not have all the information necessary to determine a path yet—unknown forces may still be at work. The only thing to do then is exercise patience, focus on the present moment, and allow further options to naturally materialize.

Estha McNevin

Notes:

January 5
Monday

2nd ♈

☽ → ♉ 10:46 am

Color of the day: Gray
Incense of the day: Narcissus

Feast of Befana

Befana is an Italian Crone goddess, and this is her feast day. She is a kindly old woman dressed in patches, riding a broom, delivering treats to good children and coal to naughty ones. Here is a spell to invite Befana's blessings into your home. At dusk, lay your broom next to your threshold. Leave an offering of bread, honey, and cumin seed as a gift to Befana. Light a stick of frankincense incense nearby where it will be safe. Then say:

> Befana, Befana, Befana flying
>   the night,
> Bless this home as you pass
>   on your flight
> Befana, Befana, Befana whisk
>   troubles away

Leave your blessings and
good luck we pray.

As her spirit passes your threshold on this her feast night, she'll gather sustenance from your offering and leave her blessings of luck on your doorstep. Leave treats for children in your home in her name.

Mickie Mueller

Notes:

ball of string (if possible) and hold it out above the paper. Unravel the string down onto the paper as you chant three times:

> *Mystery, mystery, unravel*
> *like string, seek the answers*
> *that you bring.*
>
> *Clues come fast like falling*
> *snow. Mystery, mystery*
> *time to show.*

Unravel until the string is on the paper. Put the pencil tip to paper and allow it to roam, automatic-writing style. Leave for 24 hours. The mystery should be solved, or the clue you need shown in the design of the string or the pencil marks.

Nancy Bennett

Notes:

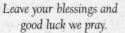

January 6
Tuesday

2nd ☉

Color of the day: Red
Incense of the day: Bayberry

Solve a Mystery Spell

Today is the birthday of fictional master sleuth Sherlock Holmes. To solve your own mystery, find a ball of string, a pencil, and paper. Create a circle to work in by sweeping a broom while walking clockwise. While sweeping, think about a mystery you want to come to light. Put the broom down and clear your mind. Place the pencil through the

Holiday lore: Twelfth Night and the night following it are when wassailing used to take place. The word "wassail" comes from the Anglo-Saxon words *waes heil*, meaning "to be whole or healthy." People drank to each other's health from a large bowl filled with drink such as "lamb's wool," which was made of hot ale or cider, nutmeg, and sugar with roasted crab apples. In some parts of Britain, trees and bees are still wassailed to ensure a healthy crop. Having drunk to the tree's health, people fire shotguns into the branches. Different regions sing different wassail songs to the tree. Here's one from Worcestershire:

> Here's to thee, old apple tree,
> Whence thou mayest bud,
> Whence thou mayest blow,
> Whence thou mayest bear
> apples enow.

workshop on a subject that interests you, would be fine. Repeat this ritual each month and review your list. As you accomplish your goals, write a sentence or two about how you felt when you achieved your objectives.

James Kambos

Notes:

January 7
Wednesday

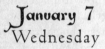 2nd ♉
☽ → ♊ 1:11 pm

Color of the day: Yellow
Incense of the day: Lavender

A Time For You Spell

The holidays are over and now is the perfect time to take some time just for you. It's a good time to think about what you wish to accomplish during the coming year. First, brew a cup of your favorite herbal tea to help you relax. Light a vanilla-scented candle. Settle into a comfy chair with your tea. Have some pretty stationery and a nice pen on hand. As you sip your tea, write a list of twelve things you want to do in the year ahead. They don't have to be major. Just simple things, such as reading a certain book or taking a

January 8
Thursday

2nd ♊

Color of the day: Green
Incense of the day: Myrrh

Connect to Your Inner Fool

Go to a place in your home where you have fun. Wear the clothes you enjoy and bring bells, the colored comic pages from the newspaper, a mirror, and lipstick in an unusual color. Ring the bell and sing, "Without rhyme or reason, it's time to ring in the silly season." Hold up the mirror and tell yourself a joke and laugh. Read the comics and laugh. Take the lipstick and draw on your face, creating a smile and cheeks of color. Guffaw and laugh. Read the comics until you find one completely

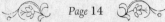

silly and funny. Close your eyes and see yourself dressed as a fool. Connect to this energy and feel the bubbles of laughter fill your being. When you are done, go out into your life with a smile.

Gail Wood

Notes:

(Change the last word as needed to "truck," "van," etc.) Wrap the toy car in a piece of cloth—preferably silk, but cotton would do. Carry it with you in a pocket or purse. Do not leave it in your car, if you have one. Repeat the anointing and chanting every three days until you find your new vehicle.

Magenta Griffith

Notes:

January 9
Friday

 2nd ♊
☽ → ♋ 1:14 pm

Color of the day: White
Incense of the day: Mint

Attract a New Vehicle

Get a small toy car or truck that resembles as much as possible the vehicle you wish to own. Be realistic; don't use a Jaguar if what you're likely to get is a Chevy. Mix a drop of motor oil with a drop of your own saliva and anoint the toy car, saying,

> Come to me, come near to
> me, come next to me,
> transport me, convey me,
> carry me, be my chariot, be
> my carriage, be my car.

January 10
Saturday

2nd ♋
Full Moon 10:27 pm

Color of the day: Brown
Incense of the day: Pine

Isilnarvinyë

In *Tië eldalieva*, the Elven Path, this Moon is called *Isilnarvinyë*, the Moon of New Fire, reverent to the year's newly increasing light. It is aligned with Aulë the Smith, who lives in the ground and resonates with metals, gemstones, mining, blacksmithing, and other forms of creation and crafting. He loves teaching his craft and even created the Dwarven race for this purpose. He can represent technology, which streamlines production to bring wanted results when properly tempered. To meet Aulë, light a black, gray, or brown candle, and hold rocks, crystals, gemstones, or metal items. Sitting comfortably, close your eyes and visualize being underground in what seems to be a cave. The walls glow, and you see the beauty of the exposed metals and gemstones are indeed reflecting the light from the fires inside *Arda*, our Earth. You then approach Aulë, who is crafting in these fires yet another awe-inspiring metal jewelry piece, bathed with magical intention. He asks you what you wish to manifest this year. Upon hearing your goals, he has created symbols of these goals, which he then engraves onto this most wondrous item. He shows you each symbol and its respective meaning and then continues working. Your jewelry piece is now complete, and he gives it to you. It can immediately be worn and you see its beauty and feel its strong powers of manifestation. Open your eyes and thank Aulë, knowing your goals will indeed become real.

Calantirniel

Notes:

January 11
Sunday

3rd ♋
☽ → ♌ 12:41 pm

Color of the day: Yellow
Incense of the day: Eucalyptus

Recycling Sexual Fluids

Things like sex and masturbation are often put to shame in our Christian-founded society. But not so for us Pagans! Sexual energy is an extremely powerful force, one that every animal on the planet possesses. We, as Witches and magicians, can use this energy to help connect us to the Earth and her cycles. Though it's cold in most Western places this time of year, take this day to either sow your "seed" or feminine juices to the Earth. Whether you have to travel as near as your backyard or as far as a forest many miles away, find a safe and undisturbed area of nature. Perform sexual magic by masturbating or making love with a partner, and, after channeling orgasmic energy to the Earth, bury your sexual fluids. Declare:

> With this I connect my very
> essence to that of
> Earth and her cycles.
> May this represent my
> devotion and attunement
> to the magical arts.
> So mote it be.

Raven Digitalis

Notes:

sent from the Eiffel Tower for the first time. With magic, your message can reach across the miles, too!

Nancy Bennett

Notes:

January 12
Monday

 3rd ♌

Color of the day: Lavender
Incense of the day: Rosemary

Send Me a Message

Today is National Handwriting Day, a great day for messages. Is someone you love lousy at staying in touch? Place in an envelope a piece of paper with the name of the person you wish to contact you, along with their picture. Imagine them thinking of you. Take a feather and a straight pin and hold at arm's length. Focus on the person and say:

> May this feather tickle thee
> May this pin prickle thee
> 'Til your thoughts return to me
> Contact me quick, so mote it be!

Chant this three times and then seal the items, paper, and picture in the envelope. Place near the phone or mailbox. Many years ago on this day, a long-distance radio message was

January 13
Tuesday

 3rd ♌
☽ → ♍ 1:33 pm

Color of the day: White
Incense of the day: Ylang-ylang

Computer Spirit

Computers often attract spirit elementals. A computer is basically a material housing for an elaborate construct of the mind. Most of what makes a computer useful exists in a whole different dimension! Just as you might summon a fire elemental for your hearth or perhaps an earth elemental for your garden, it's a good idea to summon a spirit elemental to help keep your computer running smoothly. You'll need a silver candle and something symbolizing your computer, such as a floppy disk or a photo. Light the candle and say:

Light of the mind,
Go forth and find
A spirit to aid my spell.
Let it be had;
Let it be glad
In my computer to dwell.
Spirit of thought,
What I have wrought
From now on guard
  and keep well.

Visualize a helpful spirit elemental entering your computer symbol. Let the candle burn out; keep the symbol near your computer.

Elizabeth Barrette

Notes:

you desire success. Visualize obstacles and imagine them dissolving in the candle flame. Chant the following as many times as you like:

I will succeed
my goal is near.
I will succeed
my way is clear.

Allow the candle to burn out.

Ember

Notes:

January 14
Wednesday

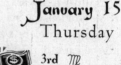

3rd ♏

Color of the day: Brown
Incense of the day: Lilac

Candle Spell for Success

To dissolve blockages standing in your way at work, school, or in your personal life, find a yellow, gold, or white candle. With a toothpick or crystal point, carve a symbol into the wax that identifies the area where

January 15
Thursday

3rd ♏
☽ → ♎ 5:30 pm

Color of the day: Turquoise
Incense of the day: Clove

Job Interview Spell

January is a great time to seek employment, due to many companies renewing their budgets for workforce expansion. On a computer, create a mock business card with your desired company, your name, and the anticipated position. Bring this together with an Ace of Pentacles tarot image (a real card or one printed from a computer). Light an orange candle sprinkled with cinnamon or nutmeg, and fully visualize your confidence in the interview. You look fabulous and answer all questions with ease. Imagine you are exactly who they are looking for, and they even show you your working area. See yourself happily doing the work you want and receiving excellent compensation. At this point, say out loud your name, your company name and your anticipated position as if it were already here. When interviewing, wear your mock business card, and sprinkle some cinnamon or nutmeg on the soles of your shoes.

Calantirniel

Notes:

rosebud. Next, place your palms on the ground in front of you and pour your anxiety, fears, and negativity into the Earth. Return to the rose visualization; this time see the bud opened slightly. Next, gather the three buttons and about 12 inches of floss. String the first button on the floss and say the following as you tie a knot, securing them together, "With this knot I tie, I learn from my past loves and relationships." Second button/knot; "With this knot I tie, I learn to be in the moment, to love who I have become right now." Third button/knot; "With this knot I tie, I learn to open my heart to a healthy and brilliant future love." Close your eyes again and see the rose open and fully bloomed. Afterward, tuck your button and floss charm under your mattress.

Gwinevere Rain

Notes:

January 16
Friday

3rd ♎

Color of the day: Pink
Incense of the day: Rose

Release Blockages to Finding Love

You'll need crimson-colored embroidery floss and three gold-tone buttons. Start by visualizing your heart chakra as a small

January 17
Saturday

 3rd ♎
4th Quarter 9:46 pm

Color of the day: Gray
Incense of the day: Sandalwood

Law of Attraction Charm

For this spell, you'll need: a blank sheet of paper, a blue piece of paper, 1/2 cup flour, 1/8 cup honey, two small twin pieces of mirror, and a blue ribbon. On the blank paper, write out what you would most like to draw into your life. Remove the vowels and repeated consonants of your written aspiration and rearrange the remaining consonants into a shape or sigil that appeals to you. Keep the meaning of your sigil to yourself. On both sides of a piece of blue paper, draw your personal aspiration symbol in dark-blue ink. Take a moment to charge your sigil with the intention of attracting your aspirations to you. See this as effortlessly allowing the universe to deliver the means and options that will put your goals within striking distance. Combine the flour and honey, chanting, "This is the glue of life which binds." When the mixture is even and smooth, apply it lightly to the back of one mirror. Place the blue parchment sigil in the glue. Tie a knot on either end of the ribbon, which should be twice as long as your mirrors. Coat half of the ribbon in glue and center it vertically on the back of the first mirror with one knot just below the bottom edge. Apply some mixture to the back of the second mirror and seal the two together back to back. Press the mirror edges together until they are flush and wipe away any excess glue. Finally, coat the mirrors in dry flour to seal the edges and allow three to five days' drying time before hanging. A knot should dangle from the bottom of the mirrors and the remaining ribbon should be used to hang the mirror over the most used space in your house.

Estha McNevin

Notes:

January 18
Sunday

 4th ♏
☽ → ♏ 1:20 am

Color of the day: Gold
Incense of the day: Juniper

Multipurpose Quick Witch Spell

This spell works best if you are in a rush and don't have the time to write your own or search through a collection of spell books. It uses the following simple ingredients: 1/2 teaspoon olive oil, white candle, appropriate candleholder, piece of paper and pen, and 8 inches of satin ribbon in a color you feel matches your goal's intent. Gather your supplies and begin by visualizing your goal. Rub the olive oil on the candle while saying this incantation:

> I consecrate this oil
> upon this blessed night.
>
> May thy candle work
> its magic right.
>
> Hear my words and power
> in this and every hour.
>
> So mote it be!

Light the wick and proceed to write down your desire on the piece of paper. When you are satisfied, roll the paper into a scroll and tie it with your satin ribbon. Keep the scroll beside your candle.

Gwinevere Rain

Notes:

January 19
Monday

Martin Luther King, Jr. Day

4th ♏

☉ → ♒ 5:40 pm

Color of the day: White
Incense of the day: Hyssop

Cleanse Your Space

Early in a new year is a good time to physically and magically clean your personal space. Your space may be your home, a specific room, a workplace, or car—anyplace where you spend a good deal of time. First, clean the area of clutter, dust, etc., and arrange things the way you like them. Next, make a mixture of water and herbs, either in a mist bottle or in a bowl. Combine 1 cup of water, 1 teaspoon of lemon juice, and a pinch each of dill weed, rosemary, and mint. Depending on the size of your space, you can double or triple the mixture (you can use dried kitchen herbs). If possible, allow the mixture to sit in the sunlight or a warm location to blend for a few hours, then spray the mist around your area or sprinkle it with your fingers or a brush as you visualize the area being fresh and clean.

Ember

Notes:

January 20
Tuesday

Inauguration Day

 4th ♏

☽ → ♐ 12:30 pm

Color of the day: Black
Incense of the day: Geranium

Penguin Meditation

Today is Penguin Awareness Day. Penguins as a totem teach us to shift into other worlds with graceful swiftness as they dive in and out of the waters of awareness and emotion. To meditate on the magic of Penguin, make yourself comfortable and shift into a meditative state. Find yourself in the land of ice, water, and sunlight. As you stand on ice, feel yourself shift into penguin shape. Feel your penguin-ness as you walk towards the edge and dive into the water. Feel the water flow around you and see the troubles in your life flow past. As you swim ahead into the water's embrace, you see swimming toward you ways to change your troubles into positives. You capture those solutions in your flippers and meld them into your heart. When you are done swimming, move back onto the ice and shift back into your human form, warmed by the shining light. With a deep breath, return to the here and now, thanking Penguin for wisdom and guidance.

Gail Wood

Notes:

January 21
Wednesday

4th ♐

Color of the day: Topaz
Incense of the day: Bay laurel

Feud Spell

Today we have a waning Moon and it is a Wednesday, the day associated with Mercury and communication. Here is a spell to help end the feud between two people. It helps to banish troubles and hurt feelings and will soothe any hard words that may have been spoken. Light an orange candle for Mercury and for extra energy to help in our task. Then repeat the charm:

> By the speed of Mercury, all
>   troubles will pass,
> Now let the squabbling end and
>   our friendship last.
> I send my apologies to you with
>   my sincerity,
> Let's put this all behind us, with
>   the power of three times three.

Now give your friend a call, and start a positive dialogue. Clear the air and

 Page 22

apologize. Also be sure to accept their apology with compassion and grace.

Ellen Dugan

Notes:

Holiday lore: Feast Day of Saint Agnes of Rome. Since the fourth century, the primitive church held Saint Agnes in high honor above all the other virgin martyrs of Rome. Church fathers and Christian poets sang her praises, and they extolled her virginity and heroism under torture. The feast day for Saint Agnes was assigned to January 21. Early records gave the same date for her feast, and the Catholic Church continues to keep her memory sacred.

January 22
Thursday

4th ♐

Color of the day: Crimson
Incense of the day: Nutmeg

St. Vincent of Saragossa

St. Vincent of Saragossa is the patron saint of vintners. He was imprisoned, tortured, and murdered around AD 304 in Valencia, Spain, when he refused to deny his Christianity and allow his sacred texts to be burned. Winemaking is an avocation that is both art and craft, requiring knowledge and patience. Guarding knowledge in books is a way to preserve ancient arts and crafts. Take a look at your life. What aspect of it would benefit from a bit of tender nurturing? Is there anything that needs to be put aside for a while to ferment? Anything that needs a little mixing up? Light a white candle in honor of St. Vincent. Give the neglected areas in your life a bit of tending. In a year's time, look back at your progress and renew projects that were put on the shelf.

Cerridwen Iris Shea

Notes:

January 23
Friday

 4th ♐
                   ☽ → ♑ 1:18 am

Color of the day: Rose
Incense of the day: Thyme

Snow Traction

Those of you who live in cold northern regions are facing snowy driving conditions at this time of year. One way to deal with slick driveways and roads is to improve the traction. You can create a mixture for use where needed to keep your vehicle from skidding in the driveway or get it unstuck if you wind up in a snowdrift. First, fill a large container (like an empty detergent jug) with equal parts of rock salt, kitty litter, and sand. Next, concentrate on the elemental energies of Earth. Pour that into the mixture, saying:

> Salt of the Earth, hold
>   fast against the cold!
> Clay of the Earth, keep
>   traction firm and deep!
> Sand of the Earth, grip
>   and let nothing slip!

Seal the jug and store it in your vehicle. To use, sprinkle the mixture on the ground and repeat the incantation.

Elizabeth Barrette

Notes:

January 24
Saturday

4th ♑

Color of the day: Blue
Incense of the day: Patchouli

Spell for Prosperity

Ekeko, the South American god of prosperity, is honored today. To ensure a year of prosperity, fashion a representation of Ekeko out of clay or salt dough. He is always pictured as a small, pot-bellied man with an open mouth and a mustache. He wears a hat, trousers, and a poncho and is loaded with baskets. Fill his baskets with money, grains, candy, and any other symbols of prosperity that you wish to manifest this year. As you work, visualize the good fortune you will experience in the coming year. When you have finished the god, set him in a comfortable place in your home and place a lighted cigarette in his mouth for his pleasure. As the cigarette burns, ask Ekeko to bless you with abundance and a year of prosperity. Each successive January 24, replenish his baskets with money and food and light him another cigarette.

Lily Gardner

Notes:

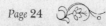

January 25
Sunday

4th ♑
☽ → ♒ 1:56 pm

Color of the day: Amber
Incense of the day: Frankincense

Spiritual Re-alignment Spell

Perform this spell to re-align your sense of spirituality and connect with the higher powers. You'll need a fresh-cut purple flower and about twenty-five onyx gemstone chips (the inexpensive type used in jewelry making). To begin, make sure you have a quiet space to work and you're ready to focus on the spell. Start by placing the flower in the center of your workspace. Begin chanting the names of the elements, "earth, air, fire, water." Continue this repetition as you place the onyx gemstones in a circle around the flower. When the circle is complete, say this prayer:

> Divine ones, I call to you
> Please bless me and guide me
> through this journey
> As I open my soul to receive
> your light and wisdom.

Take time to meditate and write in your Book of Shadows.

Gwinevere Rain

Notes:

January 26
Monday

Chinese New Year (ox)

4th ♒
New Moon 2:55 am

Color of the day: Silver
Incense of the day: Lily

Energy for New Starts

What an auspicious day January 26 is this year! It is the start of Chinese New Year, a New Moon, and a solar eclipse! There's energy for fresh starts with the New Moon and New Year energies. The ox represents strength and endurance. What you begin now has the capacity to last for a long time. The solar eclipse lends positive, active energy to the change. List three goals you wish to achieve in the coming year and beyond (because of the ox energy, this is also a good time to make five-year and ten-year plans). Under each goal, list three active steps you can take toward each goal. Charge this list with the energies of the ox, the New Moon, and the Sun. Keep it safe. Revisit the list every month on the New Moon. See what's been accomplished, what needs more attention, and what no longer works. Make the necessary adjustments. One year from today, burn it in celebration of your achievements!

Cerridwen Iris Shea

Notes:

January 27
Tuesday

 1st ♒

Color of the day: Maroon
Incense of the day: Ginger

Obtain/Maintain Good Credit

Before doing this spell, obtain your real credit report from a service like www.freecreditreport .com. Then, create a "mock" report, visualizing what you wish to see! Light a gold, purple, or white candle. Use the Magician tarot card from the major arcanca, along with the Ace, Six, Nine, Ten, and King (or Queen) of Pentacles, all empowering your image and the reality that you have plenty of money and are therefore entirely trustworthy for an extension of credit. When the spell is cast, do your research (and the important follow-up work) to clean up and improve your credit. Now, get ready to receive money or other means to pay off debt, as well as a new credit score!

Calantirniel

Notes:

January 28
Wednesday

1st ♒
☽ → ♓ 1:12 am

Color of the day: White
Incense of the day: Marjoram

Meditation for Magical Strength

The development of greater magical ability requires the development of a stronger association with the self. If your own self-awareness and self-development are not on track, your magical practice will not be on track either. It's important to spend a bit of time better connecting with yourself each day. Before starting your day, take the time to do a short meditation. Light a candle (tealights work well) and settle yourself comfortably. Take "inventory" of your internal self. Focus on the colors at your main chakra points; they should be clear and glowing. If not, take time to clear and re-energize that chakra area. Next, take time to reaffirm your grounding and shielding. Strong grounding and good, elastic shielding help keep you balanced. Lastly, focus on your positive intentions for the day. Focus magical energy toward areas you feel could be troublesome. Focus energy on a day accomplished in right relation with the universe and its inhabitants. Focus on learning something new today, just for you. Take a moment to wind down, extinguish the candle, and go into the day focused, balanced, and in harmony with yourself.

Winter Wren

Notes:

candle; try not to let the flame go out. Visualize each room energized by the Sun's warmth. Place the candle on a table or altar. End this ritual by scrying as you gaze into the flame. What do you see?

James Kambos

Notes:

January 29
Thursday

1st ♓

Color of the day: Green
Incense of the day: Carnation

Let the Sun Return

Winter may still own the land, but there are signs that we are moving closer to spring. Daylight lingers a little longer in the evening, and some early snow crocuses begin to bloom about now. The ancient belief is that the Sun should be encouraged to return at this time of year through rituals and spells. Here is one method. After dusk has turned to night, light a white taper candle. Open your front door and step outside. Whisper these words, "Candle burn, Sun return." The candle flame represents the Sun illuminating the darkness of winter. Now walk through your home carrying the

January 30
Friday

1st ♓
☽ → ♈ 10:25 am

Color of the day: Purple
Incense of the day: Vanilla

Spell for Peace

We know that the very first signs of spring are just around the corner, and it's time to breathe a deep sigh and release any stress carrying over from winter. Bring peace to your heart. Light a blue candle and your favorite incense. As you gaze into the flame, feel yourself letting go of any stress you are holding. Now you are open to bring peace into your heart for the days ahead. Hold a tumbled rose quartz to your heart and feel the loving vibrations it fills you with.

*Spirit of peace, find a home
within my open heart
Peace, I carry with me now,
serenity finds a start*

You can keep the stone with you. Anytime you have a stressful day, sit somewhere quietly and hold the stone close to your heart, remembering the magic of this peaceful January day.

Mickie Mueller

Notes:

January 31
Saturday

 1st ♈

Color of the day: Brown
Incense of the day: Magnolia

Cleansing in the Shower

When we awaken for the day, our energies are ethereal and our minds saturated with the energy of the dreaming. Begin your day by hopping into the shower or bath, yet don't let it be a physical or bodily cleansing alone. We are blessed to have access to clean and purifying water and should pay attention to this, honor this, and utilize it for the most spiritual purposes possible. As the bathwater is draining, or as the water from the showerhead cleanses you for the day, meditate on water and what it represents as an element. Water is attuned to emotions, the psychic body, and the astral plane. Allow the morning routine to be a profoundly cleansing, spiritual process to prepare you for the day. While cleansing, say something like:

I connect to the undines and the element of water. May this cleansing purify my body and mind, preparing me to dance with the spirals of reality throughout the day. I honor water, and this cleansing ritual between the dreaming and waking life. So mote it be.

Raven Digitalis

Notes:

February is the second month of the Gregorian calendar, and the year's shortest month. Its astrological sign is Aquarius, the water-bearer (January 19–February 18), a fixed air sign ruled by unpredictable Uranus. In colder regions, February is a month of deep snow and fierce storms. February's Full Moon was known as the Snow Moon. Frost may etch the windowpanes and icy winds may howl, but Mother Earth begins to stir with new life. You can see it as the buds on trees begin to swell, and the tips of green daffodil foliage pierce the frozen Earth. In old England it was believed that the Sun awoke in February. The Pagan holiday of Imbolc on February 2 is a day of purification and a time to honor the turning of the year toward spring. Corn dollies or an ear of corn from last year's harvest may be placed on the hearth to draw fertility and protection. For Christians this day is Candlemas, a time when all Yule greenery must be removed and burned. Valentine's Day on February 14 is a day for flowers, candies, and love magic. February days may appear gray and bleak, but new life is pulsing deep within the Earth. To call forth the promise of abundance, place a new houseplant or potted crocus near a window. Light a solitary white candle while meditating on the coming warmth.

February 1
Sunday

1st ♈

☽ → ♉ 5:08 pm

Color of the day: Yellow
Incense of the day: Almond

Sacred Preparations

Instead of waiting until the last minute and then running around frantically to put together your Imbolc preparations, use today as a Sacred Preparations Day. Sit down with your favorite beverage, pen, and paper. Make a list of everything you need. Beside each item, note if you have it or need to buy or borrow it. Hunt down all the items you think you have and put them in a designated area. You will find that the Stuff Gremlins have spirited away several things you were positive you had. Run your errands with a refreshed list, picking up the items that need to be bought or borrowed. Once you return, you have time to polish, iron, bake, and arrange. That means when the holiday dawns, you can greet it with a true sense of celebration!

Cerridwen Iris Shea

Notes:

February 2
Monday

Imbolc – Groundhog Day

1st ♉

2nd Quarter 6:13 pm

Color of the day: Gray
Incense of the day: Narcissus

Spell for New Beginnings

In the morning, rise and light a white candle. Place it on your altar along with three coins. Sweep the circle and call the directions. Facing the candle, chant:

> Oh Mother Brigid, whose
> eternal flame burns
> within us all.

> Oh Mother bright and
> beautiful, hear my call!"

Then say:

> I ask for new beginnings
> My wish is for_____

State your wish. Visualize it. Hold the coins up to the flame and say:

> One coin for my past,
> One for my present,
> And one for my future.

> These I give as offerings to you.

Repeat your wish. Open your circle and breathe in deeply. Keep the candle burning as long as safely possible. Later, take a walk outside and place the coins one by one in or near a water source, such as a pond or river, while you whisper Brigid's name in thanks.

Nancy Bennett

Notes:

H oliday lore: On Imbolc, a bundle of corn from the harvest is dressed in ribbons and becomes the Corn Bride. On February 2, the Corn Bride is placed on the hearth or hung on the door to bring prosperity, fertility, and protection to the home.

February 3
Tuesday

 2nd ♉

☽ → ♊ 9:14 pm

Color of the day: Red
Incense of the day: Cedar

Speak your Mind

M any of us have found ourselves feeling tongue-tied when it comes to speaking our minds, either with public speaking or in personal conversations. Here is a spell on this day for "Blessing of the Throats"

that will clear up blockages from your throat chakra and allow you to bravely express yourself. First dip your finger in a dish of water and draw a pentagram at the base of your throat, saying this blessing:

I hereby bless my throat in the name of the God and Goddess.

May they guide me to express my thoughts well, communicating with strength and conviction, always tempered with wisdom.

By my word, so mote it be.

Now hold your hand over your throat as you visualize a bright-blue light swirling around in your throat, destroying your fear of speaking your mind. Remember, your words and thoughts have value.

Mickie Mueller

Notes:

February 4
Wednesday

2nd ♊

Color of the day: Yellow
Incense of the day: Bay laurel

The Impulse of Empathy

Using a thick needle, poke a hole in both ends of an egg and drain out the contents by blowing on one end (exhaling with your mouth to the hole). Allow the shell to dry. Open a bottle of champagne and pour some into a bowl. Place your fingertips into the bowl and feel the bubbles tickle your fingers. Chant the following 64 times to evoke the energies of Venus: "Love tickles my soul." Submerge the shell within the bowl until it is almost full of this enchanted champagne. When done, plug the holes with your fingertips and carefully dry and seal the ends of the shell with candle wax. To evoke the subtle magic of empathy, shake the egg and feel the bubbles reach out to you through the shell. Know that this is a tantalizing layer of emotion charged with all the associations of passion and raw love and that, like human empathy, it delicately communicates with us on the subtle vibratory planes. Shake your egg throughout the day until the energy is depleted, then bury it in a special spot before bedtime.

Estha McNevin

Notes:

February 5
Thursday

2nd ♊

☽ → ♋ 11:05 pm

Color of the day: Turquoise
Incense of the day: Apricot

Enjoying the Moment

Today is Hank Aaron's birthday (b. 1934), baseball's home run king, who believes baseball is not about breaking records but about playing the game. To work a spell to stay joyfully in the moment and bring a project all the way home, gather together some soil for steadfast grounding, a small lavender candle, a piece of hard candy in your favorite flavor, some sandalwood incense for concentration and success, a fireproof bowl, a small piece of paper, and a pen. Light the candle and the incense and chant, "Pleasant and joyful is my day, keep my attention all the way." Breathe deeply and write your goal on the slip of paper and burn it in the bowl, lighting it from the candle. As the paper burns away, eat the candy and let it slowly melt in your mouth while concentrating on staying in the moment and the sweetness of success. Bury the ashes in the soil. Let the candle burn all the way down and place the remains in the soil. When your project is done, return the soil to the outdoors, thanking the Spirit for it all.

Gail Wood

Notes:

with the bad habit you would like to break by writing the habit on a piece of paper and fastening it to the twig. Cast a circle, if you wish, and stand facing east with the ends of the twig in your hands. Loudly declaim, "I break the habit of smoking" (or whatever habit you wish to break) as you break the twig. Next, bury the broken twig. Putting it in compost is okay, but don't put it in regular garbage. As the twig rots, the habit will go with it.

Magenta Griffith

Notes:

February 6
Friday

 2nd ♋

Color of the day: White
Incense of the day: Violet

Breaking a Bad habit

It's easy to make New Year's resolutions, such as giving up smoking, on January 1. But are you keeping them? This would be a good day to revisit those resolutions to break bad habits. If you haven't kept to your resolutions as well as you would like, here's a spell to help you. Find a twig of some kind. Name it

February 7
Saturday

 2nd ♋
☽ → ♌ 11:43 pm

Color of the day: Black
Incense of the day: Ivy

house Blessing

The Japanese have celebrated this day as the beginning of spring for more than a thousand years. Begin this spell, as the Japanese do, with a good house cleaning. As you vacuum and dust your floors and

furniture, visualize the winter doldrums vanishing with the dust and being replaced with good energy. As you clean, chant: "In with good luck, out with the demons." When you're finished cleaning the room, scatter dried beans on the floor, imagining you're hitting the demons that represent low energy, illness, and depression. The beans themselves represent good fortune. Light new white candles throughout your home and place a bowl of white flowers on your kitchen table. Gather the scattered beans in a white ceramic bowl and place on your altar. End the spell with a prayer of thanks that the back of winter is finally broken.

Lily Gardner

Notes:

who have suffered and died for the practice of their beliefs or simply for being accused of those practices, as well as to thank the universe for those who work tirelessly for legal recognition of our beliefs. Set up a white candle for remembrance, a pink candle for healing, and a blue candle for mental clarity. Light the white candle, honoring in memory and remembering with loving thoughts those who have paid the ultimate sacrifice for being called "Witch." Light the pink candle, focusing on those who continue to work for the rights of those who practice "alternative" spiritual paths. Send them healing energy, strength, goodwill, and blessings of love in spirit of light to counteract the hatred and anger they face. Light the blue candle, focusing positive energy into the world for all to open their minds to the ideals of acceptance and tolerance. Send these thoughts out into the universe as you complete your meditation.

Winter Wren

Notes:

February 8
Sunday

2nd ♌

Color of the day: Orange
Incense of the day: Heliotrope

Spell for Remembrance and Hope

This day marks the anniversary of the start of the Salem Witch debacle. With that in mind, this is a good time to remember those

Holiday lore: Today is the Buddhist Needle Memorial. On this day, as part of the principle of endless compassion espoused by the Buddhist faith for all sentient and nonsentient beings, all the sewing needles that have been retired during the year are honored. That is, needles are brought to the shrine and pushed into a slab of tofu that rests on the second tier of a three-tiered altar. Priests sing sutras to comfort the needles and heal their injured spirits.

February 9
Monday

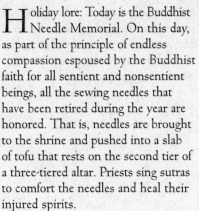

2nd ♌
Full Moon 9:49 am

Color of the day: Lavender
Incense of the day: Neroli

Full Moon

We will witness a total lunar eclipse this February Full Moon. During an eclipse, we experience the energy of the entire month as we watch the Full Moon darken to a crescent, fall into complete shadow as it does at New Moon, and grow full again, all in a matter of minutes. The lunar eclipse symbolizes the Crone, not as the embodiment of wisdom but as the Lady of Passage. It is said that chanting a mantra during a lunar eclipse has one hundred times the power. Check your almanac for viewing time, then prepare your sacred space so the Moon is visible as you cast your spell. Make sure your altar includes three candles: a white candle symbolizing the Maiden crescent, a red candle for the Full Moon Mother, and a black candle for the waning Crone. Spend time contemplating what you wish to manifest to bring about a good change in your life. When the Moon is full, cast your circle and light the three candles. Focus on your desire. As the Moon passes into darkness, light a stick of incense and visualize your prayers rising along with the smoke up in the air to the Crone. She gathers your desire into herself. Hold this visualization until you see the Crone pass your desire to the emerging Maiden crescent. Continue your prayer as you witness the Maiden growing gibbous with your desire and transforming back into the Full Moon, the Great Mother. Blessed Be.

Lily Gardner

Notes:

February 10
Tuesday

 3rd ♌
☽ → ♍ 12:38 am

Color of the day: White
Incense of the day: Cinnamon

Spontaneous Poetry as Spellcraft

There are many types of poems. Some are stylized in specific patterns and rhythms; others are more free form and less structured. Poems can be rhyming or rhythmic (these types are especially effective in spellwork), they can be stories or tales, or they can be a string of words and symbolic imagery written "off the top of the head." In the latter, abstract and arcane imagery become the essence of the work. I see this as a form of spiritual channeling or automatic writing, in which the writer acts as a conduit for words of the divine. I believe that all writing, to one degree or another, includes channeled musings. Is the writer or artist really "in control," or is there something greater at work? Today, dedicate yourself to moments of spontaneous poetry writing. Keep a pen and paper with you throughout the day and take frequent breaks. Allow the words to "write themselves" with you as the conduit. Write down anything that comes to you, letting it flow smoothly. If you write a seemingly nonsensical string of words, take time in the evening to sit at your altar and meditate on their deeper meaning. You may also wish to construct the day's poetry into a greater, longer piece of work.

Raven Digitalis

Notes:

February 11
Wednesday

3rd ♍

Color of the day: Brown
Incense of the day: Honeysuckle

Kick the Cold Tea

This time of year can bring more than its fair share of colds and flu. Mix together equal parts of peppermint, elder flowers (or berries), cinnamon, ginger, nutmeg, orange peel, and rose hips (approximately 4 ounces total dried herbs), and place them into a special glass jar. Before placing the lid, hold your right hand over the dry tea mixture and say:

> Warmth now I hold,
> Away with you, Cold!
> I find myself strong,
> All Season long!

Brew a cup of the tea with honey and lemon once or twice a day all through the spring season to stave off those "nasty bugs."

Calantirniel

Notes:

February 12
Thursday

3rd ♍
☽ → ♎ 3:33 am

Color of the day: Green
Incense of the day: Balsam

Diana's Day

This is a day that was sacred to the Roman Maiden goddess of the hunt, Diana. Here is a call to Diana and a request for the courage and cunning to face any challenges you may encounter this winter. Diana is pictured as a young, athletic woman wearing a silvery tunic and carrying a bow and arrows. She was crowned with a crescent Moon on her brow and was typically accompanied by her hunting hounds. Try lighting a silver candle for Diana, and ask for her assistance:

> Diana, you walk the woods
> unafraid and stand tall
> and true.
>
> Hear my plea and grant me
> courage, in all that I say
> and do.
>
> The candle's flame is a symbol
> of my confidence spell.
>
> For the good of all, with
> harm to none, may it
> turn out well.

Ellen Dugan

Notes:

Holiday lore: Lincoln is called the Great Emancipator and is thought of as one of our greatest presidents. Know this, however: Lincoln was an almost unknown figure until the age of forty, when he first entered the Illinois state legislature. His later assassination threw the country into widespread mourning, inspiring Walt Whitman to write:

Coffin that passes
through lanes and street,
through day and night
with the great cloud
darkening the land . . .
I mourned, and yet shall
mourn with ever-
returning spring.

Honor them, thank them for what they passed down to you through the generations, ask for their advice. Listen to them; don't assume you know what the ancestors will tell you. Store them in black cloth or a secure box. Take them out to honor the ancestry they represent on family holidays, during the Samhain ancestral rituals, and at future Parentalia celebrations.

Cerridwen Iris Shea

Notes:

February 13
Friday

 3rd ♎

Color of the day: Coral
Incense of the day: Rose

Parentalia

The Roman feast of Parentalia was to honor ancient ancestors. Not just the grandparents you can remember or the great-grandparents about whom you've heard stories, but ancestors from centuries before who have been forgotten. Make two small poppets, one male and one female, to represent the gender of each ancestral line. Dress them, decorate them, stuff them with favorite herbs (such as rosemary, lavender, angelica, mullein, and basil) as well as batting. Prepare an ancestral altar with items special to your family. Light one black, one white, and one red candle. Talk to your poppets.

February 14
Saturday
Valentine's Day

 3rd ♎
☽ → ♏ 9:50 am

Color of the day: Blue
Incense of the day: Rue

The Art of Love

Using a nontoxic marker or ink, write on your body (in symbol and word) sixty-four things that you love. These things can include anything imaginable. Place them on your body in levels of importance or function. Place the things you love the most and experience strongly near your heart, head, and shoulders. Sexual pleasure should be place on your hips or thighs and types of food near your stomach. Position skills or abilities you love, as well as gifts or possessions, on the arms and hands, and assign activities and interests along the legs and feet. When you are finished, take a moment to recall all of the things that you truly love and let them fill the space all around you and within you. As you go through your day, talk about the things on your list with others and take this day to honestly express your love and passion for the things that matter most to you in life.

Estha McNevin

Notes:

February 15
Sunday

3rd ♏

Color of the day: Gold
Incense of the day: Marigold

Nirvana Day

Today is Nirvana Day, a Buddhist holiday celebrating the death of Buddha and his attainment of total nirvana. Nirvana represents the end of all suffering, the achievement of bliss, and reunion with the divine. Buddhists celebrate this holiday by visiting temples and monasteries. They may bring donations of food or money. Although not everyone seeks to attain nirvana, the teachings are still widely useful because they help people to reduce feelings of want and suffering. Spend some time meditating today. Light a stick of Asian-style incense. Focus on a statue or picture of Buddha if you have one. Meditate on peace and nonattachment.

Elizabeth Barrette

Notes:

February 16
Monday
Presidents' Day (observed)

 3rd ♏

4th Quarter 4:37 pm

☽ → ♐ 7:53 pm

Color of the day: White
Incense of the day: Rosemary

The Call of the Owl

In rural areas, the frigid stillness of February nights is shattered by the mating call of the Great Horned Owl. It is an eerie, unearthly sound. Some cultures feared the owl as a harbinger of tragic events and death. But many shamans considered owls to be intelligent and would listen for their calls so they could time their magical work accordingly. The owls are creatures of the night and you may invoke their power to aid you in dream work, visions, and works requiring creativity. To call on the owls, select a night when you'll be alone. Light a single black candle. Decorate your altar with tokens of winter, such as pine cones. Gaze into the flame while you visualize an owl flying gracefully and silently through the frozen woodland. See it lead you to your goal. Return slowly from your vision of the owl to the here and now. Tonight, you'll likely have a vivid dream relating to your quest.

James Kambos

Notes:

February 17
Tuesday

 4th ♐

Color of the day: Black
Incense of the day: Basil

Jigsaw Puzzle

Find a jigsaw puzzle that is all one color, or one that has a picture suitable to your problem. Alternately, find a puzzle with as few pieces as possible; a jigsaw puzzle made for a young child would work. Think about your problem as you lay out all the pieces on a flat surface, design-side down (unless you are using a one-color puzzle). Put together the puzzle, thinking about your problem while you work. Leave the last piece out. You may want to cover the puzzle, especially if you have pets or small children. Spend a little while thinking about something else, perhaps listening to music or reading. Go to sleep. In the morning, put in the last piece. The solution to your problem will also fall into place soon after you complete the puzzle.

Magenta Griffith

Notes:

Allow the paper to soak until the words have vanished. Then, pour the water on the ground or into a potted plant and bury the strips of paper.

Ember

Notes:

February 18
Wednesday

 4th ♐
☉ → ♓ 7:46 am

Color of the day: Topaz
Incense of the day: Lavender

Vanishing Spell
Using a pencil, write on small strips of paper several things you want to be rid of in your life. These can be bad habits, specific troubles, debt, etc. When you've finished writing, place the papers in a dish of water and chant:

> Water, water take away
> These things that I must keep
> at bay.

February 19
Thursday

4th ♐
☽ → ♑ 8:25 am

Color of the day: Crimson
Incense of the day: Mulberry

Removing Obstacles to Abundance
Sometimes we can't figure out why we're having trouble bringing abundance into our lives. What's blocking the path to abundance? Removing those obstacles now, before planting season begins, will allow your finances to grow

unobstructed during the fertile season to come. On a slip of paper, write habits, doubts, or fears that may be preventing the bountiful abundance you seek. Fold this slip of paper several times, dip it in water, and freeze it. This represents the barriers on the path to your abundance, locked in ice. Build a fire in your fireplace or barbecue grill. Toss the frozen slip of paper into the flames and say:

> Remove these obstacles from
>   my path,
> Clear the way as abundance
>   comes back,
> By ash and soot, flame
>   and steam,
> Abundance now freely flows
>   to me!

As spring approaches, plant your seeds of abundance unhampered by obstacles of the past.

Mickie Mueller

Notes:

February 20
Friday

 4th ♑

Color of the day: Pink
Incense of the day: Mint

Chase Away the Winter Blues

Dress in green clothes and place four spring-colored candles (pastel, yellow, rose, and green) on your altar. Bring in a blue bowl and place in it snow from outside or ice from your freezer. Light the candles and walk in a clockwise circle while you chant:

> Winter's snow, born of the blue
>   cold, the time is fast
>   and fading.
> Soon the springtime comes
>   renewed
> Life return! Your time is waiting!

Keep the candles lit and let the ice or snow melt. Once it has, take one of the candles to each of the four directions and blow it out. This spell is even better if you can do it outside or through an open window. Use the water to nurture a houseplant or to water starter seedlings planned for your spring garden.

Nancy Bennett

Notes:

February 21
Saturday

 4th ♑
☽ → ♒ 9:06 pm

Color of the day: Indigo
Incense of the day: Sage

Transportation Appreciation

In our hectic day-to-day lives, it can be hard to remember to truly appreciate some of the commonplace things. Today, let your thoughts center on your means of getting about. Start with the most used method of transportation—your feet. Take time to give your feet a special treat today. This could be a simple soak and lotion or a spa visit for a good reflexology session or perhaps some new socks or shoes. Send healing and rejuvenating energy to each part of your feet. Next, consider your mode of getting about—public transportation, a bike, your own car, whatever it may be. Send thanks and blessing energy to that source for giving you the means to accomplish your tasks. Strengthen protections around your vehicle or take time to smile and thank your bus driver or train conductor. If it's time to change your mode of transportation, send out energy into the universe that you may find what is right for you, something that both meets your needs and is kind to the environment.

Winter Wren

Notes:

February 22
Sunday

4th ♒

Color of the day: Amber
Incense of the day: Hyacinth

Spell to Shine Brightly

Today is the birthday of Edna St. Vincent Millay (1892–1950), whose famous poem talks of her candle burning at both ends and giving out a lovely light. To shine brightly without burning yourself out, bring together a piece of paper, a pencil, an eraser, and a yellow crayon along with frankincense oil for faith in yourself. Draw a picture of yourself (an outline will do) and draw a heart on the left side of the chest. Write on the figure all the roles, jobs, qualities, and things that you do, corresponding with the appropriate body part. Take a good long look at it. Close your eyes, and anoint yourself with the oil and say, "Here I am shining bright, how can I best show my light?" With a deep breath, open your eyes and look at the figure. You will see the light shining behind some words and through others. With the eraser, remove all the words that block the light. With the yellow crayon, color in the light that you see with your spiritual eye. Anoint the picture with the oil and keep it on your altar, thanking the Spirit for your wonderful shining light.

Gail Wood

Notes:

Holiday lore: We all know the lore about our first president—cherry tree, silver dollar, wooden teeth—but the truth behind this most legendary of American figures is sometimes more entertaining than the folklore. For instance, did you know that once when young George went for a dip in the Rappahannock River, two Fredericksburg women stole his clothes? This story was recorded in the Spotsylvania County records. Picture then the young man scampering home flustered and naked, and the icon of the dollar bill becomes just a bit more real.

February 23
Monday

4th ♒

Color of the day: Silver
Incense of the day: Hyssop

Boundaries

Try this spell to encourage harmony and dispel any negativity in your neighborhood. Find a clear quartz crystal cluster if possible and dedicate it to peace and harmony. Place the stone outside, either in a garden or potted plant, or simply on your porch, deck, or patio—even a window box would work anywhere outside, especially near a fence, property line, or other boundary marker. Say the following: "We create the boundaries that divide us, let there be peace and harmony between us, beyond the boundary." Place a small offering of food near the stone, such as birdseed. If you know your neighbors well, use this opportunity to invite them to dinner or bring them a gift of bread, cookies, etc. If you aren't comfortable with issuing an invitation, simply project harmony and hope for peaceful coexistence with those around you.

Ember

Notes:

February 24
Tuesday
Mardi Gras (Fat Tuesday)

 4th ♒
𝄪 → ♓ 7:59 am
New Moon 8:35 pm

Color of the day: Gray
Incense of the day: Ylang-ylang

Mardi Gras New Moon

This year Mardi Gras falls on the New Moon. The New Moon is a time for manifesting all the positive things that you would wish to have in your life. Here is a spell that incorporates the traditional Mardi Gras colors of purple for justice, green to represent faith, and gold to represent power. For this spell, you will need one purple candle, one green candle, and one gold candle (any size or style) and three candleholders. Line up the candles and drape Mardi Gras beads and coins around them if you wish. Once you have things arranged as you like, light the candles and repeat the charm:

> This year, Mardi Gras has
> fallen on a New Moon night,
>
> And now I cast this spell,
> with magic and candlelight.
>
> The purple candle brings
> justice with all possible speed,

> While the green candle
> renews my faith, in my time
> of need.
>
> The golden candle is burned
> for power, may it shine
> so bright.
>
> Let the good times roll, with
> harm to none, on this Mardi
> Gras night.

Allow the candles to burn out in a safe place.

Ellen Dugan

Notes:

February 25
Wednesday
Ash Wednesday

 1st ♓

Color of the day: White
Incense of the day: Marjoram

Bath Time Spellcraft

Both the Sun and the Moon are in Pisces today, which is the ultimate water sign in my opinion! Why not take a magical bath? Baths are both physically and spiritually cleansing, and are essential for any Witch or magician. Bathing is purifying on many levels, and the ritual of bathing can quite easily become a magical act. This evening, plan to take a magical bath. Take time to gather certain salts, oils, and herbs (perhaps put these in a muslin bag) to add to the bathwater. You may wish to choose a natural food coloring to add to the water, or use "Colour Bath," which is sold in many metaphysical stores. Choose some candles, the colors of which should be aligned with your metaphysical purpose for the ritual. Choose also some incense that is spiritually aligned. As you lay down in the warm water, say something like: "I now enter the warm and cleansing womb of the Great Goddess. I enter sacred space to purify my body and mind." Follow this with a ritual, meditation, or resonating chant. You may wish to call upon spirits of healing, connect to the undines, or cleanse and realign your chakras.

Raven Digitalis

Notes:

February 26
Thursday

1st ♓

☽ → ♈ 4:24 pm

Color of the day: Purple
Incense of the day: Myrrh

Mojo Bag for Prosperity

Work this spell if you'd like more abundance in your life. You'll need a 10-inch square of dye-free muslin fabric (cotton may be substituted), a piece of green ribbon, three dimes, and at least two of the following herbs: patchouli, mint, cinnamon, cinquefoil, or pine. To begin, lay the fabric flat and pile about two tablespoons of each herb in the center of the fabric. Drop the three dimes on top and hold your palms over the mixture as you say this incantation:

> By coin and herb my voice
> be heard.
>
> I draw into my life more
> prosperity.
>
> With harm to none, my will
> be done.

Visualize your life with happiness and prosperity. Pull the edges up and tie the mojo bag closed with green ribbon. Keep the mojo bag by your purse or wallet.

Gwinevere Rain

Notes:

for easily feeling emotion, gratefulness, and ability to give; the blue one for crystal-clear expression of your truth; the indigo for trusting your intuition; and the violet one for allowing your connection with Spirit. Think about how the Goddess loves you, and since you are a perfect expression of the Goddess, know that you love yourself! If you don't have a date elsewhere, make a date with yourself—watch a movie, read a book, and pamper yourself!

Calantirniel

Notes:

February 27
Friday

1st ♈

Color of the day: Rose
Incense of the day: Yarrow

Self–Love Bath

To bring love in your life, you need to love yourself! Draw a warm bath and add Epsom salts, baking soda, and/or sea salt. Light tealight candles around the tub and bathroom and bring your favorite crystals and shells to bathe with you. Before entering, add a few drops of several essential oils: vanilla, sandalwood, ylang-ylang, rose geranium, and/or patchouli. Rose, jasmine, and neroli are costly, so go easy if you have them. Roll a towel behind your neck, moisten it, enter the bath, and relax! Visualize the Goddess cleansing away all old energy, and opening all of your chakras—the red and orange ones for passion and sensuality; the yellow one for self-esteem and the ability to receive; the green/pink one

February 28
Saturday

1st ♈
☽ → ♉ 10:33 pm

Color of the day: Brown
Incense of the day: Sandalwood

Freshen Up Your Nest Spell

At this time of year, the birds in my yard are searching for nesting sites and will soon begin to build their nests. Let's take a tip from nature and begin to magically freshen up our own homes. After a good physical cleaning, our homes need a spiritual cleansing also. If you have a fireplace, toss a few whole garlic cloves into the fire to release their cleansing properties. Remove a few bristles from your trusty broom and burn or smudge them in a heat-proof dish. Carry the dish around your home and fan the smoke about with a feather. This will please your household spirits. Then treat yourself to some spring flowers. Floral shops should have pots of spring-blooming flowers now. Tulips, crocuses, and hyacinths are good choices; they'll cleanse any space. Now you're ready for spring.

James Kambos

Notes:

March is the third month of the Gregorian calendar, and it was the first month of the Roman calendar. The month is named for the Roman god of agriculture and war, Mars. Its astrological sign is Pisces, the fish (February 18–March 20), a mutable water sign ruled by Neptune. In March we witness the power of the life-force. Plants begin to emerge from the cold Earth; from the bud will come the leaf. The winds still roar, but now they bring the promise of life renewed. In the old days, March's Full Moon was called the Storm Moon, a time when the icy grip of winter began to weaken. Ostara is the major Pagan celebration of the month, when we pause to celebrate the Goddess as she arises from her winter sleep. And now the light begins to overtake the darkness at the Vernal Equinox—the first day of spring. Signs of the season are everywhere. Robins begin building their nests and rabbits frolic in the grass. Daffodils brighten suburban lawns, and garden centers are stocked with soil, mulch, and new plants. For fertility magic, try dyeing eggs in pastel colors or decorating them with magical symbols. For a little March magic, grate some fresh ginger root and bless it by holding it beneath the rays of the Storm Moon. Then incorporate it into any love or success spell.

March 1
Sunday

1st ♉

Color of the day: Gold
Incense of the day: Marigold

New Day Spell

Work this spell at sunrise and take a moment to embrace all the magic and possibilities of a brand-new day. There are no accessories needed, just yourself and the sunrise. Turn and face the east. Feel the warmth and power of the Sun wash over you. Ground and center yourself, then repeat the charm when you are ready:

> As this new day begins, I
> stand and greet the dawn.
>
> May I help and heal others,
> and bring no one harm.
>
> I rejoice in the promise of a
> new magical day.
>
> Bring me love, success, and
> health in the best possible way.

Ellen Dugan

Notes:

Holiday lore: On March 1, Roman matrons held a festival known as Matronalia in honor of Juno Lucina, an aspect of the goddess Juno associated with light and childbirth. Some records indicated that her name was derived from a grove on the Esquiline Hill where a temple was dedicated to her in 375 BC. Whenever a baby entered the world in Roman times, it was believed that the infant was "brought to light." Women who worshipped Juno Lucina untied knots and unbraided their hair to release any entanglements that might block safe delivery.

March 2
Monday

1st ♉

Color of the day: Lavender
Incense of the day: Narcissus

Day of Knowledge

Knowledge is one of our most important tools of growth. Those who oppose growth want to keep knowledge out of our reach. Everyone has the right to take a day off occasionally to appease the hunger of the mind. Instead of taking a "sick day," take today as a "well day." Use the day to indulge and improve your mind. Go to the library or the book store. Take your time and browse. Pick whatever book appeals to you most, especially if it is something you wouldn't normally read. Spend the rest of the day reading your book in a quiet space, such as the library, an almost-empty café, a park, or curled up in your favorite chair. You can dedicate the day to Hypatia, a woman who taught mathematics, astronomy, and astrology in ancient Greece; Athena, the goddess of wisdom; or the muses. You will return to the world tomorrow refreshed.

Cerridwen Iris Shea

Notes:

simple or quite elaborate. Dolls represent the past, both in terms of your own childhood and your ancestors. Did you play with dolls or action figures in your youth? Which were your favorites, and why? Did you imagine that your dolls could move or talk? Sometimes spirit guides or other guardians take the form of a doll so they can interact with children. Honor the dolls of your past by displaying them or pictures of them. If you can afford it, buy a nice doll for a needy child who might not otherwise have one.

Elizabeth Barrette

Notes:

March 3
Tuesday

 1st ♉
☽ → ♊ 2:59 am

Color of the day: Maroon
Incense of the day: Bayberry

Doll Festival

Today is Hina-matsuri, the Japanese Doll Festival. Girls in Japan lay out a red cloth and arrange dolls that represent the Emperor and Empress, their attendants, the girl's own ancestors, and other worthy personages. These displays can be

March 4
Wednesday

1st ♊
2nd Quarter 2:46 am

Color of the day: Brown
Incense of the day: Lavender

Celebrate Life Spell

Happy Birthday to You" was first published on this day in 1924. Time to throw yourself and your friends a celebration of life spell!

Have each person you invite bring a picture of themselves when they were young and any others from important times of their life. Place the pictures on the altar and, while calling the directions, say:

> From our beginning to our
> end, we celebrate our lives
> and our achievements.
>
> Great Goddess, we give thee
> thanks for all the lessons
> learned, all the richness
> of experience and the joys
> bestowed upon us.
>
> May our life continue to be a
> celebration of life. Blessed be.

Later, have each person write a secret wish on a birthday card and place them in a sealed envelope. In the next year to come, revisit these wishes with your friends, opening the cards and sharing stories. End the celebration with a birthday cake.

Nancy Bennett

Notes:

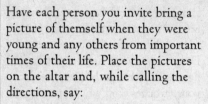

March 5
Thursday

 2nd ♊
$\mathcal{D} \rightarrow$ ♋ 6:07 am

Color of the day: Green
Incense of the day: Jasmine

A Spell for Study and Art

Today the Moon is in Gemini, which is ruled by Mercury. Mercury is aligned to a number of deities, such as the Egyptian Thoth, the Greek Hermes, the Roman Mercury, and the Norse Woden. Any of these deities can be called upon to aid in study, research, and the creative arts. For this mini-spell, you may wish to call upon your deity of choice or simply invite the air spirits. Air is aligned to the mental plane, which is that of creation and creativity. Consult your favorite magical herbal and select some dried herbs that are attuned to the planet Mercury and/or the element air. Light a charcoal briquette (only the kind that's designed for indoor use as an incense burner) and have it in your study or art space. Get a yellow candle to represent air, the east, and the mind. When you sit down to get creative, surround the yellow candle with the mixture of herbs, putting some of them on the lit charcoal to create a cloud of intellectual smoke that can drift pleasantly throughout the room. Say:

*Great God _____, I call
upon your Mercurial power
as I ready myself to connect
with the mental plane. Great
spirits of air . . . flying
sylphs . . . mighty guardian
Raphael . . . I invite your
presence into the space to
bless my work and set the
pace. As research and art are
sacred acts, so then are my
creations. Be with me in love
and in light. So mote it be.*

Raven Digitalis

Notes:

packet and light the pink and green
candles. Repeat the following chant
as many times as you like:

*Green and growing
Life is flowing
Seeds I'm sowing
Bring new life.*

Find a suitable area for the plant or
plant the seeds, either indoors or
outside when weather permits.

Ember

Notes:

March 6
Friday

2nd ♋

Color of the day: Pink
Incense of the day: Orchid

Plant Blessing

This is a good time of year to
bless seeds or a plant for your
home. Place the seeds or plant on
your altar or table and decorate the
space with bright spring colors,
especially pastel green and pink. Tie
ribbons around the plant or seed

March 7
Saturday

2nd ♋
☽ → ♌ 8:24 am

Color of the day: Blue
Incense of the day: Magnolia

Hematite Elemental Connection

Collect eight pieces of hematite
stone. Spend the day with them
in your pocket or in a sachet around
your neck. Fondle them gently and
carefully once each hour of the day.
Feel the smooth and cool energy
emitting from them. Allow that
energy to seep into your fingertips
and palms. Feel your warmth and

the energy of your body leaving you and entering the stone in exchange. Throughout the day, sense the stones warming in response each time you touch them and become aware of the hematite energy fusing with your own in balance and harmony. When the day is done, take yourself to a river, lake, or pond. Lovingly remove the stones from your pocket one at a time and exchange energy one last time. Toss the stones into the water, envisioning with each stone its total journey from your hand to the bedrock beneath the surface of water. When all the stones have left you, sense their presence, feel them beneath the waters and become aware of your energy with them, cradled within water: the blood of the Earth. Know that your energy has intertwined with the stones. Through you, they have connected with life, and through them, you are connected to the moving, invigorating flow of the energies of Earth.

Estha McNevin

Notes:

Holiday lore: Although the month of June is named for Juno, principal goddess of the Roman pantheon, major festivals dedicated to her are scattered throughout the year. For instance, today marks Junoalia, a festival in honor of Juno celebrated in solemnity by matrons. Two images of Juno made of cypress were borne in a procession of twenty-seven girls dressed in long robes, singing a hymn to the goddess composed by the poet Livius. Along the way, the procession would dance in the great field of Rome before proceeding ahead to the temple of Juno.

March 8
Sunday

Daylight Saving Time begins 2 am

2nd ♌

Color of the day: Amber
Incense of the day: Juniper

Vacation Spell

With solar energies on the upswing, it's time to start thinking about your summer vacation. Even if you aren't sure you'll have time or money for a vacation, why not cast a vacation spell? Gather whatever information you have about places you'd like to visit. Gather your travel books and brochures, along with printouts from the Internet for airplane flights, rental cars, hotels, and attractions. Lay them on the floor in a circle around you. Stand in the center and cast the circle by thinking or saying aloud places you would like to go in the four directions. Picture yourself at the place that seems most attractive to you, lying on the beach, seeing the sights, or doing whichever activity is most appealing. For as long as you can, concentrate on that image, then say, "So mote it be," and release the energy.

Magenta Griffith

Notes:

Holiday lore: While most holidays across the world celebrate the lives and achievement of men, March 8 is one day wholly dedicated to the achievement and work of women. Originally inspired by a pair of mid-nineteenth-century ladies' garment workers' strikes, today the holiday is little known in its country of origin; though this day's legacy is clear in March's designation by the U.S. Congress as Women's History Month. Throughout the month, women's groups in many American towns hold celebrations and events,

concerts, exhibitions, and rituals that recall heroic and gifted women of every stripe.

March 9
Monday

2nd ♌
☽ → ♍ 11:34 am

Color of the day: Gray
Incense of the day: Neroli

Find a New Home Spell

Find pictures of what you want your new home to resemble. Visualize the yard or garden as well as the city, area, neighborhood, schools, your ideal commute to work, and everything you find important. Combine these pictures with a Four of Wands tarot image. Light a green candle sprinkled with rosemary and sage and visualize yourself and your family living in that very house. Actually feel the happiness exuding from all of you. Then say:

Of all the places on this beautiful Earth,

This enchanting home we shall call our own hearth!

To Hestia, we plea to make our dreams real,

*And while we are wishing,
please make it a great deal!*

Finish by visualizing the timing imagined and know it will happen!

Calantirniel

Notes:

March 10
Tuesday
Purim

2nd ♏
Full Moon 10:38 pm

Color of the day: Black
Incense of the day: Basil

Full Moon Closure

Full Moon is a time of closure and thanks as the energies begin their downward cycle. This is the final Full Moon before the start of spring, so tonight is an excellent time to look back over what you have pondered during the winter season. Reflect on your intentions in the fertile seasons ahead. Take the time to thank yourself for the energy you have committed to your own growth and change. Thank the Lady for her energy, guidance, and blessings upon your season of rest and renewal.

*Lady Moon, beautiful light
Glorious you shine in the
    dark of night
Sharing my path and lighting
    my way
Marking the passage of each day
I bless your presence in my life*

*Lady Mother, mistress so fair
Keeper of earth, water, fire,
    and air
I thank you for the energy
    you give
And honor your blessings in
    how I live
I bless your presence in my life*

So mote it be.

Winter Wren

Notes:

March 11
Wednesday

3rd ♍

☽ → ♎ 2:46 pm

Color of the day: Yellow
Incense of the day: Lilac

Festival of Colors

On this day, Hindu people celebrate Holi, the Festival of Colors. It is a time of revelry, pranks, and general silliness. But the most distinctive part of this holiday is the custom of throwing colored powders and water on each other. This represents the brilliant hues of spring flowers. Celebrate Holi with your friends by obtaining some colored powders (powdered chalk, tempera paint, etc.) and/or colored water (use a few drops of food coloring or Easter egg dye). Wear white or light-colored clothes that you don't mind wrecking—or at least re-coloring!—and splash each other generously. Now here's the magical part: Charge each batch of powder or water with color energy. Red is physical energy, blue is spiritual, green is healing, and so on. Bless your friends with the color of the energy you believe they need most at this time. This is a fun family ritual to perform with small children, too.

Elizabeth Barrette

Notes:

March 12
Thursday

3rd ♎

Color of the day: White
Incense of the day: Clove

Spell for Good Health

Anemones, also known as windflower or Ladies Flower, bloom this month. Anemone was a nymph favored by the wind god Zephyr and turned into a flower by the jealous goddess Flora. The frail-looking flower can withstand March's cold temperatures and blustery winds. Windflowers close their petals and droop their heads at night or in wet weather. The fairies favor windflowers, choosing to curl up and sleep within their closed petals at night. An old proverb says:

> March windflowers so frail
> and pure,
> Keep infection from your door.

Gather the first blooms in a square of red cloth and sew the edges together. Sleep with the sachet under your pillow or wear it on your person to ensure good health. You can also plant the red anemones by your front door to guard the house from disease and infection.

Lily Gardner

Notes:

March 13
Friday

3rd ♎

☽ → ♏ 8:22 pm

Color of the day: Coral
Incense of the day: Alder

Freya Friday Spell

Hurray, it's Friday the thirteenth, a good-luck day for Pagans and Witches everywhere! The day Friday is named after and sacred to Freya, the Norse goddess of magic and prophecy. Let's see what kind of wonderful things we can conjure up with Freya's help! Now, you may burn a pink candle for Friday or an amber-colored candle to honor the goddess Freya. It's completely up to you. Light the candle and repeat the charm:

> Freya's day is Friday, and the thirteenth is today,
>
> Let's work with these energies in a magical way.
>
> Freya, mistress of magic, bless us with your wisdom,
>
> As the candle burns away, the good luck spell begins.
>
> This good luck candle spell is spun from the heart,
>
> Worked for the good of all, with a Witch's art.

Ellen Dugan

Notes:

March 14
Saturday

3rd ♏

Color of the day: Indigo
Incense of the day: Rue

Banish Negativity

Now is a good time to rid yourself of anything negative that is bothering you. This could be something from the past you can't let go of, a negative attitude in general, or regrets. Or perhaps you feel someone is acting negatively toward you. Use this spell to break that negative energy. You will need a black candle and a small piece of string or sewing thread. Light the candle. Visualize the negative aspect you wish to dispel; the string represents this negativity. Now imagine yourself free from it and hold the string at each end, pulling it tight in the middle. Pass the center of the string through the candle flame as many times as it takes to burn through it. Once the string is severed, bury the pieces of string in separate locations. Allow the candle to burn out.

Ember

Notes:

March 15
Sunday

 3rd ♏

Color of the day: Yellow
Incense of the day: Almond

Spell for Good Fortune

Roman citizens celebrated the festival of Unfailing Years for the goddess Anna Perenna on this day. They picnicked in the country and made offerings of cake and wine to the Crone goddess in the hopes of assuring that the circle of the year would be completed happily. If you live in a climate where picnics in March are out of the question, bake a cake made with banana, hazelnuts, and a pinch of nutmeg for good fortune. Bring a large piece wrapped in green paper and a bottle of wine to your garden or a park in your neighborhood. Leave your offering beneath a tree of your choosing. As you pour the wine into the ground say:

From spring to summer,
 unfailing
From summer to autumn,
 unfailing
From autumn to winter,
 unfailing
From winter to spring,
 unfailing
Love and peace,
 unfailing
Good health, well-being,
 unfailing
Abundance, inspiration,
 unfailing
The sacred ring,
 unfailing.
Goddess, make it so!

Lily Gardner

Notes:

Holiday lore: Why is March 15 so notorious? On this date in 226 BC, an earthquake brought the Colossus of Rhodes—one of the Seven Wonders of the Ancient World—to its knees. But a more famous event likely accounts for the notoriety of the "Ides of March." Julius Caesar's rule, somewhere along the way, became tyrannical. In February of 44 BC, Caesar had himself named Dictator Perpetuus—Dictator for Life. Brutus assassinated him on

March 15. Caesar's murder was foretold by soothsayers and even by his wife, Calpurnia, who had a nightmare in which Caesar was being butchered like an animal. Caesar chose to ignore these portents and the rest, of course, is history.

this sacred ground." You and your tree are now connected.

James Kambos

Notes:

March 16
Monday

3rd ♏

☽ → ♐ 5:21 am

Color of the day: Ivory
Incense of the day: Clary sage

A Magic Tree Spell

Now the trees are flourishing with the promise of new life. Buds are swelling and the sap is rising. Trees are frequently used in magic and now is a good time to select your very own magic tree. This will be a tree you'll wish to use in your magical work. For example, if a spell calls for a leaf, a bit of bark, or a twig, this will be the tree that will provide that item. Take a walk in a secluded area and see if there is a tree to which you are drawn. Then, make an offering to the tree. You may bury a coin near the trunk or sprinkle some birdseed. Now you've formed a pact with your tree. Seal your pact by saying: "Magic tree, I offer a humble gift to thee. From root to leaf, I bless

March 17
Tuesday
St. Patrick's Day

3rd ♐

Color of the day: Red
Incense of the day: Ginger

Celtic heritage Day

Celtic music fills the air, cauldrons of faerie gold are displayed, and everyone's wearing colors of the sacred Earth. Today, we modern Pagans can honor the ancient Celtic tribes, knowing we are proof of their perseverance, reclaiming the traditions of our spiritual ancestors. Ireland's a land of faerie mounds and lay lines; add its power to your magic with this journey. Close your eyes, chanting nine times:

Emerald isles, you call me in light and mirth,

Unto the bright lands of my spiritual birth.

Visualize yourself soaring over a land of rolling hills and standing stones. As you soar across the land, it hums with life. You and the land are one. Returning from your journey, bring the magic and power of the land with you, knowing you can return there anytime you wish. The ancients bless and smile upon you as you remember the old ways.

Mickie Mueller

Notes:

H oliday lore: Much folklore surrounds St. Patrick's Day. Though originally a Catholic holy day, St. Patrick's Day has evolved into more of a secular holiday today. One traditional icon of the day is the shamrock. This stems from an Irish tale that tells how Patrick used the three-leafed shamrock to explain the Trinity of Christian dogma. His followers adopted the custom of wearing a shamrock on his feast day; though why we wear green on this day is less clear. St. Patrick's Day came to America in 1737, the date of the first public celebration of the holiday in Boston.

March 18
Wednesday

3rd ♐
4th Quarter 1:47 pm
☽ → ♑ 5:18 pm

Color of the day: White
Incense of the day: Honeysuckle

Travel Protection Charm

T raveling can be stressful and nerve-wracking. Use this charm to boost your protective energies. You'll need a pen, a piece of paper, and sandalwood oil. Sign your full name in the center of the paper, then draw a large pentacle on top of your signature. Hold the spell sheet in your hands and visualize yourself in a bubble of white, protective light. Next, put a drop of the sandalwood oil on the tip of your finger and slowly trace the edge of the sheet. Work in a clockwise manner and go all the way around the paper. Use additional drops of sandalwood if necessary. When you're finished, say this incantation:

> By foot, by car
> by train or plane
> protected I shall always remain.

Fold the paper up into a small square and keep it in your wallet or purse.

Gwinevere Rain

Notes:

March 19
Thursday

4th ♏

Color of the day: Purple
Incense of the day: Carnation

Festival of Quinquatrus

This is a Roman festival, named and placed because it begins on the fifth day after The Ides of March. The festival is sacred to Minerva and is considered an auspicious day for divination. Set up a quiet space with candles, incense, and your divination tool of choice. Offer up thanks to Minerva for her guidance. Use this time to explore options in regards to important issues that have weighed on you in the past days and weeks. Instead of doing a quick "check-in" type of divination, use some of the longer spreads or meditations. Explore questions in more depth than you usually get the chance to do. Even better, use today as a chance to celebrate with a friend who also practices divination by swapping readings. That outside eye sometimes helps place things into perspective and opens up possibilities you might not have noticed on your own.

Cerridwen Iris Shea

Notes:

March 20
Friday

Ostara – Spring Equinox –
International Astrology Day

4th ♏

☉ → ♈ 7:43 am

Color of the day: Rose
Incense of the day: Cypress

Vernal Equinox

Today is the Vernal Equinox, the first day of spring in the Northern Hemisphere and the New Year in many ancient traditions. It is the time of new growth and new beginnings. Eggs are one symbol of this festival since they represent new life. To celebrate, decorate an altar or small table with a green cloth and place on it spring flowers, Pussy Willows in vases, or sprouting bulbs in pots. Place a bowl of hard-boiled eggs in the center. Cast a circle and call the quarters: east for the spring, now with us; south, for the summer that is to come; west, for the autumn far away; and north for the winter that is ending. Hold up an egg and say, "I dedicate this egg to new beginnings in the coming season." Meditate for a little while on your hopes for spring, then take that energy into you by cracking and eating the egg.

Magenta Griffith

Notes:

March 21
Saturday

4th ♑
☽ → ♒ 6:06 am

Color of the day: Black
Incense of the day: Pine

Spring Goddess Meditation

The wheel is turning and spring is imminent, though it is hard to feel that way after a long, hard winter. To feel the connection to the birthing of spring, dress in fresh, pastel colors. Light candles of yellow, sky blue, and lavender. Light orange-scented incense and settle into a meditative state. Close your eyes and feel your deep connection to Mother Earth. Find yourself in a fresh meadow full of white and yellow flowers. The Sun is shining and the birds are singing. Very still and sitting in the grass is a lovely young woman whom you know instinctively to be a goddess. She looks at you and smiles; you follow the direction of her eyes and see young animals frolicking in the grass. You smile and feel the delight of youth, birth, and freshness. You walk to her and she holds your hand. She whispers a word, something you need to know right now to connect to the zestfulness of new life. Then you take a deep breath and open your eyes back in the here and now. Write the whispered word on a yellow piece of paper and keep it as a reminder of your connection to the eternal youthfulness inside you.

Gail Wood

Notes:

March 22
Sunday

4th ♒

Color of the day: Orange
Incense of the day: Heliotrope

Releasing Toxins

Our bodies are sacred reflections both of our species' genetic pattern and of our individual spirits. We must strive to keep our bodies and minds healthy and aligned. In this culture, it's almost entirely impossible to live a completely pure, unpolluted lifestyle. It's essential to cleanse one's body of toxins that have built up over a period of time. An ideal way to do this is to perform a juice fast for a couple days or engage in a different type of fast. If performing any sort of physical fast or bodily detoxification, light a yellow candle to represent burning away unhealthy energy, both physical and metaphysical, as the two are

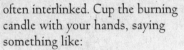

often interlinked. Cup the burning candle with your hands, saying something like:

> As this candle burns, I
> perform this physical detoxi-
> fication. May the alighting
> of this yellow wax signify the
> mutual cleansing of my body,
> spirit, and mind. Hail be,
> ever-changing universe. I ask
> that I be aligned to health,
> healing, and constant
> spiritual sustenance.
> So mote it be.

Though you have performed a physical and metaphysical detox, continue to be mindful of what you consume, as well as the situations you surround yourself with—mental health is just as important. Remain mindful of the origins of your food; you may even choose to eat only organic foods after researching genetic food modi-fication and its politics, or you might become vegetarian or vegan after researching the reality of the welfare of our animal allies.

Raven Digitalis

Notes:

Holiday lore: Cybele was the Great Mother of the gods in Ida, and she was taken to Rome from Phrygia in 204 BC. She was also considered the Great Mother of all Asia Minor. Her festivals were known as *ludi*, or "games," and were solemnized with various mysterious rites. Along with Hecate and Demeter of Eleusis, Cybele was one of the leading deities of Rome when mystery cults were at their prime. Hila'aria, or "Hilaria," originally seemed to have been a name given to any day or season of rejoicing that was either private or public. Such days were devoted to general rejoicing and people were not allowed to show signs of grief or sorrow. The Hilaria actually falls on March 25 and is the last day of a festival of Cybele that commences today. However, the Hilaria was not mentioned in the Roman calendar or in Ovid's *Fasti*.

March 23
Monday

4th ♒
☽ → ♓ 5:08 pm

Color of the day: Silver
Incense of the day: Lily

Selene Dream Spell

Today is Monday, and we are in a waning Moon. Mondays are associated with all lunar magic. This is an excellent time to banish any nightmares that may have been troubling you. Call on Selene, the Greek Goddess of the Moon. Selene is very fond of Witches and is well known for her practical magic. For this spell you will require a small moonstone. Hold the moonstone in your projective hand and repeat the charm three times:

> By the silver light of
>   Monday's waning Moon,
> I now ask Selene, for a
>   magical boon,
> Ward off bad dreams, allow
>   me to rest and sleep,
> A token of your magic, with
>   me I will keep.
> By the magic of three
>   times three,
> As I will it, so must it be!

Now keep the stone with you—on your person during the day and near the bed at night while you sleep. Sweet dreams!

Ellen Dugan

Notes:

March 24
Tuesday

4th ♓

Color of the day: White
Incense of the day: Geranium

Escape Spell

Today is the birthday of Harry Houdini (1874–1926), the famous magician and escape artist. To escape from a situation that binds you, gather together a sharp cutting knife, a length of cord with the ends tied together, a small black candle, and dragon's blood incense. Breathe deeply and ground yourself. Contemplate the situation that binds you but don't get caught up in the emotion of it. Light the black candle and the dragon's blood incense. Gather the cord in your hand and wave it through the incense and chant, "Banish suppression and oppression" three times. Do the same with the black candle. With the knife, cut the cord in three places, and chant with each cut, "By the power of the sword, I gain freedom with cut cord."

Place the cord in front of the candle, stretch out your arms and shout at least three times, "I am so happy now that I am FREE!" Bury the remains of the cord and dispose of the candle wax and incense ash in the same way.

Gail Wood

Notes:

March 25
Wednesday

4th ♓

Color of the day: Topaz
Incense of the day: Bay laurel

Banish Destructive Forces

Construct a paper doll image of the issues or people causing destruction in your life. Make dolls to represent all of the inadequacies and frustrations that you feel. Talk to your dollies and communicate with them. Tell them how they make you feel and recite to them the ways in which they cause destruction. In a large bowl, light each doll on fire and spit on it with the intention of separating yourself from the destructive energy depicted by the doll. Before the flames subside, drown them with wine. Empty the

dregs into freshly tilled soil or into an unused planter.

Estha McNevin

Notes:

March 26
Thursday

4th ♓
☽ → ♈ 1:03 am
New Moon 12:06 pm

Color of the day: Crimson
Incense of the day: Nutmeg

New Moon Spring Spell

Spring is the season of new life, beginnings, and growth. So too, the New Moon is a time of renewal and rebirth; it represents the Maiden goddess. This is an auspicious time to start projects, till gardens, and otherwise begin things that will take a while to reach fruition. The Moonflower (*Ipomoea alba*) vine grows up to fifteen feet high. Its fragrant white flowers bloom at night, attracting moths. This plant manifests lunar energies and makes an ideal centerpiece for a Moon garden of white, night-blooming plants. For the best results, soak Moonflower seeds overnight in a bowl of water left where moonlight can shine on it. Cultivate soil to 1/2-inch depth, sow seeds, and cover loosely. Pour the bowl of water over them. Then say:

> Maiden of the silver Moon,
> Show your flower face
>   here soon.
> Let them grow so swift
>   and high,
> Like a ladder to the sky.
> Perfume from your palace fair
> Hangs in sultry evening air.
> When the owls begin to sing,
> Bring white moths upon
>   the wing.
> Goddess, gloriously bright,
> Bless me now by New
>   Moon light.

Keep the soil moist until your flowers sprout. Use your Moonflowers as a focus for lunar work throughout the growing season.

Elizabeth Barrette

Notes:

March 27
Friday

1st ♈

Color of the day: Purple
Incense of the day: Vanilla

Enchanted Chocolate Strawberries

Strawberries are in season now. To make your love blossom, we will draw upon the energies of Friday for love, spring for growth, and chocolate, for, well, chocolate! You will need 2 pints of clean dry strawberries, 1 bag of chocolate chips, 1 tablespoon vegetable shortening, and wax paper on a cookie sheet. Melt the chocolate chips and shortening in the microwave. When completely melted, dip each strawberry in the chocolate and while coating, say:

> Close are we, my love and I,
>   As chocolate and strawberries
>   side by side,
> Enchant for me this
>   magical feast,
> Passionate love shall
>   be unleashed!

As each strawberry is coated, lay them out on the wax paper. When you're done, put them in the fridge for one hour. Make sure you tell your love that you have an enchanted and passionate dessert to share after dinner. Let the magic of your love be awakened!

Mickie Mueller

Notes:

March 28
Saturday

1st ♈

☽ → ♉ 6:09 am

Color of the day: Blue
Incense of the day: Patchouli

Yestarë

Yestarë is the Elven New Year—the first of seven Elven feasts mentioned by Professor J. R. R. Tolkien in the appendices of *The Return of the King*, the last volume of The Lord of the Rings trilogy. In the *Tië eldaliéva* tradition, it is aligned with Vairë the Weaver. She resonates with the weaving of the threads of time: past, present, and future. Because of this, we can see her "cutting" the fabric of the old year and beginning this year anew. To meet Vairë, light a white or gray candle and visualize yourself facing west, crossing a great ocean. You see a lovely island, the Blessed Realm. On the shores, you see a wondrous hall of gray stone. Vairë greets you here and shows you the stories woven into the fabric of your life thus far and even points out the fabric of your future. She shows you how to change it if it is not to your liking—fabric can be unraveled and rewoven. After you reveal your future goals, she now creates a special piece in what appears to be shimmering black and white threads, and gently places it on your shoulders. It is light and heavy at the same time and you are overwhelmed with emotion. She tells you it is representative of your destiny, and she wishes you well. Come back to where you are, knowing Vairë's strength and constitution. Allow the fabric of your life to unfold.

Calantirniel

Notes:

March 29
Sunday

1st ♉

Color of the day: Gold
Incense of the day: Eucalyptus

The Festival of Ishtar

Ishtar, sometimes known as the sacred prostitute of Babylon, is the Babylonian goddess of fertility, sexual love, and war. She was a temperamental and fickle lover. That being said, allow yourself today to reflect on embracing your own sexual being. On a piece of paper, list things about your body and your sexuality that make you uncomfortable. Then, light a pink candle and send pink, healing light to any parts of yourself with which you have emotional discomfort. Embrace your sexual self for who you are and find peace within. After spending time for yourself, consider your own sexual relationships. Focus energy on things within them that are not right and comfortable for you. Send healing to those areas as well. Your sexual relationships should bring joy and pleasure into your life. Remember to be safe in them as well. Thank Ishtar for her presence in your life. Finish your meditations and enjoy the vibrancy of the day.

Winter Wren

Notes:

March 30
Monday

1st ♉
☽ → ♊ 9:36 am

Color of the day: White
Incense of the day: Rosemary

A Spell to Protect Your Health

It's National Doctors' Day and a good day for a health spell. Add sea salt to a bowl of clear water. Make a talisman with a smooth stone painted with a snake symbol. (You should use permanent paint or markers for this.) Place the stone, water, and a white candle on your table. Call the four directions and, facing center, say the following:

> Hygeia, goddess of healing,
> Hygeia, she of well-being,
> Grant me good health from
> this day,
> Sickness, ailments held at bay.
> With this stone I do ignite
> All the powers to keep me right.

Place the stone through the flame three times and then dip it in the water. Dry it with your breath. Carry the stone with you or leave it by your bedside to improve your health.

Nancy Bennett

Notes:

March 31
Tuesday

1st ♊

Color of the day: Gray
Incense of the day: Cedar

Banish Negativity Spell

The soft light of a March evening is the perfect time to perform spells banishing negativity or fear. The sudden jet-black nightfalls of winter have passed; they are replaced now with the lingering, pale light of March evenings. Begin this spell out of doors facing west as the Sun begins to set. If it's windy, even better. Truly look at the fading light of the dusk. What colors do you see? Imagine the colors of the evening sky cleansing any problem you have. Breathe deeply. You should feel your burdens leaving you with each exhalation. They're being harmlessly neutralized by this magical time known as twilight. As the fingers of dusk glide over the horizon and the Sun sinks lower, visualize your problems fading. Now your tensions will feel lighter. Walk silently away and just enjoy the earthy scents of the spring night.

James Kambos

Notes:

April is the fourth month of the Gregorian calendar and the first month of the astrological calendar. Its astrological sign is Aries, the ram (March 20–April 19), a cardinal fire sign ruled by Mars. The name of the month comes from the Latin *aprilis*, which derives from *aper*, or "boar," as April was thought to be the month of the boar. The sights and scents of April lift our spirits. Lawns are lush again, and tulips of every color dazzle the eye. Pink and white flowering trees burst into bloom, and the air is sweet with the fragrance of crab apple and freshly mown grass. It is easy to understand why colonial Americans referred to April's Full Moon as the Pink Moon. The month begins with April Fools' Day—a day of practical jokes, but also a day to honor the Trickster. Earth Day is observed on April 22 to help make us more aware of our environment and how we can better care for it. In the countryside, farmers return to their fields as plowing begins. At home, gardeners begin to plant early crops such as lettuce, onions, and spinach. During April in ancient Rome, Cybele the great Mother goddess was honored in one of the most important celebrations of the Roman calendar. She was regarded as the creator of everything and the ruler of the eternal cycle of life, death, and rebirth. To honor her, bring fragrant cut flowers into your home. They'll cleanse your living space.

April 1
Wednesday
April Fools' Day

 1st ♊

☽ → ♋ 12:30 pm

Color of the day: Brown
Incense of the day: Lavender

Smart Witch Study Spell

Use this spell to promote productive study sessions. You'll need an envelope, several bits of a lemon rind, dried rosemary, and a resealable bag. To begin, visualize a calming blue mist around your body. See it flow through your aura and feel it dissipate any anxiety. After a few deep breaths, open your eyes and run your fingers through the rosemary. Think of the subject you are studying and say, "Rosemary will help me remember." Smell the herb. Again, think of the subject, run your fingers through the lemon rinds and say, "Lemon will help my mind stay awake and sharp." Then smell the rind. Next, place the herb and lemon rind together in the envelope. Seal it closed and hold it up against your temple. Speak this incantation:

I cast this spell and cast it well
To aid me in my task
Mind remember, make it last.

Put the date on the envelope and place it in the resealable bag. Keep it close by whenever you study. Open up the bag and smell the lemon and herb mixture as needed to remind you of your goal.

Gwinevere Rain

Notes:

April 2
Thursday

 1st ♋

2nd Quarter 10:34 am

Color of the day: Green
Incense of the day: Apricot

A Grass Spell

Before human or beast walked our Earth, the wild grasses were growing and they were already ancient. Grass provides our planet with life-giving oxygen. Fresh green grass is one of April's most beautiful sights, and it's a good spell ingredient to use when you want to make a wish come true. Here is one such spell. On your altar light one yellow and one green candle. Between them place an ordinary rock and a few blades of common lawn grass. Concentrate on your desire. Then rub the grass on the rock until there is a green stain. Bury the grass and rock together and sprinkle the spot with water. Recite this charm: "Rock and grass, I return you to Mother Earth. What I want shall come to pass." Grass is the essence of the life force and will give energy to any spell.

James Kambos

Notes:

cycle? What has grown out of the winter's turn inward? Treat yourself with fresh flowers. Prepare a cake, cookies, or a casserole, and give it to a friend or neighbor. Send a note or an e-mail to someone with whom you've been out of touch for a while. Call your mother and catch up on the news. Use today to reconnect with the world.

Cerridwen Iris Shea

Notes:

April 3
Friday

2nd ♋
☽ → ♌ 3:32 pm

Color of the day: White
Incense of the day: Violet

Prosperpina's Rise

Some calendars mark today as the day of Prosperpina's rise from Hades to rejoin her mother and bring spring back to the world. Other calendars place it earlier or later in the cycle. Use today's energy to return the light to dark corners of your own life. Do you feel an awakening? Do you feel the need to reconnect, to come out of your winter's hibernation? What energy do you want to bring out into the world for the next

April 4
Saturday

2nd ♌

Color of the day: Indigo
Incense of the day: Ivy

Day of Isolation and Pampering

The Moon is in Leo. There's no better sign under which to pamper and spoil ourselves. Leo is, in fact, the most fabulous sign of them all . . . or is that just my subjective Leo nature speaking? Either way, Leo rules—at least it rules the energies of this spell! Today, isolate yourself from any and all human communication.

No contact with anyone but pets, period. This day of isolation will allow the fullness of your energy to emerge. Plan this day carefully! If you live with roommates, alert them of your intention ahead of time, and operate without interacting or looking at them the whole day through. Don't get on the Internet and don't write letters to other people. Simply take the day to positively isolate yourself from everyone. Choose carefully your day's activities. Spoil yourself! Here are some ideas: Cook an intricate, delicious meal for you and you alone. Walk naked around the house. Drink some wine. Take a bath. Create some art. Paint your nails. Perform a self-created ritual. Dress up and take photos. Sing! Whatever you do, let it be fabulous and self-empowering. The day is yours, and you must choose to truly respect and love yourself.

Raven Digitalis

Notes:

April 5
Sunday
Palm Sunday

2nd ♌
☽ → ♍ 7:01 pm

Color of the day: Orange
Incense of the day: Frankincense

Stick-To-It Spell

When it gets tough to stay on track for your goals (and you know that accomplishing these goals are in your highest good), light a green or brown candle, sprinkled with black or red pepper, and use the Chariot and Strength tarot images. With the Chariot card, see yourself having discernment, authority, and mastery over your tasks and yourself. See the Chariot, which is actually you, reaching your goals. With the Strength card, allow the Spirit to cut away any negativity and replenish you with the strength you need to accomplish everything you wish. Know this will happen, and feel good about yourself when the goals are completed!

Calantirniel

Notes:

April 6
Monday

2nd ♏

Color of the day: Lavender
Incense of the day: Hyssop

Dreaming up Inspiration

Have you had trouble finding the inspiration for a creative project? Using Monday's lunar energies, here's an opportunity to do some dream work for inspiration. Set a glass of water next to your bed, as well as a notebook and pen. Write down anything you can think of relating to the creative project you wish to work with. Repeat three times:

> I journey to the dreamtime,
> To search for what I seek,
> Inspiration shall come to me,
> My creative mind shall speak.

Place the paper in your pillowcase and drink all the water in the glass. When you awaken, you will probably recall some very vivid dreams about the project you are working on. Write them down immediately in the notebook, as dreams can be fleeting and dissipate the longer you are in the waking world.

Mickie Mueller

Notes:

April 7
Tuesday

2nd ♏

☽ → ♎ 11:22 pm

Color of the day: Red
Incense of the day: Ylang-ylang

A Meditation for healing

Dress in blue today to represent the ocean and/or green to represent Mother Earth, because today is World Health Day. Find a quiet place where you can be undisturbed. Picture in your mind the Earth slowly spinning. See the Sun rise above it, showering it in strong light. Breathe in deeply and then begin to chant:

> The world spins round
> the Sun rises bright
> soon will be found
> a way to make it right.
>
> The world spins round
> the wind blows free
> a way will soon be found
> to heal her and me.

As you chant, imagine the world cleansed of disease and despair. Picture rich forests, happy people, and clean water. Saturate yourself in these images. When you are done with your meditation, stand up and go outside. Breathe deep and send your healing energy out to the world with open arms.

Nancy Bennett

Notes:

April 9
Thursday
Passover begins

 2nd ♎
Full Moon 10:56 am

Color of the day: Turquoise
Incense of the day: Mulberry

Moon Magic

We sometimes forget that moonlight is simply the light of the Sun, reflected and softened for us to look at with the naked eye. How fortunate we are to have this mirror of light. When we honor the Moon, we also honor the Sun. Both celestial bodies are important to our lives. Find a place where you can see the Moon, either indoors or outside. Capture the moonlight by reflecting its image in a bowl or glass of water. Gaze upon the reflection for as long as you like, meditating, thinking of what you need: healing, strength, confidence, or just general well-being—anything you wish to manifest in your life. When you are ready, chant the following:

> Reflected light, sunlight
> at night,
> Gift of Earth's stone satellite;
> Silver, shining, sister Moon,
> I receive this light; the light
> of life.

April 8
Wednesday

2nd ♎
Color of the day: Yellow
Incense of the day: Honeysuckle

Cultivating Love with Pendulum

Spinning a pendulum clockwise in front of your chest, open your heart chakra. Feel the path of the pendulum draw out the light energy of your heart. As you do this, slowly chant ten times:

> I rightfully open the core of
> my being to give and receive
> love, freely without cause or
> expectation.

When you feel full of energy, spin the pendulum counterclockwise and chant slowly ten times:

> I seal love and light within
> me and all around me. So
> mote it be.

Estha McNevin

Notes:

Drink the water, imagining you are drinking the liquid light of the universe, of life itself. Feel your body being energized, healed, filled with magic, your spirit renewed. Leave a few drops and pour it on the ground or into a potted plant as an offering of thanks.

Ember

Notes:

April 10
Friday
Good Friday

3rd ♎

☽ → ♏ 5:23 am

Color of the day: Pink
Incense of the day: Thyme

hot Cross Buns

> *Good Friday comes this month, the old woman runs,*
>
> *With one-a-penny, two-a-penny, Hot Cross Buns.*
>
> *Whose virtue is, if you believe what's said,*
>
> *They'll not grow moldy like common bread.*

The Anglo-Saxons originally made these sacramental cakes to honor the spring goddess, Eostre. The early Christian church tried to ban the little cakes with no success, so they cut a cross on top of each bun and called them Hot Cross Buns. They are considered very lucky when eaten on Good Friday. Householders tucked a piece of a Hot Cross Bun in the rafters of their homes and barns to protect them from fire, mice, and other pests. Sailors brought a bun onboard to keep themselves safe from shipwreck. A piece of the bun crumbled into milk will cure stomach ailments. Recipes for Hot Cross Buns can be found on the Internet and in most cookbooks. What better way to respect the rhythms of the year than by observing this ancient practice?

Lily Gardner

Notes:

April 11
Saturday

3rd ♏

Color of the day: Blue
Incense of the day: Rue

Reflection on the Magical Life

Some thoughts for consideration as you begin your day: To simply practice magic does not make one a Witch. You must also live as a Witch. Walk with responsibility for your failures as well as your successes. Celebrate the cycles of the Moon and seasons, not because it is expected, but because it keeps you in tune with nature and the life force. All life is sacred; all acts are ritual. Do not take more from the Earth Mother than you need to live. Walk in right relation to the Mother and her creatures. Power is a sacred gift; use it wisely and with humility. Pride in power will bring failure. It should never be used to flaunt your ability or be lorded over others. Be certain of your intentions when performing any act of magic. Know that words are sacred, and use them wisely. Knowledge is the heart and soul of the Craft. You can never know too much about your art.

Winter Wren

Notes:

April 12
Sunday
Easter

3rd ♏

☽ → ♐ 2:00 pm

Color of the day: Yellow
Incense of the day: Almond

Easter

Easter Sunday is a day of rebirth and renewal in the Christian calendar. Even if you no longer observe this holiday (or never did), you can tap into the collective energy of the day. Millions of people throughout the world are concentrating their minds on rebirth. Some are wondering how much the hat cost the woman in the third row, but many are facing and mulling over the concepts of rebirth and renewal. You can see and feel the vibrations. You don't have to agree with the details of the concepts that produced the energy in order to make use of it. Where do you need rebirth in your life? What commitments need renewal? Use the positive aspects of today's energy to renew your commitment to your own growth and positive participation in your community. Ground and center at both ends of the day to prevent an energy hangover.

Cerridwen Iris Shea

Notes:

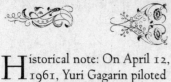

Historical note: On April 12, 1961, Yuri Gagarin piloted the first manned spaceship to leave the pull of our planet's gravity. This achievement is given much less attention than it deserves. Part of that is politics, since Gagarin was a cosmonaut for the Soviet Union. Part of it, too, is time; today, space pilots live and work for months aboard space stations, so a simple space flight seems routine. Still, Yuri Gagarin's 108-minute flight in space represented a triumph of science and engineering, and also broke a psychological barrier. It was literally a flight into the unknown. "Am I happy to be setting off on a cosmic flight?" said Yuri Gagarin in an interview before the launch. "Of course. In all ages and epochs people have experienced the greatest happiness in embarking upon new voyages of discovery . . . I say 'until we meet again' to you, dear friends, as we always say to each other when setting off on a long journey."

April 13
Monday

3rd ♐

Color of the day: Gray
Incense of the day: Lily

Spring Cleaning

Spring is in full swing, so it's a good day for spring cleaning. Physical cleaning is as important as psychic or spiritual cleaning. Get a stick of incense, preferably something aromatic like cedar or copal, or use a sage smudge. Gather your tools: brushes and brooms (remember the broom is a symbol of Witchcraft), rags, mops, and cleaning products. Put them in the middle of the kitchen or some other clear spot. Use the broom to draw a circle around them. Run water in a pail or bucket, add a pinch of salt, and recite, "Bless this water for cleansing, bless this salt for purifying." Sprinkle the blessed water on the cleaning supplies. Light the stick of incense and draw another circle around everything, reciting "Blessings of air and fire on these tools." Put the incense in a holder and allow it to burn down while you start to clean your home.

Magenta Griffith

Notes:

April 14
Tuesday

3rd ♐

Color of the day: White
Incense of the day: Ginger

Bird Augury

In many cultures, birds served as messengers between gods and humanity and later as bearers of truth. In ancient Rome, the augur divined the future from the activity of birds or the kinds of birds sighted. Bird lore abounds. It is said that hearing a cuckoo's song today signals a prosperous year ahead. If a blackbird builds a nest on your roof, good luck is yours. Make a wish when you see the first robin of the season for a year of good fortune. Doves are the messengers of Venus, for whom April is dedicated, and if you hear their song, love is on the way. Sparrows are the patrons of a happy home. A flock of chirping sparrows indicates rain is imminent. If you disturb a swallow's nest, your work will be unsuccessful. Learn to observe birds as a reflection of the divine in nature.

Lily Gardner

Notes:

April 15
Wednesday

3rd ♐

☽ → ♑ 1:27 am

Color of the day: Topaz
Incense of the day: Bay laurel

Reduce a Stressful Situation

When facing a particularly stressful situation, use this spell in conjunction with mundane efforts to help ease the tension. You'll need a well-ventilated area, a piece of paper, pen, fireproof cauldron, a calming essential oil (such as lavender or ylang-ylang), and a cotton ball. Write down things that you have been stressed about, pouring them into your letter. Then, tear the paper into tiny pieces and place them in your cauldron. Light the last piece of paper on fire and drop it in with the other papers. As you see them burning, visualize the stressful situation leaving you. Once the fire is completely out, retreat to a calm area of your home. Place one or two drops of oil onto the cotton ball, inhale the scent and say, "All is well." Meditate, write in your journal, or listen to soothing music to further reduce your stress.

Gwinevere Rain

Notes:

April 16
Thursday

Passover ends

3rd ♑

Color of the day: Purple

Incense of the day: Balsam

Planting Seeds Spell

Today marks the end of Passover and the beginning of spring for those of the Jewish faith. What better time to do a ritual around growing things! Gather your gardening tools, soil, seeds, and small containers. Place them on your altar and call the directions. Breathe deeply and say:

> Goddess Ceres, Mother of the Harvest.
>
> Goddess of the plants, of the time of growing.
>
> Ceres, I ask your blessings upon these items.
>
> May my garden spring forth, strong and bountiful.
>
> May my flowers scent the air and warm the senses.
>
> May my vegetables grow large and tasty.
>
> And may my plot be free of weeds.
>
> For this I ask your blessing, Ceres!

Even if you do not intend to have a garden, this is a good day to plant some seeds in a pot for your windowsill. Ask Ceres' blessing!

Nancy Bennett

Notes:

April 17
Friday

Orthodox Good Friday

3rd ♑
4th Quarter 9:36 am
☽ → ♒ 2:19 pm

Color of the day: Rose
Incense of the day: Mint

Honoring Animals

The American Society for the Prevention of Cruelty to Animals (ASPCA) was founded on this day in 1866, and it's a perfect day to honor creatures of fur, fin, hoof, and wing. Create a small outdoor altar made of found objects. Include some animal food and water on the altar. Bring feathers and other animal objects you may have. Sit before your altar and go into a light meditative state. Find yourself in a wild outdoor place. Take in the details of the area. In the north, you see a strong woman seated on a large rock surrounded by

the animals of the world. You know this is the Great Lady of the Beasts. Go before her and kneel. As you look into her face, you see the animals shift in her visage. Place a bowl of water at her feet and say, "May they never thirst." Place a bowl of food at her feet and say, "May they never hunger." Place leaves and grass at her feet and say, "May they always live life according to their nature," and then a rock, saying, "May they always be protected from cruelty." She accepts these gifts and blessings with thanks. She raises you to your feet, kisses you on both cheeks, and honors you as one of her creatures. In a twinkling of an eye, she is gone. Take a deep breath and return to the here and now.

Gail Wood

Notes:

April 18
Saturday

 4th ≈

Color of the day: Black
Incense of the day: Magnolia

Bill Banishing Spell

Many of us pay our bills on the weekend, so put this activity to good use. Remember that a bill is an extension of trust because the biller believes you can pay! Light a red, gray, or black candle with patchouli oil, and pay your bills as usual. However, when you are done, go through the invoices again. Get some old checks (or make blank ones) and write "void" in small letters so no one accidentally negotiates them! Then, write the "check" not for the monthly amount of the bill but for the entire balance due. If your car payment is $300, but your total balance is $8,645, write the "check" for $8,645, and then write "paid in full" and sign your name. "Pay" all of your balances, even one-time payments you haven't been able to afford yet. And definitely write a "check" to pay off the mortgage on your house, or, if renting, write a check for the amount of a house you want. Keep these "checks" in a pile, while feeling free of all debt and paying only with cash from now on. Burn the "checks," knowing this energy is launched. Expect miracles!

Calantirniel

Notes:

April 19
Sunday

Orthodox Easter

 4th ≈

☉ → ♉ 6:44 pm

Color of the day: Gold
Incense of the day: Marigold

Sowing Seeds of Change

Convert a large glass bottle into a small terrarium. Place a layer of stones along the bottom of the bottle to allow drainage and cover with enough dirt to provide 2 to 3 inches of soil. Add seeds by pressing them into the soil and covering them with a long chopstick or spoon. As you do so, chant, "I now sow these seeds of change." On the outside of the bottle, write or draw symbols of the ways in which you would like to grow in the season to come. Place your terrarium in a partially shaded window or light-filled room. Tenderly water and care for your bottle of life to ensure that your progression manifests with tender perfection.

Estha McNevin

Notes:

April 20
Monday

 4th ≈

☽ → ♓ 1:55 am

Color of the day: Silver
Incense of the day: Clary sage

Washing Away Negativity

Today is a Monday and we are in a waning Moon, so let's use the "April showers" that are traditionally occurring at this time of year to wash away any negativity that may be hanging about. If it isn't raining today, this spell could be easily adapted to work in the bathroom shower! Get out in the rain, or under the water, and repeat the charm three times:

> *April showers bring May flowers, we know that is true,*
>
> *Let us speak this Witch's rhyme to wash away the blues.*
>
> *April showers wash away all negativity,*
>
> *By the powers of the waning Moon, now must it be!*

Ellen Dugan

Notes:

April 21
Tuesday

4th ♓

Color of the day: Black
Incense of the day: Geranium

Conquer Fear

Most of us have hidden fears or anxieties about something. This is a good day to begin overcoming any of these that have become a burden to you. Use a red candle and any stones of your choice. Write down your fears and worries on a small piece of paper and place it in the bottom of a candleholder. Place the candle on top of the paper and light the wick. Next, begin using the stones to build a circle around the candleholder. Imagine you are building a fortress of strength. As you put each stone in place, repeat the following: "Fear is crushed, fear is conquered." As the candle burns down, visualize it conquering the fears you addressed. Allow it to burn completely. Discard the wax and paper.

Ember

Notes:

April 22
Wednesday
Earth Day

4th ♓
☽ → ♈ 10:09 am

Color of the day: Brown
Incense of the day: Marjoram

An Earth Day Spell

The Earth does not belong to us; rather, we belong to the Earth. This is a truth I learned many years ago on my grandparents' farm. From the Earth come the crops, and from the crops come the food that fuels our bodies. The Earth, in fact, has fueled all civilization for centuries. Let this spell return you to the power of the Earth. With your hands, scoop up a small amount of soil. It may contain a bit of grass, rocks, bark, or any natural object. Press the soil into a small ball and let it dry upon a piece of coarse cloth, such as burlap. Then, tie up the corners of the fabric. Keep this sacred Earth bundle as a token of the powers of the Earth. Place it upon your altar when you need some Earth energy for spellwork. If possible, go to a local farmers' market and purchase some produce or bread. As you eat the natural products, stop and think about where they came from. Reflect, and give thanks to the Earth and to the ancient farmers who first tended the soil. Without them, our civilization would not exist. Blessed be.

James Kambos

Notes:

Pour the salad dressing in the shape of your chosen symbol and say:

> Green leaves, new growth,
> In self and world both.
> This spell's complete:
> You are what you eat.

As you eat, concentrate on taking in the quality you desire.

Elizabeth Barrette

Notes:

April 23
Thursday

4th ♈

Color of the day: White
Incense of the day: Carnation

Spring Salad Spell

Spring makes everything sprout new growth. Seeds put out shoots; trees put out new leaves; bulbs put out the first flowers of the season. Of course, you are what you eat. This spell uses spring greens to cultivate personal growth. Decide on a quality you want to improve and a symbol for it, such as a peace symbol for holding onto your temper or a Gebo (X) rune for generosity. Prepare a salad with mixed-leaf lettuces and your favorite vegetables or fruits, perhaps including some edible flowers. If you grow your own herbs, they should be greening now, so toss in a few of those new shoots.

April 24
Friday

4th ♈
☽ → ♉ 2:46 pm
New Moon 11:22 pm

Color of the day: Coral
Incense of the day: Rose

The Sound of Silence

This evening's New Moon will assist with this exercise, and you may wish to incorporate it into your Dark Moon esbat. Sit in complete darkness, in a comfortable, meditative position. Meditate for as long as you'd like. In the meditation, try to hear the "sound of silence." Bring

your ears' attention to the silence around you. Eventually, you will begin to hear a light "hum." This is vibration. Keep your ears focused on this "noise" and nothing else. Focus on it until it takes you over. When this happens, the silent "sound" will seem deafening. When this sensation becomes too overwhelming, snap yourself out of the trance by inhaling loudly, bringing your audile focus elsewhere. This profound act takes time to hone and is difficult to describe. Once you experience the sound of silence, you will know exactly what I mean. Bringing yourself into a meditative state, perhaps before a ritual or spell, immerse yourself in the essence of this vibration. It will help attune you to the now— this reality, this stitch in time.

Raven Digitalis

Notes:

April 25
Saturday

1st ♉

Color of the day: Blue
Incense of the day: Sandalwood

Cover Your Assets Spell

They say the Romans had a god for everything. Well, today's New Moon also falls on the festival of Robigus, the Roman god who banishes mildew! You can't make this stuff up! The ancient Romans petitioned Robigus to prevent mildew from ruining crops of grain. Not a problem you have in your modern life? The wheat crops were the wealth of the Roman people and determined their prosperity. A modern equivalent could be a spell to ward and protect your assets. Carve a hole in a dinner roll big enough to fit a votive holder. Carve a dollar sign and an equal-armed cross on a red votive (red is sacred to Robigus). Anoint the candle with patchouli oil. Place the holder in the roll and light it. This arrangement represents your finances connecting to the ancient grain harvest.

> Protect the harvest of
> my assets
> Teach me frugality at
> its best,
> Shield my account from
> overspending,

Safe from scams or foolish lending.

Draw small equal-armed crosses on your checkbook and bankcard to ward them. This spell combined with common sense should protect your assets from draining away, and yes, even from mildew!

Mickie Mueller

Notes:

April 26
Sunday

1st ♉

☽ → ♊ 5:02 pm

Color of the day: Amber
Incense of the day: Hyacinth

Weather Spell

Many Pagans are interested in weather magic. However, it's a good idea to study something carefully before attempting to manipulate it. The changeable spring season is an ideal time to learn about your local weather. Pay attention to the forecasts and keep a record of how well they match the actual weather. By attuning yourself to the weather, you will increase your mystical influence. Say a rain blessing for every storm and the weather will quickly learn the sound of your voice. For example:

> *Sister Wind, thank you for traveling here.*

> *Brother Cloud, thank you for shading the sky.*

> *Sister Rain, thank you for watering the thirsty ground.*

Later, when you begin working magic for a desired type of weather, it will be easier to understand and therefore accomplish.

Elizabeth Barrette

Notes:

April 27
Monday

1st ♊

Color of the day: Ivory
Incense of the day: Neroli

Planting Flowers

Today is another excellent day to plant flowers around your home to be part of your shields. They can also provide an indicator of negative energy: if your plants die suddenly and without apparent cause, it may indicate harmful influences in the vicinity. Even a window box or a few plants on a windowsill can provide both inspiration and protection. If you aren't used to gardening, start with easy plants. Marigolds are excellent for protection, their scent tends to keep away harmful insects, and their orange and yellow blossoms are very cheerful. Get a packet of seeds and dirt or potting soil. Put the dirt in a pot, add the seeds, and cover with dirt as indicated on the seed packet. Then, bless a container of water, saying, "I bless this water for beauty and strength," and use it to water the seeds.

Magenta Griffith

Notes:

April 28
Tuesday

1st ♊

☽ → ♋ 6:38 pm

Color of the day: Gray
Incense of the day: Cedar

Flower Blessing

Today is the festival of Flora, the Roman goddess of flowers. Call on Flora to bless your gardens and all the pots of flowers and container gardens you've just planted. Flora is pictured as a lovely young woman carrying flowers. She wears a floral robe with garlands of flowers adorning her shoulders. The best way to contact Flora is to toss a few fresh flower petals in the air and call her name out loud. Then repeat this charm three times. Happy Floralia!

Today is Flora's festival day,
may it dawn bright and fair

Lady, please hear my call as I
toss these petals to the air

Bless my flowers, help them
grow healthy, strong, and true

May your power charm these
plants, blessing all I do.

Ellen Dugan

Notes:

April 29
Wednesday

 1st ♋

Color of the day: White
Incense of the day: Lilac

Taliesin Meditation

History purports this date as the birthday of Taliesin, the legendary Bard of Britain. In honor of him, let today's thoughts focus on creativity. Allow yourself a generous amount of uninterrupted time. Gather up a small blue candle, your favorite incense, a sheet of nice paper, and a pen or pencil you truly enjoy writing with. Settle yourself in a comfortable place for writing. Prepare for reflection and meditation in your usual manner. Light the candle and incense. Focus your mind on your creativity, whatever it may be. (There is creativity in all of us in some form.) As your mind cycles through your creative processes, note upon the paper what it is your creativity gives to you. Write down the creative things you are generating, and also write down thoughts about future creative endeavors. Keep your thoughts positive; the inner critic has no voice here. Let your dreams generate themselves on the paper in whatever way comes naturally. When you feel you are done reflecting, place the paper in a secure place where you see it often to remind you of your creative soul.

                              Winter Wren

Notes:

April 30
Thursday

 1st ♋
☽ → ♌ 8:56 pm

Color of the day: Crimson
Incense of the day: Jasmine

Beauty Ritual

Tonight is May Eve, and one of the customs for maintaining beauty is to wash your face in the morning dew of May Day. May Eve is a perfect time to seek peace and beauty. Spend the evening doing things that please you and bring you happiness. Rose scents promote a feeling of beauty and pleasure, and lavender promotes peace and joy. Breathe deeply and relax. As you get ready for bed, use rose-scented soap to wash your face. Gaze into the mirror and touch your chin and say, "Beautiful is my chin," then touch your lips and say, "Beautiful are my lips." Repeat for all parts of your

face, paying attention to details of skin, eyes, brows, and more. When you are done, bow to yourself in the mirror and say, "I honor the beauty within, and as within and so without. I honor the beauty of myself." Blessed be and sweet dreams.

Gail Wood

Notes:

May is the fifth month of the year. Its astrological sign is Taurus, the bull (April 19–May 20), a fixed earth sign ruled by Venus. The month is named for Maia, a Roman goddess and mother of the god Hermes. May is a month of fertility and abundance. This theme is celebrated on May 1, which is Beltane or May Day. On Beltane the union of the Goddess and God is celebrated. Customs for this day include placing flowers outside your front door and erecting a maypole. Traditionally, a maypole was the trunk of a fir tree with the side branches removed—a symbol of fertility and the God aspect. The Earth that supports the maypole represents the Goddess. The beauty of May is like a spring tonic. We are surrounded by color and fragrance. Dogwood trees bloom, pansies add a cheery touch to flower beds, and wild blue violets carpet dooryards. In some regions black locust trees bloom with honey-scented clusters of white flowers. Early settlers honored the floral display of May by calling this Full Moon the Flower Moon. May is also a month to remember the ancient fertility symbol of the Green Man. He brings abundance back to nature after winter's rest. Fashion a small doll from twigs or grass, and release the figure into a body of water. By doing so you're giving thanks for the bounty Mother Earth returns to us.

May 1
Friday
Beltane

1st ♌

2nd Quarter 4:44 pm

Color of the day: Purple
Incense of the day: Thyme

Beltane Magic Spell

It's Beltane day and we are at the halfway point between spring and summer. Today is a day for lover's trysts, beauty magic, and communing with the faeries. Gather some flowers from your garden or pick some up from the florist and arrange them in a vase in your home. Share a glass of wine with your loved one and sprinkle the bed sheets with fragrant rose petals. Light red and white candles to encourage love and magic and to bring the energies of the sabbat into your boudoir. You can keep it simple or really go for some drama, just as long as you set a magically romantic and passionate mood. Light your candles and repeat the charm. Blessed be!

Beltane is a day of magic, ardor, and love,

May the old ones now bless us all from up above.

A night for enchantment where faeries circle around,

Let my magic bring romance and let passion abound.

Ellen Dugan

Notes:

May 2
Saturday

2nd ♌

Color of the day: Gray
Incense of the day: Pine

Healing a Broken Heart

Our hearts get broken into pieces both big and small. Big love affairs cause big hurts and small slights cause minor fractures. To heal the heart broken by many small things, gather together a piece of red or pink fabric, scissors, paper, felt-tipped pen in red or pink, glue, a green candle for healing, and lavender incense for peace. Light the incense and breathe in the peaceful feeling. Draw a heart on the paper and cut out a similarly sized heart shape from the fabric. As you think about the small hurts that have fractured your heart, cut a piece from the heart-shaped fabric. When you are finished, take a deep breath and look at the pieces. Light the healing green candle and say, "By my magic and by my love, I mend my fractured heart." Start gluing the fabric pieces onto the heart shape on the paper. Fill in gaps with the colored pen, all the while concentrating on mending and re-knitting the fabric of your emotions and your heart. When you are done, hold the mended heart to your own heart and say, "Patched and healed, love revealed," until you feel wholeness again. Keep the patched heart in your journal as a testament to your ability to heal and to love again.

Gail Wood

Notes:

May 3
Sunday

2nd ♌
☽ → ♍ 12:37 am

Color of the day: Gold
Incense of the day: Heliotrope

Solar Success Spell

Cast this spell during the day, preferably at noon, to infuse your life with fruitful, successful energies. You'll need a yellow candle,

appropriate candleholder, bergamot oil, a piece of paper, and a pen with green ink. In front of a window with sunlight, hold the candle between your palms and visualize your goal. Rub a few drops of oil on your candle and place it in the holder. Light the wick and say this incantation:

> Oh dynamic Sun
> I draw down your solar energy
> Power of light and goodness
> To summon forth success
>   and prosperity
> And bind it to my name
> With harm to none, may it
>   be done
> So mote it be.

Finally, write your name with three dollar signs on the paper. Fold it up and keep it near the candle. Relight and visualize your goal a few days at noon until the candle is burnt down.

Gwinevere Rain

Notes:

May 4
Monday

2nd ♏

Color of the day: Lavender
Incense of the day: Clary sage

Megalesa

Depending upon which calendar you follow, the Megalesa games in honor of Cybele fall in either early April or early May. Unlike games to prove athletic prowess, these were considered "scenic," such as plays and tableaux in honor of the goddess. If you wish to celebrate with others, get together and discuss the basic outline of your play, pull together some simple props and costumes, and improvise the rest. Use the attitude of "I have a barn (yard, garage, living room), let's put on a play!" Invite friends and neighbors, or just invoke the goddess herself to observe. If you prefer to celebrate as a solitary, create a table display or diorama in honor of Cybele. Light candles and make offerings of honey and grain. Either way, make sure your table is abundant with festival food and drink, since Cybele is a primitive Earth goddess.

Cerridwen Iris Shea

Notes:

May 5
Tuesday
Cinco de Mayo

2nd ♏
☽ → ♎ 5:51 am

Color of the day: Gray
Incense of the day: Basil

Increasing Personal Prosperity

Gather a green seven-day candle, parchment, a pen with green ink, a pen with gold ink, and a malachite stone. Cast a circle in your usual manner. Say three times: "I have a right to prosperity. I draw to me the prosperity that is mine." While speaking this phrase, draw on the parchment symbols that represent prosperity to you (dollar sign, four-leaf clover, etc.). Say three times: "Prosperity surrounds me. Prosperity is mine." While speaking this phrase, trace over the green symbols with the gold pen. Fold the paper seven times and place it under the green candle in such a way that the malachite stone can also be placed atop the paper. Light the candle and say: "This candle lights the way for prosperity to come to me." Allow the candle to burns itself out. Each time you pass the candle and paper, repeat the chant. Once the candle is out, place the malachite stone in your purse or the pocket where you keep your cash or wallet.

Winter Wren

Notes:

Holiday lore: Don't confuse Cinco de Mayo with Mexican Independence Day on September 16. Cinco de Mayo marks the victory of the brave Mexican army over the French at the Battle of Puebla. Although the Mexican army was eventually defeated, the *Batalla de Puebla* became a symbol of Mexican unity and patriotism. With this victory, Mexico demonstrated to the world that Mexico and all of Latin America were willing to defend themselves against any foreign or imperialist intervention.

May 6
Wednesday

 2nd ♎

Color of the day: Yellow
Incense of the day: Bay laurel

Employment Satisfaction
If you're already happily employed, use this spell to achieve added success or increased job satisfaction. If you're searching, this spell can help you find a job that's right for you. It's important to keep an open mind, even if you think you know the perfect job. If you're searching, you should have some jobs in mind and be actively pursuing them. Just remember that sometimes the universe knows best and will lead you in an unexpected direction. Place one green candle and one orange candle together in a large dish or bowl. Sprinkle sage around the candles. Visualize your intent as you light the candles and invoke Janus, god of beginnings, for a literal new beginning or to approach your existing job with a new perspective.

> *Janus, bring me what I need*
> *In my career to succeed.*
> *Give me strength to know*
> *   and build*
> *The work to keep my life*
> *   fulfilled.*

Ember

Notes:

May 7
Thursday

2nd ♎
☽ → ♏ 12:48 pm

Color of the day: Turquoise
Incense of the day: Nutmeg

Learning to Trust Your Senses

On a solid white scarf or strip of fabric, write out "I do not need my eyes to see what is around me." Tie this around your head with the words facing you and then tie on a second, darker scarf. Practice blindly getting a sense for your environment alone at first. Explore your home and feel with your hands the shape, size, and texture of things and where they are in relation to your body. This exercise builds the power of the senses and helps the mind operate on a more astral level. In many ways, the eyes attach us to physical reality and can bind the other senses with overstimulation. Once you feel adept at defining and traveling within your physical space mentally, try doing small tasks blindfolded. As you perform actions, visualize them in your mind. Learn to rely less on your eyes as a sensory faculty and more on your other senses. If persistent, you may even delight in venturing out into safely enclosed spaces, such as a backyard or fenced garden. As your skill improves, your fingers will become adept at creating mental images.

When you have explored this for yourself with some success, try sharing this exercise with a magical partner or partners. Take turns wearing the blindfold to strengthen the bonds of trust and ensure personal safety if you wish to perform this exercise in open, populated, or wild spaces.

Estha McNevin

Notes:

May 8
Friday

 2nd ♏

Color of the day: Rose
Incense of the day: Violet

Spell for Luck

*With Hal-an-Tow! Jolly
Rumble, O!
For we are up as soon as
any day, O!
And for to fetch the
summer home,
The summer and the May, O!
For Summer is a-come!
And Winter is a-gone, O!*

Festivals throughout Great Britain celebrate the return of the Green Man and Flora. On this day, known as Furry Day, the celebrants dress in their best clothes, gather green boughs to decorate their houses, and wear sprigs of Lily of the Valley. It's considered a breach of conduct to work today; rather, they visit friends and dance through their houses and gardens, eventually spilling out into the streets. Plan a dinner party, or better yet, a dance party. Fill your house with greenery and flowers and raise a toast to Flora and the Green Man for a year of good fortune.

Lily Gardner

Notes:

May 9
Saturday

2nd ♏

Full Moon 12:01 am

☽ → ♐ 9:49 pm

Color of the day: Blue
Incense of the day: Sage

Full Moon Lemuralia

Lemuralia falls on the Full Moon this year, the Roman Feast of Lemures, who were the restless spirits of the dead that may have taken up residence in Roman homes.

Drawing upon the power of the Full Moon, now's the time to exorcise unwanted energies not in accord with your will and fill your home with bright, Full Moon energy. Set up your altar with white candles and flowers. Also include a dish of black beans sprinkled with sea salt in the middle of the altar. Barefoot, smudge your whole house with incense or sage. Any dark energies will be drawn and attached to the beans. Over the beans, repeat three times:

> Shadows of dark, to beans
>   of black,
> From whence you came,
>   return ye back
> By the Full Moon's power I
>   banish thee
> With these beans, I redeem
>   mine and me

Toss the beans out your front door and bang a cooking pot or ring a bell three times:

> Shadows flee, you
>   don't belong,
> Never to return, now
>   be gone!

Now feel your home clean, blessed, and brimming with Full Moon energy!

Mickie Mueller

Notes:

May 10
Sunday
Mother's Day

 3rd ♐

Color of the day: Amber
Incense of the day: Juniper

happy Moments Reminder

Find a picture or photograph that reminds you of a wonderful time in your life. This could be a scene from your childhood, a picture of a professional or athletic achievement, or a family portrait. It could be a famous painting you have always loved or a sketch bought at an art show. Frame the piece (or have it matted) so that it will stay in good condition. Put the picture where you can see it frequently. Once you have the picture in place, pick a time when you will be undisturbed. Face the picture and think of all the fond memories it holds for you. If you wish, invoke other senses: play music, smell oils or incense, touch cloth such as velvet or silk, taste a favorite food. Concentrate on the sensations and fix them to the sight of the picture so that whenever you see it, you can summon those feelings of that happy, successful moment.

Magenta Griffith

Notes:

May 11
Monday

3rd ♐

Color of the day: Silver
Incense of the day: Lily

Dancing Faeries

If there's one thing faeries are good at, it's dancing. They are light, airy, graceful creatures with an innate sense of music and motion. They infuse every dance with joy and beauty. You can call on the Fey to help improve your skill at any type of dance. For best results, invoke them regularly while practicing and also before dancing at a ritual or other public event. This spell is anchored to a green ribbon strung with bells. Tie the bells to your ankle or wrist, and say:

> Faery charm and Faery grace
> Guide my every step and pace.
> Lithe and lively be my feet
> As they're tapping out the beat.
> Laughing faeries twirl
>   and prance:
> Let their beauty fill my dance.

Turn on the music and dance the night away! You'll be as alluring as a faery yourself.

Elizabeth Barrette

Notes:

May 12
Tuesday

3rd ♐

☽ → ♑ 9:09 am

Color of the day: Red
Incense of the day: Cinnamon

A Garden Protection Spell

Now gardeners are beginning to plant their flower and vegetable gardens. After all your hard work, it's a good idea to protect your garden from pests. Here is a spell that may help without harming any cute but pesky little critters. In a small glass jar, mix about 1/4 cup each of vinegar and olive oil. Add a clove of finely chopped garlic, black pepper, and a dash of cumin. Shake well and let steep for a day. Sprinkle here and there around the edge of the garden plot or borders. End the spell by saying in a strong voice:

> *Creatures of the land*
> *And creatures which take flight,*
> *This garden is protected*
> *Both day and night.*
> *So mote it be.*

Repeat as needed.

James Kambos

Notes:

May 13
Wednesday

3rd ♑

Color of the day: Brown
Incense of the day: Honeysuckle

Discipline Your Memory Spell

A Capricorn Moon is excellent for any application of discipline and focus. Light a yellow candle sprinkled with lobelia. Visualize an image of your brain and visit the part that retains memory (you don't have to know where it is, just ask to see it). See what in there is keeping you from remembering and clear it out. If you can, stretch or expand this space, making "filing" areas for easy retrieval. To clear out the channels, go to the central nervous system, making sure the nerves (especially the optic nerves, if reading) are bringing and retrieving information properly. Now, picture yourself reading a book you are studying and see how easily your whole system retains and recalls information. Know your memory problem is solved.

Calantirniel

Notes:

May 14
Thursday

 3rd ♑

☽ → ♒ 10:01 pm

Color of the day: Purple
Incense of the day: Clove

A Blessing of a Lifetime

The planet Saturn rules Binah on the Kabbalah Tree of Life. This sephiroth is perceived as black in color, which has many other associations with the planet. Saturn also rules Capricorn, the sign the Moon is in today. This is a great day to work magic concerned with life's greater picture. This spell is actually a meditation. This evening, sit yourself in candlelit darkness, within a fully cast circle if you prefer. You may wish to perform this meditation in the bath because water is highly spiritual. When you are comfortable, call upon your own spiritual guides and guardians. If you don't have a personal relationship with them, simply ask that they be present, knowing that they exist regardless of your specific awareness of them. Take a very long time to mentally review your past, present, and future—in this incarnation only. Beginning by thinking the number 0, envision yourself in your mother's womb. Continue slowly, counting up in years, remembering or discovering anything about these years of your life that comes through.

Continue to the present moment and project into the future, enjoying any future visions you receive. As you envision or perceive experiences in your life, surround them in your mind with a white, healing, and accepting light, sending a vibration of peace through your past, present, and future.

Raven Digitalis

Notes:

May 15
Friday

 3rd ♒

Color of the day: Coral
Incense of the day: Vanilla

Friendship Spell

Today is Aio Matsuri Hollyhock festival in Japan. Place on your altar a large bouquet of red hollyhocks, water with sea salt, a bell, and some red ribbons. Light incense and call the directions. Then say, "Oh honored gods and goddesses. Hear my wishes." Sprinkle salt water to each direction and breathe deeply. After invoking each god or goddess, ring the bell.

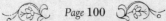

*Benten, goddess mother of
luck and love, may the keepers
of these flowers know love
and good fortune.*

*Fukurokuju, god of long life
and wisdom, may the keepers
of these flowers know good
health and knowledge.*

*Hotei, god of wealth and
laughter, may the keepers of
these flowers know joy and
freedom from worry.*

Ring the bell three times. Tie each
hollyhock with a red ribbon and
deliver to a friend. Make sure to give
one to yourself.

Nancy Bennett

Notes:

year on a positive note. Light soothing
incense and then light a blue candle
for clarity and openness. Put on
some gentle music and settle yourself
in a comfortable place. Relax, breathe
deeply, and let your tensions and
concerns leave your body with each
exiting breath. Once your mind is
settled, take time to reinforce all your
positive thoughts about your course-
work. You have done your work,
taken your notes, paid attention
in lectures. You know the material
before you. You are ready for your
exams. Meditate for about ten minutes.
Then make yourself a refreshing cup
of your favorite tea and return to
your studies refreshed, reassured, and
confident of the outcome. And don't
stay up too late studying!

Winter Wren

Notes:

May 16
Saturday

3rd ≈≈

Color of the day: Indigo
Incense of the day: Patchouli

The Exam Spell

With the end of the school
term upon us, today seems
a good time to focus on ending the

May 17
Sunday

3rd ♒
4th Quarter 3:26 am
☽ → ♓ 10:17 am

Color of the day: Yellow
Incense of the day: Marigold

A Vow of Silence

Silence is profound. Too often, we are immersed in conversation and verbal interaction, rarely having time to settle down, become quiet, and simply observe. We must make time for this. Sometimes it takes reserving an entire day of silence for the lesson to hit home. When you decide to do this, write a small note card to carry around that says something like: "I am undertaking a one-day vow of silence as a dedication to the gods." Throughout the day, if you are prompted to interact with anyone, you may choose to act in charades or write occasional messages on a sheet of paper. Many truths having to do with the energy exchange of human communication will reveal themselves throughout the day, as you are forced to remain silent, observe, and keep your energy relatively within yourself. You may wish to plan three to seven full days to perform a vow of silence; the lessons that this difficult and often humorous method of fasting can present are absolutely profound. Upon waking the morning after the end of the dedication, situate yourself in front of your altar and vocally chant a word or words of power to break the fast in a sacred manner.

Raven Digitalis

Notes:

May 18
Monday

4th ♓

Color of the day: White
Incense of the day: Narcissus

Banish the Blues

Mondays—or any time you have to return to a regular routine after time away—get a lot of people down. Start the day by drinking a glass of cool water. Bend down and touch your toes, then reach for the sky and stretch. Take several deep breaths. Get some sunlight if you can. You have at least one good reason to be glad today: you're alive! Repeat the following: "I'm thankful for today, for who I am and what I have in my life." Keep repeating, "I'm thankful for today," like a mantra. Words are powerful. Life is precious. Remember that today is the first day of the rest of your life. Make it a good one. And just so you don't forget, do something memorable today; wear a special ring, write yourself a note, or draw a smiley face on your hand, anything that will remind you. Make Mondays a regular day for a ritual of gratitude.

Ember

Notes:

for some extra magical fortification, garden Witch style. Once they are potted up and watered, enchant them for protection and courage with the following verse:

> May these red snapdragons
> ward and protect me well,
>
> Will it charm you or snap
> back, you can never tell,
>
> Let the courageous energies
> now circle 'round,
>
> No more negativity will ever
> be found.

Ellen Dugan

Notes:

May 19
Tuesday

 4th ♓
☽ → ♈ 7:30 pm

Color of the day: Black
Incense of the day: Geranium

Snapdragon Spell

Today is a Tuesday and the Moon is in a waning phase. We have an opportunity to go with the day's astrological energy of Mars, which brings courage and passion into the mix. This is a great time of year for snapdragon magic. The snapdragon is a protective flower associated with Mars and the element of fire. Why not plant a small container of bright-red and colorful blooming snapdragons? Add them to your porch or patio

May 20
Wednesday

 4th ♈
☉ → ♊ 5:51 pm

Color of the day: White
Incense of the day: Lavender

Leadership Spell

To enhance your leadership ability, gather together three or more of the following herbs in powder form: basil, garlic, orris root, poppy, and

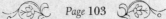

sunflower. Mix them together as you envision others following your effective lead. Visualize your leadership in the most positive terms. Place the powder on your altar and light patchouli incense and a red candle. Wave the powder through the incense and the candle, envisioning your responsibilities and rewards growing in strength. When you are done, sprinkle the powder in the shoes you will wear as you step into leadership and say, "Let others see in every deed, I have the power to lead." Extinguish the candle, thank the spirit, and go out and do a fabulous job!

Gail Wood

Notes:

things she is thankful for: her new baby, the support of her husband, her friends, her dog, her cat. She varies her list from week to week. Some things she has been thankful for include wonderful weather, bargains at the store, a raise at work, or a helpful friend. She believes doing this has made her more positive and aware of the many good things in her life, and the lists give her a record to look back on when life is difficult. This is a wonderful way to bring more positive energy into your life. Every Thursday, write a list of seven things you are thankful for. You can repeat yourself from week to week, as long as you keep a record of thankfulness.

Magenta Griffith

Notes:

May 21
Thursday

 4th ♈

Color of the day: Crimson
Incense of the day: Myrrh

Thankful Thursdays

A friend of mine decided that one Thanksgiving Day a year was not enough, so she started making every Thursday into Thankful Thursday. Each week, she writes a list of seven

May 22
Friday

 4th ♈
☽ → ♉ 12:40 am

Color of the day: Pink
Incense of the day: Alder

Nost-na-Lothion

The second of the seven Elven feasts is *Nost-na-Lothion*, the Birth of Flowers festival, and it marks the beginning of the warm season, Lairë. In the *Tië eldaliéva* tradition, it is aligned with Vána the Ever-Young. Vána resonates with the new green plant growth and has dominion over flowers. Light a green candle, close your eyes, and meet the golden-haired Vána on the green hills of the beautiful hidden Elven city, Gondolin. As she walks, see the hills fill with flowers of all kinds. See the golden light of *Anar*, the Sun, showering the moist land in warmth; hear the chirping of the songbirds; and smell the collectively sweet floral aroma floating on a warm breeze. Vána invites you to plant your seeds of intention to grow amongst the flowers, and you carefully see yourself doing so. Once your seeds are planted, your heart is uplifted as you see the Elven city's residents begin to dance! You join in the revelry and thoroughly enjoy this invigorating season with the *Quendi*, the Elves. Come back to where you are and enjoy the season!

Calantirniel

Notes:

May 23
Saturday

Color of the day: Black
Incense of the day: Magnolia

Binding Ribbons for Trust

Braid vines, reeds, or tall grasses while meditating on the people who love you most. Envision the plats of each braid as symbolic of the interlaced and supportive relationships you have in your life. When they are braided, tie the ends together with a thin lock of your hair bound by knots along a strip of green ribbon or string. For each knot, vocalize a strength or empowerment that the relationship has fortified. These grass hoops may be of any size or material and can help guide us in times of depression or trial. Hanging them in places where we retreat when we feel gloomy will produce the best results. Consensually binding the ribbon with the hair of friends and family will help to empower this spell with fidelity and genuine trust. Doing so without such trust will take little time to fester and backfire.

Estha McNevin

Notes:

May 24
Sunday

 4th ♉

☽ → ♊ 2:34 am

New Moon 8:11 am

Color of the day: Orange
Incense of the day: Hyacinth

New Moon Wishes

The New Moon is a good time for making wishes that can come true within two weeks. For this spell, you need pen and paper, a small fireproof bowl, and a white or silver Moon candle. Begin your spell on the night of the New Moon. Light the candle. Take some time to meditate on what you want. Describe your wish in a single sentence. Write that sentence on a slip of paper, saying:

> This is my wish. This is my will. Magic come forth—my wish fulfill!

Fold the paper toward you, creasing it in half; turn it to the side and fold toward you again, creasing it in quarters. Touch the paper to the candle flame and quickly say:

> As the flame burns, my light shines through. As the Moon turns, my wish comes true!

Drop the paper into the bowl, letting it burn out. Extinguish the candle, but leave it on your altar. Repeat every night of the waxing Moon. At the Full Moon, revise the final verse:

> Light of the Moon so strong and chill, I thank you for working my will.

Allow the candle to burn out.

Elizabeth Barrette

Notes:

May 25
Monday

Memorial Day (observed)

1st ♊

Color of the day: Ivory
Incense of the day: Neroli

Spell for Self-Love

We all need to spend a little less time listening to our inner critic and a little more time connecting with our inner god/goddess. Work this spell to boost your self-love. You'll need soothing music, a bubble bath, red juice or wine, and a silken robe. Set up your bathroom by turning on the music and drawing the bath. Place your juice or wine within reach. Stand by the tub and visualize all the negativity draining away from you into the Earth below. When you step in the water, say aloud, "I am blessed." Let the healing waters surround you. Visualize your heart charka opening. Take a sip of your drink and say, "I take within me goddess love, goddess spirit, the essence of creation, beauty see, beauty be." Soak in the tub, play with the bubbles, and enjoy the music. Afterward, dry off and wrap yourself in the silken robe. Embrace yourself and move on with your day.

Gwinevere Rain

Notes:

Four of Wands from a tarot deck. Honor the stability you have in your life. Make a commitment to stability (not stasis) in areas where you feel it is lacking. For one Moon cycle, spend a few minutes every day at the altar and perform one small action to achieve your desires. On the fourth day of the next 12 months, spend a few minutes at the altar with the same intentions and action.

Cerridwen Iris Shea

Notes:

May 26
Tuesday

 1st ♊

☽ → ♋ 2:58 am

Color of the day: Scarlet
Incense of the day: Ylang-ylang

Stability Day

In numerological terms, May 26 adds up to the number 4—a number of stability and endurance. Since we are in the Chinese year of the ox, this year's number 4 days have special power. Four is also the number of the physical elements: earth, air, fire, water. Prepare a special altar using a brown or green cloth. Light a green candle. Place a representation of each element on the altar, along with the

May 27
Wednesday

 1st ♋

Color of the day: Topaz
Incense of the day: Marjoram

Spell for Tolerance

Tolerance is needed in the world now more than ever. The more people work in both the physical and spiritual realms for peace, the closer we can get to the world becoming whole someday. Take a section of a wire clothing hanger and push it down as deep as you can into a white seven-day jar candle, making a deep hole. Fill the hole with frankincense oil. Print a photo of Earth and glue it to the candle.

> Message of freedom, message
>   of peace,
> Intolerance is a deadly disease.
> Though we are different, we
>   are one,
> Children of Earth, our time
>   has begun.
> Send away prejudice; send
>   away fear,
> This message of hope, I pray
>   all will hear.

Allow the candle to burn and empower it every day with your intentions.

Mickie Mueller

Notes:

speech, fairness in the work place, etc. Call the directions from the center, then say:

> I call upon the powers that be
> To release within me,
> Three times three
> The morals that I wish to see
> The ideals that will now
>   spring free!

One by one pick up the papers and read aloud the ideals three times. Think how you will effect this change in yourself or your world. Open the circle and gather them, keeping your thoughts on the ideals. Place them one by one in a fire. As the smoke rises, your power rises to the cause.

Nancy Bennett

Notes:

May 28
Thursday

 1st ☋ ☾
☽ → ♌ 3:44 am

Color of the day: Green
Incense of the day: Carnation

Spell for Releasing Ideals

Make a circle on the floor and place around the edge ideals that you wish to see working in your life. These could include freedom of

Holiday lore: Opinions are divided concerning the origins of the holiday of Memorial Day in the United States. This is a day set aside for honoring the graves of American war dead. While most historians credit the origins of the custom to Southern women, there is also a rumor, historically speaking, of an anonymous German who fought in the American Civil War (no one is sure on which side). At the end of the war, this soldier was allegedly overheard commenting that in the Old World people scattered flowers on the graves of dead soldiers. In May 1868, a Union army general suggested to Commander John A. Logan that a day be set aside each year to decorate Union graves. Logan agreed, and he set aside May 30 for this ritual. His proclamation acknowledged those "who died in defense of their country" and "whose bodies now lie in almost every city, village, or hamlet churchyard in the land." This patriotic holiday was later amended to include all the dead from all the wars, and its date was shifted to a convenient Monday late in May.

Palm to palm and face to face
We work this charm in
   sacred space
To build, to weave
To keep faith in what we
   believe.

Affix a bracelet to your partner's wrist. As you are closing the clasp, have them read this statement aloud: "Around my wrist, circle spell, Powered by trust and cast well." Repeat this step as your partner puts the other bracelet on your wrist. Take the rest of your time to meditate, do energy exercises, and discuss future ritual plans.

Gwinevere Rain

Notes:

May 29
Friday
Shavuot

 1st ♉ ♌

Color of the day: Purple
Incense of the day: Yarrow

Magic Partners Friendship Spell

Do you plan on performing rituals with a friend or significant other? If so, this spell will help align your energies. You'll need two similar bracelets and a quiet space to cast a circle. Sit across from one another, lean forward, and touch your open palms. Say the following together:

May 30
Saturday

1st ♌
☽ → ♍ 6:17 am
2nd Quarter 11:22 pm

Color of the day: Blue
Incense of the day: Ivy

Spell for Our Military

Joan of Arc, the patron saint of soldiers, is honored today. Against all odds, Joan, a rural teenager, led the army of Orleans and triumphed over their enemies. Whether you wish to cast this spell for a loved one in the military or you have an issue that requires you to soldier on, Saint Joan can help you. Make a small bag of red cloth and place within it three runes: Sowelu for life force and completeness; Ehwaz for foresight, tenacity, and knowing when to act; and Algiz for emotional stability, positive personal conduct, and protection. A picture of your soldier and a likeness of Saint Joan should also be placed in the bag. Draw a figure of the fleur-de-lis, the French lily and symbol of Saint Joan, on the outside of the bag. Hold the bag in your dominant hand and say:

> Saint Joan,
> Give _____ courage and
>   strength
> As he/she faces this hardship
>   and danger.

Place the bag on your altar and repeat this prayer each day until the battle is resolved.

Lily Gardner

Notes:

May 31
Sunday

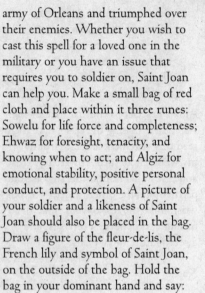 2nd ♏

Color of the day: Gold
Incense of the day: Almond

Celebrate the Green Earth Spell

At no other time during the year is the Earth so lush. Tree branches that were in bud a few weeks ago are now covered with a canopy of green, city parks and country meadows are covered in shimmering green carpets, and the mornings are alive with the chorus of birdsong. This spell will let you become one with the greening Earth. Take time to plant just one plant if possible. It could be an herb, a houseplant, or even a tree. Before you begin, write a wish on a small piece of paper about something you want to see grow in your life. It could be more family time, love, prosperity, anything. Place your wish in the bottom of the planting hole. As you water and nourish your new plant, see your wish becoming closer to reality. Your spell is alive like the Earth itself.

James Kambos

Notes:

June is the sixth month of the year. Its astrological sign is Gemini, the twins (May 20–June 21), a mutable air sign ruled by Mercury. It is named for Juno, the principal goddess of the Roman pantheon and wife of Jupiter. She is the patroness of marriage and the well-being of women. There is a sense of serenity as spring turns to summer and June settles softly over the countryside. Roses bloom heavily on garden fences; sweet clover sends out a heavenly fragrance. Dawn greets us with bird song and the sweet scent of honeysuckle. In rural areas, the afternoon is perfumed with one of the most ancient scents in the world—hay curing beneath the Sun. Country meadows are frosted with the white blooms of ox-eye daisies, and the orange flowers of wild daylilies star the roadsides. As nature reaches for maturity, the Sun ascends to its zenith, which brings us to the major holiday of the month, the Summer Solstice. The ancients lit bonfires for purification and to encourage the power of the life-giving Sun. Old-timers called June's Full Moon the Strong Sun Moon. And beneath the June Sun strawberries ripen, corn stretches for the sky, and bumblebees drift in the flower beds. Magical activities for the month may include charming away evil by hanging a sprig of valerian beneath a window or using some lemon balm in a love spell.

June 1
Monday

2nd ♏
☽ → ♎ 11:17 am

Color of the day: Lavender
Incense of the day: Hyssop

To Enhance Intuitive Awareness

Even though we all have intuition, some people have the ability to recognize it and work with this sense more than others. Use this spell to enhance your intuitive awareness! You'll need a small amethyst gemstone, 3 tablespoons of mugwort, a strand of deep-purple ribbon, and a white organza fabric sachet. Start by awakening the amethyst stone by cupping it in your hands and chanting, "Goddess, light, energy." Then hold it up to the space between your eyebrows (your third eye) and say, "With this stone, I enchant my intuition. Reveal to me all the things I wish to see." Place the gemstone in the sachet. Next, sprinkle in the mugwort 1 tablespoon at a time. As you do so, visualize a purple mist surrounding you. Finally, tie the sachet with the ribbon and inhale the scent. Keep the charm with you throughout the week.

Gwinevere Rain

Notes:

June 2
Tuesday

2nd ♎

Color of the day: Red
Incense of the day: Bayberry

Life's Little Rituals

A wise Witch once told me that life is full of little rituals. We do them without even thinking, but for every moment in life, there is magic. Is there a ritual for washing dishes? Perhaps you think of the feasts you and your loved ones share, and how the Goddess' bounty has been plentiful. Perhaps you give thanks when you wipe your plate clean clockwise. Want some others? We sweep the floor clean, and we "sweep" away the dust from our souls as well. We drive to destinations and do rituals to keep us safe while we venture forward. Even kissing a loved one goodbye is a ritual, a promise to return to our lives. Sometimes when the mundane gets me down, I recall, "For life's little moments, ever played, a little magic will be made." Honor your everyday rituals today.

Nancy Bennett

Notes:

June 3
Wednesday

2nd ♎
)) → ♏ 6:43 pm

Color of the day: Brown
Incense of the day: Lavender

Spider Web Internet Spell

If you have a Web site, you probably know how challenging it can be getting your name out there. Here is some magic to weave yourself all over the World Wide Web. E-mail a message to yourself that reads:

> Spider web of info, as I surf,
> Bring visitors to my cyber-turf
> To whom I link, link back
> to me
> As by my will, so mote it be!

Include your Web address in the message. Attach a spider image to the message and hit "send." As soon as the message arrives, do a browser search for Web sites that have links to others like yours. Find at least ten Web sites and e-mail them requesting to exchange links. Make sure you add their link to your site as soon as they agree. You have just enacted the law of return; may everything you send out return times three!

Mickie Mueller

Notes:

June 4
Thursday

2nd ♏

Color of the day: Purple
Incense of the day: Apricot

Good Marriage Spell

June is named for the Roman goddess Juno, patron of married life. Here's an old Gypsy charm to strengthen your marriage: choose an apple without blemish and cut it in half. Write on a piece of paper your name and the name of your mate and trim the paper in such a way so that it fits within the two halves of the apple. Fasten the apple halves together with toothpicks. As you skewer the two halves together say:

> Together we're bound
> Me, in love with you,
> You, in love with me.
> May all our words
> and actions
> Be a reflection of our love.
> Blessed Be.

Sprinkle liberally with sugar (love energy) and bake at 350 degrees F. until the two halves fuse together. This spell works best if both of you eat the magic apple.

Lily Gardner

Notes:

June 5
Friday

2nd ♏

Color of the day: White
Incense of the day: Mint

The Magic of Wild Roses

Some call them sweetbrier and some know them by their European name *eglantine*, but they are also known as wild roses. No matter what you call these plants, their small pink flowers and apple-scented foliage add beauty to rural areas during June. Herbalists of long ago prized them for their magical properties; for example, when their foliage is crushed, it releases an apple fragrance that was used as an aphrodisiac. For a powerful love mixture try this: Leave a handful of wild rose petals and a few leaves to dry at least a week. Pulverize them with a tablespoon of crushed blanched almonds. Place these in a small pouch and you'll have a powerful love sachet. If you want a romance to lead to marriage, old herbalists advise adding some orange blossoms to the mixture. And, for a real delicacy, purchase a jar of rose petal jam, which can be found at Greek and Middle Eastern grocers. Serve on toast or English muffins for a romantic breakfast.

James Kambos

Notes:

June 6
Saturday

2nd ♏
☽ → ♐ 4:23 am

Color of the day: Blue
Incense of the day: Sage

Habitat Day

Did you know that your yard can be certified as a wildlife habitat? Visit http://www.nwf.org/backyard/ to get the list of criteria and ideas on how you can transform your yard into a habitat. Most of the ideas are simple rearrangements with a few purchases, such as a bat house or bird bath. Take a look at the yard. Holding the list, find a space where you can meditate and talk to your garden's deva. Discuss how to make your yard eco-friendly and more of a welcoming habitat. Use today as the first day of the transformation. Garden work takes time, and changes happen over a period of years and cycles. Celebrate your yard's natural rhythms, your region's climate. However, don't try to do everything at once. Make small changes and celebrate each one. Let your land experience your loving stewardship.

Cerridwen Iris Shea

Notes:

June 7
Sunday

2nd ♐

Full Moon 2:12 pm

Color of the day: Gold
Incense of the day: Frankincense

Full Rose Moon Spell

This Full Moon is also called the Rose Moon. Let's incorporate a bit of garden witchery into your esbat celebration. The rose is sacred to Venus and encourages enchanted love and romance. You will need a glass bowl filled with water and a open fresh rose with the stem clipped off (so the flower can float upon the water). Fill the bowl and set the rose to float. Carefully hold up the bowl and allow some of the Moon's light to pass down into the water. Slowly lower the bowl and look into it, repeating three times:

On this magical night of the Full Rose Moon,

I do ask the Goddess to grant me a boon.

By the enchantment of this Full Moon night,

I ask for a love to light up my life.

Now increase romance, send a loving partner to me.

For the good of all; and by the power of three times three.

When finished, allow the rose to stay in the water until it fades. Then pour the flower and the water neatly on the ground outside as an offering to the Goddess.

Ellen Dugan

Notes:

June 8
Monday

3rd ♐

☽ → ♑ 3:59 pm

Color of the day: Gray
Incense of the day: Lily

A Spell for Safety in Travel

The Sun is in Gemini, which is ruled by the planet Mercury, the king of travel, communication, trade, study, and magic! For most of the day, the Moon is in Sagittarius, whose energy is that of movement and "getting things done." It is thus the perfect day to craft a spell for safety in travel! Gather moss, seaweed (like kelp), cotton, and a moonstone (or any combination of these). Put them in a spell bag and draw the alchemical sign for the planet and element Mercury on both sides of the bag. Cast a circle and enchant the bag at the elemental quarters. In your own way, ask each element and their guardians to bless the spell bag to protect you in all of your travels and journeys, both spiritual and physical. Next, envision the bag glowing in serene white light, spiraling and spinning ever outward. Finalize the spell by saying:

> Great God and Goddess, great
> Yin and Yang, the power of
> the divine paradox, I now
> enchant this bag with all the

power of protection and safety in travel. So mote it be.

Keep the bag when you travel, be it to physical or astral destinations.

Raven Digitalis

Notes:

June 9
Tuesday

3rd ♑

Color of the day: White
Incense of the day: Ylang-ylang

Techno Crystals

Natural objects tend to absorb natural energy, and synthetic objects tend to store synthetic energy. To affect technology, use synthetic spell components and fill them with synthetic energy. Quartz crystals are great for most magical purposes, but when working with technology, try manufactured glass, such as Austrian crystal. Glass crystals can be cleansed, charged, and programmed just like natural crystals, but the methods differ. You can clean glass crystals with glass cleaner or expose them to incandescent or fluorescent light. Charge by setting them on your computer or an appliance. For programming, visualize computer code or a menu interface. You may add an incantation such as:

> All things grow and change
>   in time:
> Blade of stone to blade of steel,
> Altar bell to boot-up chime.
> Each holds power, true
>   and real.
> Crystal facets clear and bright,
> Hold the magic that I code.
> Make it elegant and tight
> In a technologic mode.

Elizabeth Barrette

Notes:

June 10
Wednesday

3rd ♑

Color of the day: Yellow
Incense of the day: Bay laurel

Clear-headed Decisions Spell

With the Sun in Gemini, a versatile and busy mental sign, we can get bombarded with inadvertent information. A Capricorn Moon provides focus and the ability to push away everything that is not relevant when making a decision of great importance. Light an orange candle sprinkled with rosemary or lobelia, and have an Emperor tarot image on hand. Visualize your ability to, piece by piece, discern and prioritize the mental jumble intended to bring a wise decision. Rid yourself of the thoughts that are obviously unimportant, keep those you know are relevant, and visualize a "holding bin" for those thoughts that need more research. After researching and deciding to keep or discard the "holding bin" thoughts, begin to delve into the "keep" thoughts. See yourself easily assimilating and prioritizing these pieces of information, just as the pieces of a puzzle form a picture. A decision is easily reached without later regret. Know you can repeat this learned ability at any time in the future.

Calantirniel

Notes:

June 11
Thursday

3rd ♑
☽ → ♒ 4:52 am

Color of the day: Green
Incense of the day: Clove

The Festival of Mater Matuta
The Roman goddess Aurora, known among the Greeks as Eos, is honored on this day. It is she who opens the gates of heaven each day so that Helios may ride his chariot across the skies. Her tears create the morning dew. Try greeting Aurora today as she opens the gates of heaven. Walk barefoot through the grass, feeling her tears upon your skin. Connect with her eternally youthful soul. Then, as Helios begins his journey across the sky, settle yourself in a quiet place outdoors and let the light bathe your face for a short time as you meditate on the beauty you bring into your world each day. Once you finish your meditations, pay tribute to Aurora for her task of opening the gates for each new day to bring light in the world. Take with you her beauty and grace as you go about your day and tasks.

                              Winter Wren
Notes:

June 12
Friday

3rd ♒

Color of the day: Pink
Incense of the day: Rose

Receptivity
Would you just like to meet a new friend? Use this spell to create a meeting—it's important not to have anyone specific in mind, just the right person. It could be someone from your past or someone new, but the point is to make a new friend, to bring someone into your life with qualities that will benefit each of you. Gather a handful of stones of any kind. Put them in a bowl and then close your eyes and select one at random. As you're making your choice, say these words:

> If there is someone I
>   should greet,
> Allow us to find ways to meet.
> For the benefit of everyone,
> As I will so it be done.

Carry the stone with you until someone new has come into your life.

                              Ember
Notes:

June 13
Saturday

 3rd ♒
☽ → ♓ 5:32 pm

Color of the day: Black
Incense of the day: Pine

Controlling Dreams

If you are having unpleasant or dull dreams, try this trick. Keep a remote control for a TV or VCR by the bed. It doesn't matter if it works or not. Spend some time studying the controls and pick what they will represent in your dreams. "Mute," of course, turns off the sound; changing the channel would signify changing the dream; the "stop" button would wake you up; pressing "play" or tuning to your favorite channel would be the cue for a good dream. Remind yourself what the buttons are for each night, and, if you wish, keep the remote in your hand while you go to sleep. Otherwise, place it somewhere handy where you could reach it, like the bedside table. Train yourself in dreams to look at your hands and use the remote to direct your dreams.

Magenta Griffith

Notes:

June 14
Sunday
Flag Day

3rd ♓

Color of the day: Amber
Incense of the day: Juniper

Celebrate the Sun

The ancients knew what they were doing when they worshipped the Sun as a god. We would not be here if not for the Sun's light. In fact, the formation of the Sun started the birth of our galaxy and our planet. Since today is the day named for the Sun (Sunday), use this ritual to honor the Sun. Gather items that symbolize the Sun— yellow and gold candles and stones such as pyrite, citrine, or clear quartz. Put the candle or candles in the center and make a circle around them using the stones. Use yellow, gold, red, orange, and white ribbons as rays of light extending from the circle. Dedicate your ritual to a particular Sun god or goddess if you desire, such as Apollo.

Sun of light, Sun of power,
We watch your movement
mark the hours.
By your light we each do live,
Thanks to you in this ritual
I give.

Ember

Notes:

Holiday lore: It was on June 14, 1777, that Congress standardized the flag of the United States with 13 stripes in alternating red and white and 13 white stars on a blue background. Forty-one years later, in 1818, Congress voted to keep the number of stripes at 13 representing the 13 original colonies, but to add a new star for each new state. A star's addition becomes official on the Fourth of July following the state's admission. The current flag of 13 stripes and 50 stars has been in use since July 4, 1960, following Hawaii's 1959 statehood.

June 15
Monday

3rd ♓︎
4th Quarter 6:14 pm

Color of the day: Silver
Incense of the day: Rosemary

Nightmare Charm
If you've been having nightmares more frequently lately, consider

using this charm. You'll need a small plate, a piece of cream paper, a blue pen, and at least one tablespoon of the following herbs: peppermint, lavender, rosemary, and chamomile. Draw a large pentacle in the center of your paper. Hold your hand over the image and speak this incantation:

> Mean and evil dreams be gone
> with this pentacle charm.
>
> I summon forth this protection
> power through every
> midnight hour.

Visualize yourself sleeping peacefully. Next, measure out each herb individually. Inhale the herbal scent as you place it in the center of the plate. Run your fingers through the mixture and say, "Bad dreams that haunt my every night, I banish thee from my sight!" Finally, fold the pentacle paper and drop it on top of the herbs. Keep the charm near your bed each night.

Gwinevere Rain

Notes:

June 16
Tuesday

 4th ♓
℘ → ♈ 3:51 am

Color of the day: Black
Incense of the day: Geranium

Do The Work

In your favorite park or open garden space, try taking a leisurely 15-minute walk in utter slow motion, much as Zen practitioners do. As you move, relax your body so that each movement becomes a slow and fluid action. When your knees bend and your heel begins to lift from the ground, slowly roll your arch. With each step, strive for silence and a slow and steady flow. If you become distracted, simply focus again on the ground and ease back into the lull of graceful motion. Feel the grasses beneath your feet bend to bear your weight and thank them for their flexibility and endurance. From this place, clearly see time as a chosen perspective. The subtle energies of life rush around us in accordance with human drive and choice. We define time as we learn to observe it, as sustenance and need often demand. When we visit this slow fluid place, we make contact with a deeper and more subtle Earth clock. This is the true time of our physical environment. When we learn to observe Earth time, our expanding consciousness grounds and centers us in our daily lives.

Estha McNevin

Notes:

June 17
Wednesday

 4th ♈

Color of the day: Topaz
Incense of the day: Lilac

All Couples Day

In Greece, people observe the marriage of Orpheus and Eurydice by celebrating All Couples Day. It applies equally to heterosexual and homosexual relationships. Specifically, this is a holiday about the condition of marriage and the union of two individuals who thereafter function as a single unit. It's an auspicious time for magic supporting domestic bliss.

For this spell you'll need a "bride and groom" candle, either white (to sanctify married fidelity) or blue (for peace in the home). Spread an altar cloth in matching color. Light both wicks of the candle and say:

> Love is a bridge between
>   two hearts;
> Love is a song sung in
>   two parts.
> Love is a harbor safe
>   from doubt;
> What you put in is what
>   comes out.
> Love turns a house into
>   a home;
> Keep it all safe, and
>   never roam.

                        Elizabeth Barrette

Notes:

June 18
Thursday

4th ♈
☽ → ♉ 10:20 am

Color of the day: Turquoise
Incense of the day: Carnation

Keeping Your Temper

To calm your impetuous temper and fast-boiling anger, gather together a lavender-colored candle and lemon-balm incense. In your kitchen, light the candle and the incense. With focused intention and deliberate attention to every motion, boil water for tea. Continue to focus as you brew a cup of chamomile tea sweetened with a little sugar. Sit quietly with the candle, the scent, and slowly sip the tea while saying, "Spirit of tea, bring calmness to me. Spirit of sugar, sweeten my personality." Once you have finished the tea, wash the cup and spoon with the same focus. With a deep breath, find your calm connection to deep magic of herb, tea, and sweet vision. Blessed Be.

                        Gail Wood

Notes:

June 19
Friday

4th ♉

Color of the day: Purple
Incense of the day: Alder

Enchanting Your Food

The Moon is in Taurus, which is a great sign to perform magic having to do with the physical plane. As Witches and magicians, we must strive to live a fully magical and spiritual life. However, we often forget about the simple things. We are constantly eating, which gives us a constant opportunity to perform magic! Numerous cultures are indeed shocked that we in the West have forgotten the art of blessing and giving thanks for our food regularly. Next time you sit down to eat, cup your hands over the food and say a prayer in your own words. Here is an idea for a prayer you can say or chant:

> Behold, Great Spirit. I honor
> that I am permitted to take
> this food into my body and
> give thanks for the suste-
> nance it brings. I enchant
> this crop of the Earth with
> the energies of holistic health
> and balance and ask that
> these properties permeate my
> being as I consume this food.
> So mote it be.

Envision the food glowing with energy (a color of your choice), and know that the energy will carry into your body and flow through your blood, empowering you all the more.

Raven Digitalis

Notes:

June 20
Saturday

4th ♉
☽ → ♊ 1:00 pm

Color of the day: Indigo
Incense of the day: Rue

A Lavender Dream Spell

Lavender is a great herb to use if you wish to work sleep or dream magic. It is especially good if you wish to induce a psychic dream. To do this, you'll need some fresh or dried lavender (both flowers and foliage), a small square of white fabric, lavender-colored ribbon, and an amethyst crystal. Perform this spell in the evening. First, crumble some of the lavender onto the fabric and tie into a bundle with the ribbon. Place this beneath your pillow, and set the amethyst crystal near your bed.

Smolder the rest of the lavender in a dish and scent your bedroom. As you get into bed, think of your question. Expect a vivid dream. If an answer isn't revealed, wait a week and try again.

James Kambos

Notes:

June 21
Sunday
Father's Day – Litha –
Summer Solstice

 4th ♊

☉ → ♋ 1:45 am

Color of the day: Orange
Incense of the day: Almond

The Sacred Masculine

Today is Litha, the Midsummer sabbat, as well as Father's Day. It's a perfect day to celebrate the sacred masculine within all of us and to highlight the strong, warm, active power we all possess. Create an altar with yellow candles, symbols of masculinity, and images of the Sun; include pictures of male relatives and admired men in your life. Cast a circle and stand before the altar, drawing on your power and strength.

Begin by speaking your feelings to the men pictured on the altar, emphasizing the qualities you admire. Light the yellow candles and call in the Sacred Masculine Divine. When he is present, stretch your arms upward to the sky and ask him to imbue you with the qualities that you admire. Feel that energy flow into your being and feel it mingle with your own energy. Draw a deep breath and raise a cone of power in celebration of this masculine power in the universe and within you. Chant, starting softly and ending very loudly:

In the season of the Sun
I find wonder, strength,
*   and power*
Wonder, strength, and power
Power, power, power
Power
Power!

Ground the excess energy into Earth. Thank the spirits that are present and especially thank the gods and forefathers for their strength and power. Open the circle. Blessed Be.

Gail Wood

Notes:

June 22
Monday

4th ♊
☽ → ♋ 1:12 pm
New Moon 3:35 pm

Color of the day: White
Incense of the day: Narcissus

honoring the First Fruits

Several cultures, including the Romans, believed in the importance of honoring the first fruits in order to ensure continued abundant harvests. Not doing so created fears of blight, lost crops, and later famine. Sometimes the honor combined with the first harvest; sometimes it was celebrated with the first flowering. Close to Midsummer is a good time to celebrate all that is blossoming, flowering, and abundant. Place your favorite seasonal fruits, vegetables, and flowers in cheerfully painted pottery or in hand-crafted baskets. Arrange these on a brightly colored cloth. Write a blessing to celebrate the abundance that blossoms in your life. Play your favorite instrument, dance around the offerings. Make a libation with your favorite beverage and an offering from the pieces you've gathered. Prepare a meal from what is left, and, even better, invite someone to share it.

                    Cerridwen Iris Shea
Notes:

June 23
Tuesday

1st ♋

Color of the day: Gray
Incense of the day: Ginger

Crystal Recharging

Crystals are an important aspect in many magical practices. However, it is not always necessary to obtain new crystals for your workings. When a crystal is charged to a specific working, that is its purpose until the working is completed. The crystal may then be cleared and refocused for another working. Gather up your crystals from completed workings and give them a bath in sea salt water, rinsing them thoroughly after the washing with fresh water. Dry them with a cotton towel or allow them to air dry. At this point, you may also wish to smudge them. Place the cleared stones on a windowsill where they may bask in the light of the Moon for a full lunar cycle. You may need to place them in a deeper bowl if you have helpful felines. With the passing of the lunar cycle, your crystals are ready to be charged to new workings in your practice.

                    Winter Wren
Notes:

June 24
Wednesday

1st ♋
☽ → ♌ 12:50 pm

Color of the day: White
Incense of the day: Honeysuckle

A Travel Spell to the Sky Gods

In the evening, go outside. Spread out a dark blanket and stand in the center. Spread your arms wide to the sky and say:

> Great gods of the sky, those
>   of many names,
> I pay homage to you tonight
> Baal-Haddad, Zeus,
>   and Nwyrve,
> Buku, Taranus, and Obtala
> You who dwell on high!
> Cast your blessings upon me,
>   your earthly child,
> That I may feel your
>   protection and your love,
> No matter to where I wander
>   while under your sky.

Spread some white stones on the blanket and leave them to charge overnight. Gather them in a dark cloth bag as a talisman to keep you safe while you travel. The gods called upon can be changed to whichever deity you choose, depending on your travel region.

Nancy Bennett

Notes:

June 25
Thursday

1st ♌

Color of the day: Crimson
Incense of the day: Mulberry

Green Man Prosperity Spell

Green Man is the laughing spirit of abundant growth and the perseverance of nature. This day is known as Old Litha and was sometimes celebrated as the height of summer abundance. Most of us now celebrate Litha on the planetary Summer Solstice, but today would be a great time to tap into the old energies of bounty and bring some prosperity into your life. Light a green candle anointed with pine or patchouli oil, surrounded by green leaves and set before an image of Green Man. Focus on all the life force that is pulsing around the green Earth.

> Green Man smiling in
>   the wood
> Bring abundance and all
>   that's good
> Growth and bounty send
>   to me.
> As by my will, so mote
>   it be!

Allow the candle to burn all the way out. Water your trees and magical garden to thank Green Man and honor all that's green and growing.

Mickie Mueller

Notes:

May I walk in beauty and
magic all of my days.

Allow the candle to burn out in a
safe place.

Ellen Dugan

Notes:

June 26
Friday

 1st ♌
☽ → ♍ 1:46 pm

Color of the day: Coral
Incense of the day: Orchid

Personal Improvement Spell
Today is Friday, and we are in
a waxing Moon phase. It is a
great time to pull personal improvement, beauty, and glamour into your
life. As the Moon increases, so too
will positive feelings about yourself.
Today we call on Freya, the Norse
goddess of love and magic. Light a
rosy pink candle to represent the
positive and loving change that you
are working to manifest. Then repeat
the charm:

Freya, mistress of magic, hear
my call on this June night,

Allow personal improvement
to brighten up my life.

A pink candle to represent
the positive change,

June 27
Saturday

1st ♍

Color of the day: Gray
Incense of the day: Ivy

Lost Item Retrieval Spell
In Brian Froud's *Faerie Oracle*,
there is a wonderful card called
Ilbe the Retriever, and his particular
purpose is to find lost items. After
cleaning your house, place Ilbe the
Retriever (a real card or one printed
from a computer) nearby the last
place you remember seeing the item
you seek. Light a white tealight candle,
chew on some rosemary leaves, or
rub the oil on your temples and
visualize yourself remembering and
finding—even holding—the lost
item! Ilbe the Retriever can certainly
help by revealing what isn't clear—
oftentimes, we trick ourselves. We

get caught up with mundane matters and don't remember details very well. This process allows your memory to work and unseen planes to be seen again (this is one reason why you clean your house). Thank Ilbe and know you will locate your item very soon.

Calantirniel

Notes:

opposite ends of your altar or a small table. If you have a specific issue, name it, and consider both sides of the situation. Meditate on various forms of balance: light and dark, cold and heat, and so forth. Move each object halfway toward the center. Meditate a little longer, then move the objects so they are next to each other. Meditate on the two opposite forces joining, like the yin and yang symbol. When you feel like the situation is more in harmony, ring the bell to end.

Magenta Griffith

Notes:

June 28
Sunday

 1st ♍
☽ → ♎ 5:24 pm

Color of the day: Yellow
Incense of the day: Marigold

Balancing Spell

With the Sun in the sign ruled by the Moon (Cancer), and the Moon in the sign ruled by the Sun (Leo), today is an excellent day to do a spell to bring matters into balance and harmony. Get a Moon symbol, such as a small mirror, and a Sun symbol, such as a yellow, silver, or gold candle. You also need a bell. Put the Moon and Sun items on

June 29
Monday

1st ♎
2nd Quarter 7:28 am

Color of the day: Silver
Incense of the day: Clary sage

Well-Paying Employment Spell

Today honors Saint Peter and his Voodoo counterpart, the god Ogun. Both the god and the saint are invoked in matters of success. For this spell, you will need a large green candle, green and black beads, and a string for making a necklace. Dress your altar in green and black cloth. At the center of the altar, place a cauldron filled with iron screws, nails, and tools. Be sure to include two keys (the amulet for both Saint Peter and Ogun). Write a letter to Saint Peter and Ogun describing the job you desire. Place the letter beneath your candle and light the wick. String your beads into a necklace using this pattern: 7 green beads, 7 black beads, then alternate 1 green bead and 1 black bead for 14 beads (7 of each). Repeat the entire 28-bead pattern until you've achieved the desired length. Wear this necklace day and night until you've secured your job.

Lily Gardner

Notes:

June 30
Tuesday

2nd ♎

Color of the day: Scarlet
Incense of the day: Cedar

DNA Linking with Cord Magic

In a muslin bag or medicine bag, I compile samples of your hair, fingernails, toenails, and flakes of skin. Spit on these to bind them all together with your energy and tie the bag to a blue cord that measures the length of your body. This is an energetic facsimile of your emotional body. When knots are tied in the cord or energy work is performed, the result streams to your energy vibration and is channeled directly to you, not restricted to or contained by the cord. While children do outgrow these types of cords quickly, adults over thirty can continually add personal DNA to create a stronger link. Using the cord enables one to perform healing work on the self. One of the most effective uses for these types of bonded cords is to charge them with energies beyond physical reach. For example, if you are too busy to nap but feel thoroughly exhausted, your cords could be laid to bed and charged to receive the energy of rest and rejuvenation while the body follows through with its terrestrial day. As with all implements that contain one's personal energy, cords should be carefully stored when not in use and should never be used by others on your behalf without your full consent and participation.

Estha McNevin

Notes:

July is the seventh month of the year. Its astrological sign is Cancer, the crab (June 21–July 22), a cardinal water sign ruled by the Moon. An awesome majesty comes over the land now; tomatoes fatten, corn tassles out, and shaggy heads of monarda brighten the herb border. July is the high noon of summer, even though the Summer Solstice has passed. The Goddess is watching over the ripening fields and orchards. July's Full Moon was known as the Blessing Moon, and our forebears, who were close to nature, realized the importance of this time of year. They knew that if the crops were healthy in July, there was a good chance that they'd be blessed with a bountiful harvest. Independence Day on July 4 is the main holiday of the month. It's a time to be grateful for our personal freedom, and a time to count our blessings. Since July's astrological sign is associated with water, any magical activity using the element of water is very effective. Seashells, sand, and seaweed can add power to spells this month. If you can take a trip to the shore this month, look for a seashell that attracts you. Bless it and keep it as a power object. By the end of July, apples begin to blush with color and Queen Anne's lace begins to appear along the roadsides. Dusk comes earlier now. Pause, and enjoy the glory of July.

July 1
Wednesday

2nd ♎

☽ → ♏ 12:18 am

Color of the day: White
Incense of the day: Bay laurel

Storing Sun Power

This month, the Sun burns hot in the summer sky. Use this spell to capture the Sun's power for future use. You will need a large magnifying glass, a small glass lens, some tinder (such as paper), and a fireproof container. Go outside and pile the tinder in the container. Line up the magnifying glass with the Sun, adjusting until you have a tiny hot spot focused on the tinder. Continue until the tinder bursts into flame. Set aside the magnifying glass. Wave the lens above the fire three times, saying:

> Light of fire,
> Light of Sun,
> Blend together
> Into one.
>
> Lens of magic,
> Lens of glass,
> Gather power
> With each pass.

Allow the fire to burn out. Keep the lens for use in future workings that call for the power of the Sun or the element of fire.

Elizabeth Barrette

Notes:

Holiday lore: Today is the first day of the season for climbing Mt. Fuji in Yamabiraki, Japan. Mt. Fuji is the highest peak in Japan and is revered in Japanese culture. Considered the foremother or grandmother of Japan, Fuji is an ancient fire goddess of the indigenous Ainu people. In modern times, the Ainu mostly resided on the northern island of Hokkaido. The name *Fuji* was derived from an Ainu word that means "fire" or "deity of fire." Each year since the Meiji era, a summer festival has been held to proclaim the beginning of the climbing season and to pray for the safety of local inhabitants and visitors or pilgrims to the sacred mountain. The two-month climbing season begins today and ends on August 30.

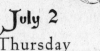

July 2
Thursday

2nd ♏

Color of the day: Purple
Incense of the day: Jasmine

Spell for the Expecting

Today is the old Roman festival date of the Feast of Expectant Mothers. Since today is a Thursday (a good day for health issues) and we have a waxing Moon phase, this is a perfect spellcasting opportunity. If you are pregnant or have a loved one who is expecting, work this spell to promote a safe pregnancy and delivery. Light a white candle for the mother and unborn child and repeat the spell verse three times:

> Juno, Roman Mother watch
>   over us/them I pray.
> Guard the mother and child
>   well, be it night or day,
> When the time comes for
>   baby to enter the world.
> May they both be strong and
>   safe, be it boy or girl.
> By the pow'r of three
>   times three
> As I will it, so must it be!

Let the candle burn out in a safe place.

Ellen Dugan

Notes:

July 3
Friday

2nd ♏
☽ → ♐ 10:10 am

Color of the day: Coral
Incense of the day: Violet

Looking Within

Understanding the complex makeup of our inner being is a continual goal in life. One method for doing so can be found through tarot. Seek out your soul card. This can be found through birth date numerology. Add together your date of birth. (July 3, 1969 = 7 + 3 + 1 + 9 + 6 + 9 = 35, 3 + 5 = 8. You want the last number to be 22 or less.) Find the major arcana card that corresponds to your soul. Study the card until you can picture it clearly in your mind, then put the card aside. Meditate on the card, seeing it life-sized before you so that you may enter into the scene and converse with the figures therein. Ask them what they can tell you to further you on your life path journey. Remember to thank them when you leave. You can repeat this meditation as often as you wish.

Winter Wren

Notes:

July 4
Saturday

Independence Day

 2nd ♐

Color of the day: Black
Incense of the day: Sandalwood

Break the Chains That Bind You

Using lengths of construction paper, write down things of which you would like to be free. They could be physical things, such as debt or a burned-out job situation, or more internal needs, such as being free of self-doubt. Form the papers into a paper chain. Light a fire in an outside area or have a container in which you can burn things. Call your directions and then chant:

> Chains that bind me from
>   my destiny
> Keep me from being all I can be.
> In this circle I respond
> Make me independent of
>   these bonds!
> Now free! Forever free!
> So mote it be!

Read each chain link and then cast it into the fire. When the ashes have cooled, gather and dispose of them by burying or offering them to the wind.

                    Nancy Bennett
Notes:

Holiday notes: On July 4, 1776, the Second Continental Congress adopted the Declaration of Independence. Philadelphians were first to mark the anniversary of American independence with a celebration, but Independence Day became commonplace only after the War of 1812. By the 1870s, the Fourth of July was the most important secular holiday in the United States, celebrated even in far-flung communities on the western frontier of the country.

July 5
Sunday

 2nd ♐
          ☽ → ♑ 10:07 pm

Color of the day: Orange
Incense of the day: Eucalyptus

See and Talk to the Fae Spell

At sunset, go outside and set up an "altar" on a tree stump or other natural organic place without pesticides or herbicides, and position yourself near a tree, a group of trees, or a faerie ring of mushrooms (don't go inside the ring). Bring as an offering a thimble of honey and something shiny (not iron). Bring a cup of chamomile tea for yourself to drink. Pick some tansy flowers and pick off a couple of leaves to swipe over your third eye (and the oils in the leaves smell wonderful). Light some candles if it's not too breezy. Rest in a comfortable place with an open mind and a light, happy heart. Observe any butterflies, dragonflies, bees, or other creatures informing you of their presence. Tell the creatures that you are a child of nature and then provide care to the plants outdoors, even tend an organic flower garden. Don't strain to see or hear, just relax and be open to experience whatever happens. You may see impressions out of your peripheral vision or hear faint, beautiful music, or you may feel "tingly." No matter what you experience, come back as you are, remembering your otherworldly contact.

Calantirniel

Notes:

July 6
Monday

2nd ♑

Color of the day: White
Incense of the day: Rosemary

home Energy Spell

Warding your home is important, both to keep out harmful influences and to retain good ones. A popular technique is to imagine strands of energy woven tightly within the outer walls of the structure. You can also visualize energy running through interior walls, especially around rooms that are important to protect, like your bedroom. These can be constructed with layers of elemental or other types of energy. If you use elemental energy, be sure to have all four elements—fire, water, earth, and air. Other sorts of energy are from the Sun, the Moon, a favorite large tree that grows near your house, or a river. More complicated techniques can be employed but can often be more difficult to visualize successfully. Visualized wards and shields should be recharged or otherwise maintained on a regular basis, as they can fade over time.

Magenta Griffith

Notes:

July 7
Tuesday

2nd ♑
Full Moon 5:21 am

Color of the day: Black
Incense of the day: Cinnamon

Magic Lunar Eclipse

This is a potent night for lovers because eclipses bring emotions to their extremes so that we can recognize and better understand them. On July 7, the Japanese observe Tanabata, a festival that celebrates the annual reunion of Shokujo, the sky princess, and Kengya, a lowly cowherd. When Shokujo's father discovered the love affair, he separated the two on either side of the great sky river, the Milky Way. Once a year on the seventh day of the seventh month, a flock of sympathetic magpies form a living bridge over the Milky Way so the lovers can be reunited. Skogugo, the Weaver Star (Vega), joins the Cowherd Star (Altair) in the sky. The Japanese honor the lovers by placing spools of colored thread on their altars. To bring a lover into your life, place red jasper, a pearl, and rose quartz in a spell box. Under the light of this Full Moon, burn a red candle and write:

> In the light of the Tanabata,
> Lover, come to my bidding,
> Come in the red light of flame,

> Come in the flooded Moon
> of night,
> Across the wide expanse of
> the Milky Way,
> In the pull of tides,
> By the light of Tanabata,
> By the power of Weaver
> and Cowherd,
> To my bidding come.

Roll the spell in a tiny scroll and tie with a colored threads. Before the next Full Moon, a new lover will enter your life.

Lily Gardner

Notes:

July 8
Wednesday

3rd ♑
☽ → ♒ 11:03 am

Color of the day: Brown
Incense of the day: Honeysuckle

Making a Dark Banishing Powder

There is always something we can banish from our lives to help us function as more complete spiritual beings. Whether it's a

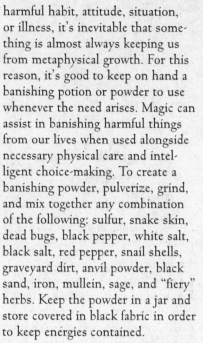

harmful habit, attitude, situation, or illness, it's inevitable that something is almost always keeping us from metaphysical growth. For this reason, it's good to keep on hand a banishing potion or powder to use whenever the need arises. Magic can assist in banishing harmful things from our lives when used alongside necessary physical care and intelligent choice-making. To create a banishing powder, pulverize, grind, and mix together any combination of the following: sulfur, snake skin, dead bugs, black pepper, white salt, black salt, red pepper, snail shells, graveyard dirt, anvil powder, black sand, iron, mullein, sage, and "fiery" herbs. Keep the powder in a jar and store covered in black fabric in order to keep energies contained.

Raven Digitalis

Notes:

July 9
Thursday

3rd ≈≈

Color of the day: Crimson
Incense of the day: Myrrh

Cleaning a Mess

Paper napkins were used for the first time on this day in 1887. To clean up a mess and dispose of it, gather together white paper napkins, paper and pencil, and a cold cup of tea or coffee. This spell is best done in the kitchen or similar space. Create sacred space in your usual manner. On the napkin(s) write down your strengths and your problem-solving skills. Take the cold cup of tea or coffee and gaze at it, sending your problem into the liquid. Pour it onto the counter and clean the spill with the napkins as you chant, "I am done with the mess, it is over without stain." Wad up the napkin and throw it away with a loud "Goodbye." Be sure to take the garbage completely out of your home, disposing of it in your usual manner.

Gail Wood

Notes:

July 10
Friday

 3rd ≈
☽ → ♓ 11:44 pm

Color of the day: Purple
Incense of the day: Yarrow

Boost Your Confidence Spell

In July, nature explodes with color. Flower beds are splashed with yellow, orange, and red. Even the vegetable garden is full of color, the first tomatoes ripen, and yellow squash peek out from beneath large green leaves. This spell draws upon the energy of the season to increase your confidence. It should be performed at noon when the Sun is at its zenith. Turn your altar toward the south and light one orange pillar candle. Decorate the altar with as many vases of bright summer flowers as you wish. As the candle burns, watch the flame. As the flame grows, imagine your self-confidence growing. Snuff out the candle after a few minutes. Go outdoors, face south, and leave a small offering to the Sun. This could be a small piece of coffee cake or any cinnamon-flavored pastry. Over the next few days, don an article of clothing that is a brighter color than you usually wear. People may compliment your appearance. When they do, you'll feel a surge of confidence.

James Kambos

Notes:

July 11
Saturday

3rd ♓
Color of the day: Gray
Incense of the day: Patchouli

Adventure Day

Is there something you've always wanted to do, but never had the chance? Today is the day to do it, a lovely summer day, using the sturdy power of the number 11! Eleven is considered a "master number" and is the number of the visionary, idealism, inspiration, and inner strength. Your adventure doesn't have to be something as extreme as jumping out of a plane. It could be as simple as riding a roller coaster, taking a lesson in something you've always wanted to try, or eating something exotic to you. In the morning, spend a few minutes communing with your guardian angel before you start the day. Spend the day doing something out of your normal routine and out of your comfort zone. Before you go to sleep, spend some time giving thanks for your day of adventure. It will open doors for you, both physically and spiritually.

Cerridwen Iris Shea

Notes:

Unwanted psychic ties
dissolve,
You'll never break my
strong resolve.

As you get in the tub, visualize unwanted cords running to you dissolving as you hit the water. Suddenly, others in the situation should lose interest in you and go their own way.

Mickie Mueller

Notes:

July 12
Sunday

3rd ♓

Color of the day: Gold
Incense of the day: Hyacinth

Cool Off Bath Spell

Breaking off any kind of relationship can be a tricky situation. If you feel that you need a little extra help separating yourself from an individual or situation, try this handy magical bath. In a 7-inch square piece of deep-purple cotton cloth, place the following: sea salt, sage, mint, 9 drops of frankincense oil, a pinch of dragon's blood powder, thyme, and a small tumbled quartz crystal. Tie the bundle closed with a black ribbon, knotting it three times. Toss into a bath full of water.

Cool off now, and leave me be,
Be gone, you have no hold
on me.

July 13
Monday

3rd ♓
☽ → ♈ 10:40 am

Color of the day: Silver
Incense of the day: Neroli

Honey Spell to Find Love

July is the month when the Dog Star, Sirius, rises with the Sun. The goddess most associated with Sirius is Demeter, the goddess of grain and fertility. In ancient Greece, priestesses offered honey and fig cakes to Demeter. Honey has long been used in love spells and as an aphrodisiac. To grant your love match, use the magical properties of honey. Light a yellow candle on your kitchen table and bake a fig cake as an offering to Demeter. While the cake is baking, lay out two strips of rice paper. Write your name on one strip and the qualities you seek in a lover on the other strip. Spread honey over each strip and place the written sides together. Pray to Demeter to grant you the gift of love. Eat the honeyed strips of paper. Thank Demeter and leave the fig cake offering at the foot of a tree.

Lily Gardner

Notes:

following until the temperature of the water increases:

> A hardened heart even water
> can wear
>
> For the candor of the anguish
> leaves us all threadbare.
>
> Life's only souvenir is the love
> that we share.

Leave the bowl on your altar or in a sacred space until you experience results.

Estha McNevin

Notes:

July 14
Tuesday

 3rd ♈

Color of the day: Red
Incense of the day: Basil

To Warm a Cold heart

Add 1 drop of rose oil and 7 drops of dove's blood ink to a large bowl of salted water. Use a rose quartz stone to sink a photo or likeness of the person to whom you would like to send love. Place your hands within the water and chant the

July 15
Wednesday

 3rd ♈
4th Quarter 5:53 am
☽ → ♉ 6:30 pm

Color of the day: Topaz
Incense of the day: Lavender

Spell for Forgiveness

At times, anger becomes a part of our lives. It can be very easy to allow that anger to remain within and fester into a dark void inside ourselves. If allowed to remain there, it can even

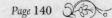

grow to become a dominant force in our lives. It is said the only true cure for anger is forgiveness, forgiveness for whoever or whatever brought about the anger in the first place. It is not easy to forgive. It takes great strength and conviction. Some positive meditation time is also optimal. With a pink candle for emotional healing and some soothing incense, the following chant to the Lady is a good starting point.

> *After loss, there is gain.*
> *After pain, there is healing.*
> *Let the anger I hold*
>   *be healed*
> *From within and without*
> *I release my anger toward*
>   _____
> *Anger has no place in my life*
>   *or power over my heart*
> *All ills are healed, all*
>   *wrongs forgiven*
> *Let there be peace for now*
>   *and all time.*
> *So mote it be.*

Winter Wren

Notes:

July 16
Thursday

Color of the day: Green
Incense of the day: Clove

Competition Spell

Today is the anniversary of the first recorded date of the Olympic Games in ancient Greece. For this competition spell, set up a white-and-gold tablecloth on your table. Surround it with laurel leaves or vines and place on it something that represents the area in which you want to compete. This could be chess pieces for a chess player or a baseball mitt for a pitcher. Call your directions and begin to circle clockwise saying:

> *This spell I cast now, three*
>   *times three*
> *To help me shine competitively.*
> *May my game be on today*
> *May I win while fair I play.*
> *While this I chant, the*
>   *spell begins*
> *This day is marked for me*
>   *to win.*

Repeat the charm three times and circle the table thrice as well. Clothe your representation in laurel leaves. Leave it in place during your competition, assuring your success.

Nancy Bennett

Notes:

Now, no more gossip or
slander will haunt my day.

Before the next New Moon, bury the jar deep in the ground.

Gwinevere Rain

Notes:

July 17
Friday

 4th ♉

☽ → ♊ 10:41 pm

Color of the day: Rose
Incense of the day: Cypress

Stop Gossip

Having people gossip about you and spread rumors behind your back can be one of the hardest social situations to handle. Use this spell in conjunction with other, more traditional means to tackle the issue. You'll need an empty jar with matching lid, broken seashells, a handful of new nails, a piece of paper, and a black marker. Fill the jar halfway with the nails. Then write "stop gossip about me" on the piece of paper. Place it in the jar and fill the rest with the broken shells. Say this incantation as you seal the container:

I suffocate and seal the bad
words sent my way
Shredding them like the
angry sea
Nailing them to the
deep darkness

July 18
Saturday

4th ♊

Color of the day: Indigo
Incense of the day: Sage

Flame of the Sun

At noon exactly, light a solid yellow candle in the middle of a warm sunny spot. Focus on all of the light spilling down around you and on the steady force of the flame projecting its own radiant solar energy to you. Regulate your breathing to slow, deep cycles. Feel your pores opening to the light, sensing your whole body being penetrated and brightened. Envision this light reaching through to the very core of your body. See the very air you breathe spread light throughout your body as you inhale and exhale. Notice your whole body relax as each nook and cranny of your internal structure begins to pulse and glow in the brilliant white light. Continue as long as you like until every fiber of your being is bathed and glowing in the light of the Sun.

Estha McNevin

Notes:

being filled with this smoke, cleansing it of any negativity. Then, speak this incantation:

By smoke and with light,
I work this spell by cloak
of night,
So forth, from this time,
This book is now protected,
Blessed by faith and rhyme.

When you are done, write your first entry and keep it on your altar for the night.

Gwinevere Rain

Notes:

July 19
Sunday

 4th ♊
☽ → ♋ 11:51 pm

Color of the day: Amber
Incense of the day: Juniper

Book of Shadows Blessing

When you start a new Book of Shadows, it is a good idea to bless it so that the book is protected and empowered. You'll need the book you'd like to bless, a sage bundle or frankincense incense sticks, and a lighter or matches. First, de-clutter your altar so you can lay the book in front of you. Light the sage bundle or incense and let the smoke hover across the book. With your free hand, slowly weave it in the smoke. Visualize every page in the book

July 20
Monday

4th ♋

Color of the day: Ivory
Incense of the day: Narcissus

Fade into the Background Spell

There are times in which it would benefit us to "shine," but there are also times where blending in, even becoming invisible, will suit our purposes better. This will not work for unethical means (i.e., to spy on someone and wrongly invade privacy). Light a gray candle. Imagine you now possess an "invisible cloak" similar to Harry Potter's. See yourself being looked over so you can do your work, or see yourself not being missed at an event that you had to forego. Hear the silence of your phone when working on a project with a deadline. You can also visualize this cloak for your car while you travel so you remain safe and unseen. Know you have access to this cloak at any time as needed.

Calantirniel

Notes:

July 21
Tuesday

4th ♋
New Moon 10:34 pm
☽ → ♌ 11:27 pm

Color of the day: Scarlet
Incense of the day: Bayberry

Eclipse Balancing Spell

Today, we have a total solar eclipse that occurs over Southeast Asia and the western Pacific. This will be the longest eclipse of the twenty-first century, with totality occurring for 6 minutes and 39 seconds. Today is

a prime time for magic, as eclipses are rare and wondrous events. Some see the eclipse as a time when the Sun god and the Moon goddess are embracing. It's a great opportunity to work with the balance of masculine and feminine energies. Even if you live in a part of the world where the Moon's shadow doesn't fall during this eclipse, you can still work magic for new opportunities and to bring change into your life. Light a white candle for the Sun god and a black one for the Moon goddess. Then repeat the verse:

As the Sun god and Moon goddess embrace today,

May new opportunities start to come my way,

During this eclipse, the Moon's shadow is cast on the Earth,

Ushering in a time of balance, magic, and re-birth.

Allow the spell candles to burn out in a safe place.

Ellen Dugan

Notes:

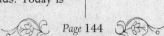

July 22
Wednesday

1st ♌

☉ → ♌ 12:36 pm

Color of the day: Yellow
Incense of the day: Lilac

Spell for Good Fortune

Bring together a red cloth, fortune cookie(s) with the prewritten fortunes removed unread, your athame or wand, a red candle, a green candle, small slips of paper and pen, coins, and paper money. Start in a very positive frame of mind, banishing all worries and bad thoughts; lavender scent helps with this. Breathe and connect with Mother Earth. Write the fortunes you desire on the slips of paper and place them inside the cookies with intention. Place the cookies atop the money. Light the green candle, concentrating your good fortune into being in the present. Light the red candle for fast action. Tap each cookie with your athame to energize the fortune inside of it. One at a time, take the slips of paper out of the cookies and read them out loud. Eat the cookie while envisioning the fortune already in your life. When you are finished, burn the slips of paper, extinguish the candles, and thank the Spirit for your upcoming good fortune.

Gail Wood

Notes:

July 23
Thursday

1st ♌

☽ → ♍ 11:22 pm

Color of the day: Turquoise
Incense of the day: Nutmeg

Stone Barrier

For this spell, you will need three or four anchor stones to place outside your home (or inside, if you don't have a yard). You can put one at each corner of your property or just scatter them, one in the front yard or on the porch, the others at the side or in the back. Set them in plain view as ornaments or conceal them beneath bushes or in flower beds. You can also use existing items in the landscape to help anchor your ward, especially large trees. Use this ward for protection and to keep out unwanted negative energy and trespassers. Visualize these stones as anchors for a protective net or screen. Touch each stone as you make a clockwise route around your home and say:

Keep trespassers at bay
Keep all danger far away
No negativity or discontent
May this ward be firmly set.

Ember

Notes:

I welcome joy within me
In my heart with every beat
May that love be extended out
To everyone I meet.

Make it a point during the following week to extend a kindness to everyone on your list in appreciation for their kindness and love for you.

Mickie Mueller

Notes:

July 24
Friday

 1st ♍

Color of the day: Pink
Incense of the day: Vanilla

Making Love Grow

It can be difficult finding true love until we learn to appreciate the love we are already given. Make a list of everyone that loves you. Search your heart and you'll realize how loved you are by members of your family, friends, even pets. Place the list under a pink candle next to the Two of Cups and Three of Cups tarot cards. Place a vase of roses and daisies nearby. While you gaze at the candle flame, think about the people listed, feeling their love filling you. Allow the love to push out negative feelings; feel warmth and love.

July 25
Saturday

1st ♍

Color of the day: Blue
Incense of the day: Ivy

A Prayer Cup Spell

Prayer cups are rarely used these days, but they produce powerful magic. First, you'll need a tea or coffee cup and saucer. Wash and bless your cup and saucer according to your spiritual path. Speak words of power over them according to your spell as you hold the cup in both hands. Next, sprinkle herbs in your cup suitable to your wishes. Raise the cup and present it to each direction, plus Heaven and Earth. Cover the cup with the saucer; set them aside and let the spell do its work. When the spell physically manifests your desire, sprinkle the herbs around your magic circle or outdoors. Then wash your cup and saucer. End by rubbing the inside of your cup with a drop of olive oil to show your thanks. Now your prayer cup is ready for your next spell.

James Kambos

Notes:

potluck, instead of the usual, "people whose last names start with A to G brings salads" method, try something different. Have people whose Sun signs are fire signs bring an entree, water signs bring beverages, air signs bring salads, and earth signs bring desserts. For music, try Irish reels or other lively folk dances, which people can dance to by joining hands and going around in a circle. Games can be anything people wish to play, but it's more fun if there are prizes, even if they're from the dollar store or someone's attic. Have fun!

Magenta Griffith

Notes:

July 26
Sunday

1st ♍

☽ → ♎ 1:25 am

Color of the day: Yellow
Incense of the day: Frankincense

Summer Picnic Day

What a wonderful day for a picnic! Weather permitting, get together with your friends for an outdoor celebratory ritual, followed by a potluck feast, games, and music. It's almost Lammas (Lughnasah), the feast of the Welsh god Lugh, which was celebrated by games and athletic contests. If you're having a large

July 27
Monday

 1st ♎

Color of the day: White
Incense of the day: Clary sage

Vocal Chakra Balancing

The Moon is in Libra, which is a great sign to aid in achieving internal balance. Hinduism recognizes the seven major chakras, or energy centers, on the human body. Before performing this exercise, familiarize yourself with Hindu concepts of the chakras and the human energy body. Discover the most common alignments for these energetic centers, such as colors, scents, vibrational tones, and common associated imagery. Be alone for this working, ensured that no one will hear your voice. I prefer to perform this exercise while driving in the car. Using your voice, hum the absolute lowest pitch you can possibly make. You will have to stretch your jaw down with your lips closed in order to create this deep tone. This resonates with your base chakra. Slowly, raise the pitch of your voice, finally reaching the highest octave to which your vocal cords can stretch: this represents your crown chakra. Continue these vocal fluxes as long as you feel is necessary. Envision your intentions for this vocal intonation so that each tone helps cleanse a certain chakra.

Raven Digitalis

Notes:

July 28
Tuesday

1st ♎

☽ → ♏ 6:56 am

2nd Quarter 6:00 pm

Color of the day: Black
Incense of the day: Ginger

Spell to Unlock Your Inner Power

Perform this spell to give your magic an extra boost and use it sparingly to maintain the overall impact. You'll need a navy-blue eyeliner pencil and flowing, comfortable clothes. When you are ready, stand in the center of your circle and assume the goddess position (arms spread high and legs apart in line with your shoulders). Speak this welcoming statement:

> *Upon this blessed night,*
> *I stand here, child of the*
> *divine surrounded by*
> *magic and light.*

Let down your arms. Using the eyeliner, draw a pentacle on the palm of your dominant hand. Hold your other (nondominant) hand over your heart and say,

> *This is my moment, all that I*
> *am, and all that I will be.*

Then, draw a second pentacle on your nondominant palm and speak this incantation:

Oh lord and lady, I ask of you,
Grant me eternal energy
to conjure my will with
harm to none.

To weave goodness in my life
and in lives of the people
whom I love.

I cast this spell to awaken
your blessed gifts
and so shall it be!

Gwinevere Rain

Notes:

to Christianity. Are you feeling oppressed in any area of your life? Today is the day to review your options and figure out the most positive course of action to dissolve negative situations and replace them with positive ones. You don't need to be violent or instigate a physical battle. Make choices, seek help, remove yourself from the situation. Use today to symbolize positive action and a fresh start. If you feel no negative situation, take a look at the organizations that work to defeat oppression. Volunteer time with them, write letters, or help organize protests. The most important thing to do on this day is to take action.

Cerridwen Iris Shea

Notes:

July 29
Wednesday

 2nd ♏

Color of the day: Brown
Incense of the day: Marjoram

Defeat of Olaf the Lawbreaker

Today is an important day in the calendar for those following the Asatru religion. Today marks the defeat, in the year 1280, of Olaf the Lawbreaker. Called "St. Olaf" in some non-Asatru circles, he was famous for the despicable ways in which he tortured and murdered those who refused to convert

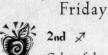

July 30
Thursday

2nd ♏︎
☽ → ♐︎ 4:10 pm

Color of the day: Purple
Incense of the day: Carnation

Ogahm Staves

Everybody loves popsicles, and popsicles leave popsicle sticks. Save yours; wash and dry them carefully. When you have twenty sticks, make a set of Ogham staves. Ogham is an ancient Celtic alphabet used in magical writing and is made by carving or painting lines on wood or stone. To make your set, first look up the letters of the Ogham alphabet, readily available on the Internet or in magical books such as *Ogam: The Celtic Oracle of the Trees* by Paul Rhys Mountfort. Use red or black paint to mark one Ogham sign on the end of each stick. Allow them to dry. Store your Ogham staves in a cloth bag for safekeeping. To learn Ogham, draw one stick from the bag each morning. Look up its meaning and meditate on the interpretation. After going through all the staves, repeat the process, trying to remember the meaning without looking it up.

Elizabeth Barrette

Notes:

July 31
Friday

2nd ♐︎

Color of the day: White
Incense of the day: Rose

Cultivate Beauty

Everyone has their own special brand of beauty, but we can sometimes forget this as we are bombarded by unrealistic images in our society. To remind yourself of your own true beauty, find ways to cultivate beauty in your life and surroundings every day. Light either one pink and one green candle or two of the same color and place a piece of jasper stone or jewelry between them. If you have a string of jasper beads, you can wrap this around the base of the candleholders. Allow the candles to burn out, then carry the stone or wear the jewelry whenever you feel you need a beauty boost.

> Venus help me to recall,
> I am your child after all,
> Help my beauty to shine through
> In everything I say and do.

Ember

Notes:

August is the eighth month of the year and named for Augustus Caesar. Its astrological sign is Leo the lion (July 22–August 22), a fixed fire sign ruled by the Sun. The harvest begins, and on August 1 we observe the ancient harvest festival of Lammas. This is the first harvest festival of the year, and a time to honor the beginning of the grain harvests. Corn is ripening, and so are peaches and tomatoes. It is a month of rich color. Black-eyed Susans, sunflowers, goldenrod, and butterfly weed provide splashes of color along country lanes. In August, the Goddess blesses us with her bounty. Farmers' markets are overflowing with fresh produce, and county fairs showcase prize-winning vegetables and canned goods. Ancient Romans paid tribute to two of their greatest goddess figures in August: Diana and Venus. And for Christians, the feast day of the Virgin Mary is August 15. Native Americans honored their life-sustaining corn crop by referring to the August Full Moon as the Corn Moon. Magical activities for the month are as simple as preparing corn bread or making a corn or wheat doll to honor the harvest. August is summer at its most mature. It is a cicada's call in the afternoon heat, and the beauty of a tiger swallowtail butterfly lingering over the joe-pye weed. It is the pause before autumn's chill.

August 1
Saturday

Lammas

2nd ♐

Color of the day: Brown
Incense of the day: Rue

A Solar Offering

In a bowl layered for open charcoal incense burning, prepare a round of coal. Blend equal parts frankincense and myrrh with six drops of ylang-ylang oil. Once stirred together, empower the resin with the following chant:

> Central star, glorious Sun
> You are the torch-bearer from
> out of the darkness
> The father of all thought
> and design
> It is your light that penetrates
> all life
> Reaching even to the depths
> of terra
> Your force knows no end
> We journey ever round
> your vestige
> Honoring your position
> For you bind us all together
> Each to the next in perfect
> synchronicity
> Without you, we simply
> could not be.

Place the resin on the charcoal round and offer up the smoke to the Sun. As you do so, accept that his light radiates through all plants and animals, sustaining us, fortifying our bodies and ensuring the survival of the grand life force, not merely the survival of humanity. Leave this offering in an open sunny place where there is no danger of fire. Let your offering rise up through the planes of Earth and beyond to meet the face of the Sun.

Estha McNevin

Notes:

Holiday lore: Lammas is a bittersweet holiday, mingling joy at the current high season's harvest with the knowledge that summer is soon at an end. Many cultures have "first fruit" rituals on this day—the Celt's version is called Lughnasadh; the Anglo-Saxon version called Hlaf-masse. In the Middle Ages, the holiday settled on August 1, taking its current form for the most part, with sheaves of wheat and corn blessed on this day.

August 2
Sunday

2nd ♐

☽ → ♑ 4:08 am

Color of the day: Orange
Incense of the day: Almond

Magical Uses of Ginger

Gingerbread cut into the shapes of men, women, children, and animals were traditionally sold at revels and hiring fairs during the month of August. Ginger biscuits, known as "fairings," often contained a piece of clove for longevity. Long considered an aid to romance, ginger cakes and cookies were a popular gift for lovers. If you add ginger to any love spell you cast, it will give the spell more power. To heat up the romance in your relationship, warm wine to just under a simmer in a nonreactive pot. Add a muslin or cheesecloth bag filled with a mixture of rose petals, peeled ginger root and 1/2 teaspoon of ground ginger. Let steep and taste every few minutes so that the ginger doesn't overpower the wine. Chill and share with your lover. Ginger is also used in money spells. Sprinkle ground ginger over a stack of dollar bills to attract more money. To attract prosperity to your household, bury a ginger root by your front door.

Lily Gardner

Notes:

August 3
Monday

2nd ♑

Color of the day: Gray
Incense of the day: Lily

Releasing Emotional Stress

The Moon is in Capricorn today, which is ruled by Saturn. Saturn oversees the darker and longer lasting aspects of the spirit and psyche; it is perfect to utilize this planet's energy for a spell to relieve stress. After the Sun goes down, walk in an area that has many rocks and pebbles. Gather a number of stones that call to you, placing each one in a black bag. With a black permanent marker or black paint, draw the symbol of the planet Saturn on each stone you wish to imbue in the spell. When the ink or paint dries, meditate on a different emotional issue and channel its energy into the stone. Perhaps you wish to think about different things you've become angry or saddened by, channeling these stresses into the individual stones. When finished, cast the stones over a bridge into running water. With each toss, say: "Cast to the abyss this stress I feel; Saturn and water, I ask you to heal."

Raven Digitalis

Notes:

Then, light a red or black candle, visualizing the protective power of the candle and flame enveloping your entire computer and providing ultraprotection. Know your computer is safe and will be during this Mercury retrograde.

Calantirniel

Notes:

August 4
Tuesday

2nd ♑
☽ → ♒ 5:08 pm

Color of the day: Red
Incense of the day: Geranium

Computer Protection Spell

During September, Mercury will go retrograde, which is known as a time that causes problems with communications of all types, including the realm of computers. Do a thorough backup of your system and delete anything extraneous. Install an anti-virus program, consider changing browsers or using programs to avoid spyware and malware, and examine firewalls in your present system. If your computer is part of a network, examine the router as well.

August 5
Wednesday

2nd ♒
Full Moon 8:55 pm

Color of the day: Yellow
Incense of the day: Bay laurel

A Corn Moon Ritual

Native Americans and early settlers called the August Full Moon the Corn Moon. It was a time of giving thanks to the Earth and feasting. Corn was the focus of early harvest celebrations, as it was considered to be the seed of seeds and the giver of life. All the products from corn can be considered holy. Cornmeal, pollen, husks, and ears of corn were all used in fertility and prosperity magic. Corn Moon magic should be a simple ritual of giving thanks to Mother Earth. In doing so, you'll create positive karma that will return blessings to you. On the night of the Corn Moon, stand outside in a field if possible. Carry an earthenware dish filled with cornmeal. Raise it to the Full Moon, then lower it to the Earth. Solemnly sprinkle the corn meal on the ground and speak the following words:

> *From seed to plant,*
> *From plant to blossom,*
> *From blossom to harvest,*
> *I thank you, Mother Earth.*

When done, be aware of the August night as the Moon casts a mellow glow over a land of plenty. Listen to the katydid scratching at the darkness. Smell the ripeness of summer's end. And silently thank the ancient ones who gave us corn, the symbol of life itself.

James Kambos

Notes:

August 6
Thursday

3rd ♒

Color of the day: Green
Incense of the day: Apricot

Good Fortune

In China, Jupiter is associated with wood. Since Thursday is ruled by Jupiter, this spell is for creating a wooden good luck talisman. Find a small piece of wood; it could be a bead, a piece of bark, or a twig. Make sure it's something lying on the ground and not taken directly from a tree or shrub. A piece of cedar wood or a cedar twig is ideal, but any wood will do. You can also make a necklace or bracelet of wood beads. Light three or four dark-purple or dark-blue candles. Pass the piece of wood carefully and quickly through the flames. If you're using a bead, make sure you don't burn your fingers; use a tool or have the bead on a wire.

> *Fire mark this piece of wood*
> *Bring fortune that is only good.*
>
> *Fire's kiss this wood will bear*
> *Good luck to find me everywhere.*

Ember

Notes:

August 7
Friday

3rd ≈≈
☽ → ♓ 5:34 am

Color of the day: Purple
Incense of the day: Thyme

Gaia Consciousness Day

It's only a few months after Earth Day, but how many of your April resolutions have you kept? Today is a day to perform every action mindfully. Whether it's brushing your teeth, feeding the dog, taking out the garbage, or traveling to work, be aware of every aspect of every action. Think about the ripple effect. If someone cuts you off on the road, are you then rude to the clerk in the deli? Instead, CHOOSE to extend friendliness and graciousness. Stop adding to negative cycles by paying forward something positive instead of something negative. That doesn't mean you can't stand up for yourself to the person who wrongs you, but don't carry that negativity forward to the next person who crosses your path. Turn every action, every breath, every gesture into something with a positive impact on Earth and on those around you.

Cerridwen Iris Shea

Notes:

August 8
Saturday

3rd ♓

Color of the day: Blue
Incense of the day: Pine

Banishing Bad habits

If old habits die hard, perhaps you could use a magical boost to help release yourself of that which doesn't serve you. Make a list of all the bad habits you wish to remove from your life. Cut a potato in half and place the list inside the potato, tying it back together with black yarn. Tie three sage leaves to the outside of the potato. Hold it in your hands as you visualize your bad habits flowing out of you and into the potato.

> All these habits are mine
> no more,
> Aspects all that I abhor,
> As rots this potato, so
> rots thee,
> Never to return to me!

Bury the potato far from your home where it will not be disturbed. As the potato and your list rot, your habits will dissipate. For extra oomph, carry a sage leaf in your pocket every day for eighteen days.

Mickie Mueller

Notes:

August 9
Sunday

 3rd ♓
☽ → ♈ 4:23 pm

Color of the day: Yellow
Incense of the day: Heliotrope

healing Spell

Perform this spell to send someone healing energies or to help
yourself if you are not feeling well.
Use it in conjunction with traditional
medical therapies. You'll need
a medium-sized bowl, one green
floater candle (a tealight may be
substituted), a handful of smooth
rocks, and eucalyptus oil. Prior to
setting up your ritual space, fill the
bowl about three-quarters full of
water. If you are performing the spell
for someone else, ask their permission
first and consider bringing a photograph of them to your workspace.
Carefully drop in the stones, letting
them line the bowl's bottom. Then
place three drops of eucalyptus oil in
the water. Stir it counterclockwise
with your index finger. "By healing
water, perfume, and candle bright,
sickness dissipate, be gone now,
you've lost your fight." Drop in the
candle and light the wick. Visualize
the sickness leaving.

Gwinevere Rain

Notes:

August 10
Monday

3rd ♈

Color of the day: Lavender
Incense of the day: Rosemary

Getting a New Job

The process of job hunting can
be frustrating and stressful.
This spell helps to focus the energies
in your favor. Create your résumé or
have it made in a positive, professional
manner. Place a copy on a small table
or shelf with a bowl next to it. Then,
place a green candle on its left side
and a gold candle on its right side.
Light the candles and chant:

> I seek my place in the world
> of work, the one that is
> meant for me, the one that
> will provide for me. I have
> done my work, so mote it be.

Meditate in silence for a few
moments about your ideal job and
then place something in the bowl
that represents that job. Each day for
the next seven days, repeat the rite,
adding an item to the bowl that further
represents the desired position.

Winter Wren

Notes:

August 11
Tuesday

3rd ♈

Color of the day: White
Incense of the day: Ylang-ylang

Day of Danaids

King Danaeus had fifty daughters. They married the fifty sons of Aegyptus I, and forty-nine of them murdered their husbands on the wedding night. Their punishment in the underworld is to eternally attempt to fill leaky barrels and jars. Originally, this was part of the festival of Hersephoria, or "dew-gathering," but it was later performed during drought. Maidens with both parents still living or who had not experienced a death in the family for one year carried water-filled jugs covered with tiny punctures. They carried the jugs around the town to sprinkle water and stimulate the rain. If you have a garden and have had a parched summer, grab your watering can or prepare a jug punctured with tiny holes. Fill it, bless it, and sprinkle the contents throughout your property. If you have indoor plants rather than an outdoor garden, perform the same ritual with them. **Note:** Only perform this ritual during a summer drought. If you had a wet season, you should perform a Sun-based ritual instead.

Cerridwen Iris Shea

Notes:

August 12
Wednesday

3rd ♈

☽ → ♉ 12:49 am

Color of the day: Brown
Incense of the day: Lavender

Pocket Rock

I've carried a pocket rock for years and years, even before the pet rock craze. (Rocks make excellent pets, especially small ones you can carry with you. True, they aren't very lively, but they don't need to be fed.) There are many books about the magical and psychic properties of various stones. Agates are good for keeping grounded. Amethysts are calming and are traditionally said to keep a person from getting drunk. Hematite and carnelian are good for protection. Rose quartz is soothing for many people. Rutilant quartz and citrine will give you more energy. Choose your pocket rocks with care. Each rock is different. Hold a rock for a while and see what it feels like to you before you decide to "adopt" it. Carry it for a few days and see what happens. You may need to rest a particular stone from time to time; you may want grounding one day and more energy another, so having several to choose from is useful.

Magenta Griffith

Notes:

August 13
Thursday

 3rd ♉
4th Quarter 2:55 pm

Color of the day: Turquoise
Incense of the day: Balsam

A Canine Spell

To keep your four-legged friend safe and happy, perform this protection ritual. Begin by gathering some of your dog's beloved items—favorite toys, leash, ball, and a picture. Place them on an altar with a clipping of your canine's hair and a small locket or box. Call the directions and say:

> Oh faithful friend with
>   wagging tail,
> To you I spell, this wish
>   prevails.

> May your life be long and
>   full of fun,
> With long walks taken in
>   the Sun.

> Dwell with your Witch in
>   her domain,
> And be free of fleas,
>   and other pains.

> Here in this place, your
>   essence be,
> Long life, good health,
>   so mote it be.

Place the hair in the locket or box and keep it near a picture of your dog.

Nancy Bennett

Notes:

August 14
Friday

 4th ♉
☽ → ♊ 6:25 am

Color of the day: Pink
Incense of the day: Alder

Spell Forecasting

Before casting a spell, you may wish to do divination to determine whether or not it's advisable to proceed. A simple tarot spread can help clarify this. Draw five cards and lay them out in a horizontal row, from left to right: 1) Validity, 2) Viability, 3) Benefits, 4) Drawbacks, 5) Outcome. The first card reveals whether or not you have sufficient reason to cast the spell. The second card explains whether or not the spell will work. The third card shows what positive results the spell is likely to bring. The fourth card shows what negative results the spell is likely to bring. The fifth card describes the most probable outcome after the spell is cast. Put five cards together to create a picture that can help you decide if you really want to proceed with casting that spell.

Elizabeth Barrette

Notes:

August 15
Saturday

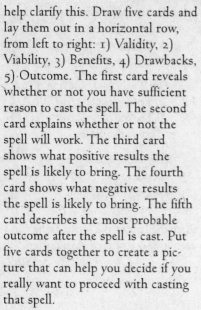

4th ♊

Color of the day: Gray
Incense of the day: Ivy

Kitchen Blessing

Today is a festival day of the Roman goddess of the hearth, Vesta. Vesta was the first of all deities to be invoked, as she represented the flame that burns at the center of Earth. Vesta is the perfect choice to protect your hearth and home. Today, most folks have the kitchen as their sacred hearth area, so let's do a bit of kitchen magic. Light a red cinnamon-scented candle for Vesta in the center of your kitchen. Red is a sacred color of Vesta and the cinnamon scent encourages protection, prosperity, and comfort.

> Goddess of fire and the
> sacred hearth flame,
>
> Now I bless my modern
> hearth in Vesta's name.
>
> Protect us well, keeping us
> happy and safe.
>
> May your fiery light shine
> forth and grant us grace.

Allow the candle to burn out safely.

Ellen Dugan

Notes:

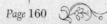

August 16
Sunday

 4th ♊
☽ → ♋ 9:13 am

Color of the day: Gold
Incense of the day: Marigold

Temperance Charm

The old saying goes, "All things in moderation." Today is a good day to work on temperance. Think about an area of your life that needs some moderation. Do you spend excessive amounts of money and feel guilty afterward? Have you accumulated too much debt? Do you consume too much unhealthy food or drink? Try to curb bad habits with the following spell. On a piece of black paper, write the areas of your life where you need temperance. Fold the paper and place it in shallow dish and cover the paper with dirt. Recite the following:

> Dispel excess that does
>   me harm,
> Earth accept this binding
>   charm.
> Help me moderate my ways,
> To meet the challenge of
>   each day.
> Guard this burden, keep
>   it safe
> In this charm I place my
>   faith.

After you have visualized your intent, bury this paper and dirt outside or in the bottom of a potted plant.

Ember

Notes:

August 17
Monday

4th ♋

Color of the day: White
Incense of the day: Neroli

House Protection

Today is the Roman festival honoring the god Portunus, guardian of gates and doors (portals). Keys were important symbols in his rituals. A very old spell for protecting your home from theft is to string three keys on a red cord and hang it above your front door. It is very important that the keys do not fit any of your locks! Say:

> Three keys I hang by
>   magic cord

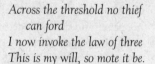

Across the threshold no thief
can ford
I now invoke the law of three
This is my will, so mote it be.

Skeleton keys can still be found at hardware stores that specialize in old house renovations. Wearing a skeleton key around your neck or in your pocket protects you from evil. If you come to a crossroads and are uncertain which direction to take, toss a bunch of keys over your left shoulder. The longest key in the bunch will point the correct way.

Lily Gardner

Notes:

August 18
Tuesday

4th ♋

☽ → ♌ 9:56 am

Color of the day: Black
Incense of the day: Cedar

Spare Spell Components

By now, you have done many spells. You probably have a variety of spell components left over—stones, beads, slips of paper, candles, threads of different colors, etc. So where do you put all this stuff? You may have a big altar cabinet. Most of us, however, need to store things more concisely. One excellent option is a tacklebox or toolbox. These come in different sizes, but all have many interior compartments to secure small- to medium-sized objects. Another choice is a parts organizer: an upright chest with tiny drawers designed for holding nuts, bolts, and other hardware. They work just as well for spell components. Plus, you can label the drawers according to contents. After you put your supplies in their proper places, dedicate the storage container for safekeeping. Draw or paint a pentacle on the top and say: "Pentacle of power spin; keep my tools all safe within."

Elizabeth Barrette

Notes:

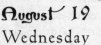

August 19
Wednesday

 4♄ ♌

Color of the day: White
Incense of the day: Lilac

Banishing Inner Darkness

Today the first "Black Cow," or root beer float, was served in 1893. To find your sweet light when you feel like you're in the middle of the dark sea, gather a dark-colored bowl, a towel, water, and some floating candles in your favorite colors. Use patchouli incense for grounding and deep inner sight. Turn out all the lights, making sure there's a little ambient light. Place the bowl on the towel. Pour water into the bowl and dip your hands in, stirring the water clockwise. As you stir, think of the things that cause you distress, anger, or other negative emotions. Keep stirring until you get it all out, then pause, and start to stir counterclockwise. For each quality, chant, "_____ I banish, from my life please banish." Keep stirring until you have chanted for all the things that cause turbulence in your life. Now slowly bring the water to a calm stillness. Breathe deeply and place a floating candle in the water. Light the candle for peace. Keep lighting candles for the qualities you wish to create in your life. Let the candles burn out. When you are finished, pour the water into the ground and bury the leftover wax.

Gail Wood

Notes:

August 20
Thursday

4♄ ♌
New Moon 6:01 am
☽ → ♍ 10:00 am

Color of the day: Crimson
Incense of the day: Mulberry

Calling on Guides and Ancestors

Being a New Moon day, this is a great time to call upon your guides and ancestors. Cast a circle as you normally would, preparing to make contact with your spiritual guides. You may wish to construct additional magical workings based on this chant, or simply repeat it in meditation and see what visions and spirit communications come to you. If you know who your spirit guides are, be they departed relatives, friends, or strictly astral beings, you may communicate with them during the ritual. Otherwise, you may be

surprised at what communications you receive. If you don't "get" anything the first time, keep trying each New Moon, altering the ritual and chanting as you deem appropriate; Witchcraft is a living and personal spiritual path, after all. Repeat three times:

> This New Moon I call to my ancestors and guides. Bless me now and appear to mine eyes. Dearly departed who stand at my side, I approach you now with honor and pride.

Raven Digitalis

Notes:

August 21
Friday

1st ♏

Color of the day: Purple
Incense of the day: Vanilla

Confidence Spell

Craft this charm to boost your confidence. It can be especially useful for public speaking or starting the school year. You'll need copper jewelry wire, jewelry glue, and a small stone of each of the following: clear quartz, carnelian, and rose quartz. Start by empowering each of the stones. Hold the clear quartz between your palms and chant, "I am light." When you're ready, hold the carnelian and chant, "I am radiant." Repeat this step for the third time as you hold the rose quartz and chant, "I am love." Using the glue, cluster the three gemstones together. After waiting a few minutes, wrap the wire around the gemstone trio. Finish by creating a loop at the top. Finally, say this incantation:

> Like honey to a bee
> I draw people to me
> I am confident and carefree.

When the charm is completely dry, you can string it on a chain and wear it as a necklace.

Gwinevere Rain

Notes:

August 22
Saturday
Ramadan begins

1st ♍

☽ → ♎ 11:12 am

☉ → ♍ 7:38 pm

Color of the day: Indigo
Incense of the day: Patchouli

Gathering Your Power

A medicine pouch is a very powerful and very personal magical charm. There is no hard and fast list of things for it to contain. All items placed within should be of strong significance to you as a magical and spiritual being. The bag itself can be a leather or fabric pouch that you stitch up yourself or purchase (leather lasts longer). It should be something you are comfortable wearing much of the time and can be as plain or fancy as you like. Once you have your bag, gather together the things you wish to place within. You may only have a few items to start, but medicine bags tend to grow over time. In your sacred space, reflect on each item as you add it to the bag. Consider once more the item's magical significance to you and the point it represents in your personal growth. When you are done, close the bag securely and begin wearing it with reverence.

Winter Wren

Notes:

August 23
Sunday

1st ♎

Color of the day: Amber
Incense of the day: Juniper

Vulcanalia Fire Spell

This is the festival of the Roman fire god Vulcan. In the dry heat of summer, the crops and food in the granaries were at greater risk of accidental fire, so bonfires were carefully created to placate Vulcan. Enjoy an outdoor fire tonight to honor Vulcan. Put some wood in the fire pit or in your barbecue grill and grab some iced tea or a glass of wine. Break apart a red taper candle. As you enjoy your fire, toss in a piece of wax occasionally. As you watch the burning wax flare up, say:

*Vulcan, lord of fire, accept
    this offering,
Blessed flame will always have
    a home with mine and me,
I light this fire for you to
    dance within the flame,*

Keeping fire where it belongs
on this your holy day.

Sometime today, check all fire extinguishers and the batteries in your smoke detector.

            Mickie Mueller

Notes:

Under bright August skies
and a waxing Moon,

Let me find a magic group
for myself soon.

I manifest a group filled with
wisdom, kindness, and fun,

As I will so now must it be,
and bringing harm to none.

Take your time and get to know the members of your group. You should feel welcome, safe, and happy at all times with any magical group.

            Ellen Dugan

Notes:

August 24
Monday

1st ♎

☽ → ♏ 3:16 pm

Color of the day: Silver
Incense of the day: Narcissus

Call for Magic Group

Today is a Monday and we are in a waxing Moon phase, a double dose of lunar magic. And as we are in the season of harvest, let's work a bit of magic to gather others of a like mind. If you are wanting to be part of a magical study group, circle, or coven, here is a spell that can help you find compatible magical folks. Get out under that waxing Moon tonight and make your request to the Lord and Lady.

August 25
Tuesday

1st ♏
Color of the day: Gray
Incense of the day: Basil

Banishing Boredom

Life sometimes gets very mundane and routine, and we become bored. To awaken interest in our lives again, collect a red energizing candle, a scarf or length of cloth in an exciting color or pattern, and a

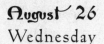

stone. Breathe deeply and connect with Mother Earth. Gather up the boredom and angst you feel inside you. Feel it well up and then hold the stone to your mouth and yell all that feeling into the stone. Take the stone outdoors and throw it away from you with all your might, shouting, "Begone!" Return and light the red candle for energy. Wave the cloth over it and wrap it around you, saying, "As I surround myself in color, texture, and pattern, I feel excitement and curiosity fill me again. I am willing myself to see new patterns and to feel my life anew. As I will so mote it be." Fill yourself with excitement and the will to see interesting new patterns. When you are finished, extinguish the candle and thank the Spirit. Wear the scarf often as a reminder that you are the excitement.

Gail Wood

Notes:

August 26
Wednesday

1st ♏

☽ → ♐ 11:16 pm

Color of the day: Topaz
Incense of the day: Marjoram

Red-Thread Clothing Spell

Do this spell first thing in the morning. Red thread is a tool of Witches; one use of red thread is to connect you to things like clothing, so you won't lose them or leave them behind. This spell will only work on a few items at a time, so choose carefully. You'll need a needle and a spool of red thread. Cut a length of thread that measures from your nose to your fingertips, and thread your needle with it. Find an inconspicuous place on the garment, and stitch a small pentagram on it, using just five stitches. As you sew, recite one line with each stitch: "Stay with me, cover me, warm me, protect me, return to me." Sew the same place until you have used up the thread, then make a very short stitch and loop the thread through it and knot it. Trim off any excess thread and burn it in a ritual fire.

Magenta Griffith

Notes:

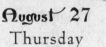

August 27
Thursday

1st ♐
2nd Quarter 7:42 am

Color of the day: White
Incense of the day: Jasmine

house Protection

If you have or know of an ash tree, harvest by hand a large bundle of the leaves and berries. At each of the four corners of your house, toss ash leaves into the air, asking them to sense and dissipate any gathered or directed negative energy within. Let them lay undisturbed on the floor overnight. Gather the leaves the next morning and place them into a sachet or medicine bag. As you take the bag out of the house, announce to the energies of your living space that all unwanted vibrations are being hauled outside and won't be allowed reentry. Hang this above your front door to counteract intruders or guests with negative intentions.

Estha McNevin

Notes:

August 28
Friday

2nd ♐

Color of the day: Rose
Incense of the day: Yarrow

Make New friends Spell

The pineapple is known as a symbol of friendship in Hawaii and other Polynesian island nations. Light a pink (or other light, pastel color) candle and use a Three of Cups tarot image. Slice a pineapple and eat some while visualizing new friends coming into your life and sharing these pineapple slices with you. See your new friends spending time with you doing things that all of you like to do. Get into the feeling of this really happening as much as you can. When the candle is burned down, place the Three of Cups image where you will see it often. Do the things you enjoy and know you will meet friends soon!

Calantirniel

Notes:

August 29
Saturday

 2nd ♐
☽ → ♑ 10:44 am

Color of the day: Blue
Incense of the day: Magnolia

Day of Thoth Spell

Today was the day the ancient Egyptian god Thoth was honored. Thoth, one of the greatest of the Egyptian gods, was believed to be the creator of the universe and all magic. He was both healer and warrior and became closely associated with the Eye of Horus, which was considered to be an amulet used to protect against the evil eye. This spell will help you invoke his power to destroy the evil eye. On a small piece of paper, draw the shape of an eye with blue ink. Put the paper in an envelope. On another piece of paper write, "I release all negativity directed at me without harm." Burn this piece of paper in the flame of a blue candle. Let the ashes cool, then seal them in the envelope along with the eye charm. Hide it in a wooden box. When you feel the time is right, burn the envelope in a ritual fire.

James Kambos

Notes:

August 30
Sunday

2nd ♑

Color of the day: Orange
Incense of the day: Almond

A Spell For Challenging Choices

We all have difficult choices we have to face. Begin this ritual the night before you are due to make a change or face some challenge in your life. Place a bowl of fruit, a snake representation, and a mirror on the table. Light a candle on each side of the mirror and turn off the lights. Choose one candle to represent Yes and one for No. Breathe deeply and focus your energy on the spell at hand. Stare into the mirror and chant:

I am in charge of my destiny
The choice is mine,
So mote it be.

As you chant, watch to see which flame flickers the most, being careful not to influence it with your breath. Blow that candle out first, then the other. Go to bed and allow yourself to dream of the right choice.

Nancy Bennett

Notes:

August 31
Monday

2nd ♑

☽ → ♒ 11:43 pm

Color of the day: Ivory
Incense of the day: Hyssop

Yarrow Love Spell

For such a common herb, yarrow has a wealth of magical uses. Hold a sprig of yarrow in your hand and it will lend you courage. If you wear it in a locket or amulet bag, it will protect you from enemies and attract friends and lovers. If yarrow is used in the wedding ceremony, it grants the couple seven years of love. Yarrow was a plant of Venus and is therefore used in many love spells. Sew a handful of yarrow in a red flannel square and put it under your pillow. Say:

> Thou pretty herb of Venus' tree,
> Thy true name is Yarrow.
> Now who my bosom friend
>   must be,
> Pray tell to me tomorrow.

You will dream of your new lover that night. If you place the serrated leaf in your nostril and your nose bleeds, the one you long for loves you:

> Yarroway, Yarroway, bear a
>   white bow,
> If my love love me, my nose
>   will bleed now.

Lily Gardner

September is the ninth month of the year. Its name is derived from the Latin word *septum*, which means "seventh," as it was the seventh month of the Roman calendar. Its astrological sign is Virgo, the maiden (August 22–September 22), a mutable earth sign ruled by Mercury. Cool misty mornings and an occasional splash of autumn color in the woodland tells us September is here. The afternoons are still warm, and the last of the garden's produce is harvested. The cidery tang of windfall apples coming in from the orchard is on the air now. Chipmunks and squirrels are busy readying their nests for winter. In the old days, September was the month that the "blizzard" pantry was stocked in preparation for bad weather. Mabon, or the Fall Equinox, is the main holiday of September. It is the second harvest sabbat and the first dark sabbat. The Great Son Mabon returns to the womb of Mother Earth for rest and renewal, just as nature does at this time of year. In September, we contemplate the dual nature of life and death. Although we are surrounded by the abundant harvest of pumpkins, apples, and grapes, at the same time nature prepares to enter the dark season. One of the most glorious sights of September is its Full Moon, the Harvest Moon. It glows with a pale golden color, and is the crown jewel of the September night.

September 1
Tuesday

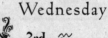

2nd ≈

Color of the day: Red
Incense of the day: Ginger

Flash Paper Magic

To get quick results from a spell, try this. Go to a store that sells supplies for stage magic and buy a package of flash paper. This is thin paper that will ignite and burn very quickly. Read the directions carefully. Think of what you want and write a few words that precisely and concisely describe your objective. Or make a sigil to express your goal. You can do this by writing your goal in as few words as possible, eliminating all the duplicate letters, and merging the letters that are left into one symbol. Copy the words or the sigil onto the flash paper. Cast a circle in your usual manner and carefully hold the paper over a flameproof dish or plate. Say, "May this happen as quickly as possible." Light the paper at one corner and drop it immediately. End the ritual by saying, "As I will, so mote it be."

Magenta Griffith

Notes:

Holiday lore: Many Greeks consider this their New Year's Day. This day marks the beginning of the sowing season, a time of promise and hope. On this day, people fashion wreaths of pomegranates, quinces, grapes, and garlic bulbs—all traditional symbols of abundance. Just before dawn on September 1, children submerge the wreaths in the ocean waters for luck. They carry seawater and pebbles home with them in small jars to serve as protection in the coming year. Tradition calls for them to gather exactly forty pebbles and water from exactly forty waves.

September 2
Wednesday

2nd ≈

Color of the day: Brown
Incense of the day: Honeysuckle

A Garden Spell

Call upon Demeter to aid you in this harvest-time ritual. Begin in early morning in your garden. Dress an altar in seasonal colors of gold and brown at the center of your plants. Call your directions and then say:

Great Demeter, to thee I call
to aid me in my harvest.

May my plants be easily
harvested, offering to me
the fruits of their labors.

May I be obliging in treating
them with respect as they
go to their rest.

Great Demeter, to thee I ask
let my work be rewarding,
let my crops be rich and
plentiful.

Begin to harvest those foods that are
ready, in clockwise order if possible.
As you harvest, thank each plant
for its efforts and pledge to share its
bounty with loved ones, as well as to
save some seed for the coming year.

Nancy Bennett

Notes:

September 3
Thursday

 2nd ≈≈
$\mathcal{D} \rightarrow \mathcal{H}$ 11:58 am

Color of the day: Turquoise
Incense of the day: Clove

Leaf Spell

Early in autumn, the leaves begin
to turn colors and drift down
from the trees. They symbolize the
passing of the old to make way for

the new and the beauty of change.
Although they come from trees,
which are grounded in Earth, the falling leaves also represent the element
of air as they float free. Find a forest
near your home where you can walk
among the trees and enjoy the drifting
leaves. For best results, go on a breezy
day to maximize the leaf activity. As
you stroll through clouds of flying
leaves, say this blessing:

High and low
Dark and fair
Autumn leaves fill the air
Orange, red
Golden, brown
What goes up must
    come down
From the trees
To the sky
Blessing me as they fly.

Listen for the leaves to whisper their
wisdom to you.

Elizabeth Barrette

Notes:

September 4
Friday

 2nd ♓

Full Moon 12:02 pm

Color of the day: Pink
Incense of the day: Orchid

Water Scrying

This Full Moon night begins the Celtic month of Muin, or Vine, which represents the powers of prophecy. Take a dark-colored bowl of water outside and add a pinch of sea salt, blessing it under the Full Moon.

> Shining mirror, white
> 　moonflower
> Please bless this dish of sea
> Fill the water with
> 　your power
> Share prophecy's gifts
> 　with me.

Take the bowl inside in a dark room lit by only two tealights. Set the candles on each side of the bowl in such a way that their light is not reflected on the surface of the water. Surround the bowl with vines or a grapevine wreath and moonflowers or moonflower seeds. Dip your finger in the water and touch it to your third eye. Ground and center and then gaze into the bowl. Look past the surface of the water, deep into the dark beyond. Concentrating on your question, you should begin to see vague images; allow them to form,

don't force them, just observe. On a paper nearby, write your impressions as soon as you can after you finish scrying. This divination technique takes practice, but with work, it can be quite effective.

Mickie Mueller

Notes:

September 5
Saturday

3rd ♓

☽ → ♈ 10:14 pm

Color of the day: Indigo
Incense of the day: Rue

Isilyavannië

In *Tië eldaliéva*, the Elven Path, *Isilyavannië* is the Moon of Yavanna and is aligned with none other than the much-loved motherly Yavanna Kementari, the Giver of Fruits. Where her sister, Vána, energetically relates to the maiden energy of new plant growth, Yavanna resonates with the maturing and ripening of fruits and the bounty of harvest. As Aulë the Smith's wife, she appears as a fair-haired woman robed in deep green, but has also been seen as a glorious tree crowned with Anar, the Sun, and golden dewdrops falling from the leaves to the ground, creating corn. To meet and honor Yavanna, light a gold or dark-green candle and visualize a green mound with a magnificent silver tree and a most beautiful golden tree. She appears and tells you the deep, beautiful stories of the Olvar, the Green-Rooted Ones, or the Plant Kingdom, that she loves so dearly. On Arda, our Earth, it is getting more difficult for the Olvar to thrive as the fires of technology suppress the green world without a care. Offer your stewardship, as the Elves once did, to learn about as well as to guard and protect their world, and the Olvar will in turn care for all of us. Come back to where you are with Yavanna's harvest for you. Then, plant a tree!

Calantirniel

Notes:

September 6
Sunday

3rd ♈

Color of the day: Gold
Incense of the day: Marigold

Fairy Magic

The Fey are powerful magical allies, if they can be convinced to aid you in your desires. They also love gifts and goodies. If you wish to attract the assistance of the fairy folk, plan to take your magical workings to the nearby woods. In addition to your magical tools, take a small plate and cup, a silver- or gold-colored coin (not copper), a small purple or blue birthday cake–type candle, seven pretty cookies, and some fine sparkling cider or juice. Walk about until you locate a fairy circle. Arrange the cookies neatly on the plate and pour the cider in the cup. Place these items in the center of the fairy circle. Next to them, place the coin and light the candle, fixing it upon the coin with a few drops of wax. Leave the circle and do your magical working just outside its borders, then go on your way. When you return the next day, if the plate and cup are empty and the coin is gone, the fairies have accepted your entreaty and joined in your magic.

Winter Wren

Notes:

September 7
Monday
Labor Day

 3rd ♈

Color of the day: White
Incense of the day: Lily

Avoid Mercury Retrograde!

Mercury goes retrograde today and will be retrograde for about three weeks, until September 29. This means that Mercury appears to be moving backwards, an astronomical illusion caused by the relative movements of the planets. Since Mercury is associated with communication, transportation, and commerce, letters and e-mails might be lost and people may misunderstand each other during this time. Mercury retrograde is also a poor time to buy or sell anything important. Here is a talisman that could help: on a small octagonal piece of paper with one point up, draw the symbol of Mercury in orange ink and decorate the border with orange ink. (The number of Mercury is eight, the color is orange.) Light a stick of lavender or white sandalwood incense and draw a circle around you. Hold the talisman and recite:

> Winged god of thought and
> speech and sign,
>
> As I my thoughts and words
> do send,

> Touch this small charm with
> light divine,
>
> So magic may all
> errors mend.

Magenta·Griffith

Notes:

September 8
Tuesday

3rd ♈
☽ → ♉ 6:17 am

Color of the day: Black
Incense of the day: Bayberry

Rid a home of Negative Energy

If you feel your home has a buildup of negative energy, this spell will help re-align it for positive energy. Gather frankincense and myrrh incense and a mixture of salt water in a spray bottle. Walk through each room and spray the water three times, then smudge the area with incense. Say this chant each time you're in a new room:

> Here and now, I work
>   this spell
> Cast well, where I dwell

> Scent and brew
> Purify through
> With harm to none
> May it be done!

When you have been all around your home, return to the starting point and say:

> I now bless this home with
>   love and light
> May it be filled with
>   positive energy
> And block harm from coming
>   this way
> This is my will
> So mote it be!

Gwinevere Rain

Notes:

or other favorite candy, a pillow or teddy bear, a mirror, and a fuzzy blanket. Use soft pastel candles and flower-scented oils or incense. Pink rose quartz will further enhance the environment. Settle deeply and comfortably into your most comfortable chair or couch. Surround yourself with the scent and lit candles. Wrap the blanket around you and hug the teddy bear. Hold the mirror up and gaze deeply into your eyes, saying:

> As I look into this glass
> I know bad feelings will pass.
> The good inside me bursts
>   out free
> As I will it, so mote it be!

Eat the chocolate, hug the teddy bear, and spend some time feeling cozy, warm, and happy.

Gail Wood

Notes:

September 9
Wednesday

  3rd ☉

Color of the day: Yellow
Incense of the day: Marjoram

I Need A hug Spell

Sometimes we need a reminder that we are okay just the way we are. You will need a piece of chocolate

September 10
Thursday

3rd ♉
☽ → ♊ 12:17 pm

Color of the day: Green
Incense of the day: Carnation

Mourning Eve

Many "holy days" begin with preparations and rituals performed on the eve of the actual event. Even if you are not a New Yorker, the deaths of nearly 3,000 people on 9/11 have an impact. September 11 is a day for families and friends to mourn the loss of their loved ones, to remember the tragic events of the day. September 10 is a day to celebrate the joys and good things the lost ones brought to so many lives. Newspapers and Web sites may print biographies of the dead. Collect them and read them out loud. Light candles, lay a place at a Dumb Supper similar to Samhain, and raise a glass to toast the LIVES of those who are now gone. Tomorrow is about the loss; today is about the enduring good these people brought to so many lives.

Cerridwen Iris Shea

Notes:

September 11
Friday

3rd ♊
4th Quarter 10:16 pm

Color of the day: Rose
Incense of the day: Cypress

Magical Makeup

The planet Mercury rules the sign Gemini, which is the sign the Moon is in all day. Mercury embodies magic, trade, study, and communication. The following simple spell, which can really be performed any day (gender notwithstanding), is for both communication and psychic sight. Hail Mercury! Get your favorite stick of eyeliner and lipstick (or purchase them if you're not accustomed to wearing them). Place them on your altar, cast a circle, meditate, or do whatever you do to put yourself in a sacred frame of mind. Enchant the makeup with the elements: put salt on them for earth, wave them in incense for air, stick them quickly in flame for fire, and drop some water on them for water. Close your eyes and envision them surrounded in glowing yellow and white, the ideal colors to represent communication. Say:

> In this night and in this
> hour, this makeup now I
> do empower.

*This eyeliner I imbue with
the power of sight, that I may
see reality right.*

*This lipstick I imbue with
clear communication, that
I may speak with truth and
clarification. So mote it be.*

Raven Digitalis

Notes:

September 12
Saturday

 4th ♊
☽ → ♋ 4:19 pm

Color of the day: Blue
Incense of the day: Sandalwood

Personal Power

Call on the strength and energy of the Sun today to increase your own power and energy. If there's a specific area you'd like to work on, visualize it. Perhaps you seek endurance for athletics or the energy to begin a new project. If you're headed back to school, this is a good time to energize yourself for the stamina students need. Collect the following: a leaf and twig (any kind found lying on the ground will do), a stone that

represents sunlight or energy (such as pyrite, citrine quartz, or amber), and any flower of your choice. Wrap these items in a small drawstring bag or tie them into a bundle of white, yellow, or gold fabric and ribbon. Place the amulet in a sunny area if possible. Recite the following:

*Leaf and twig, stone
and flower,
Increase my inner strength
and power.
Warm my body, soul,
and mind,
Help my spirit rise and shine.*

Ember

Notes:

September 13
Sunday

 4th ♋

Color of the day: Amber
Incense of the day: Eucalyptus

A Spell for Allowing Indulgences

Today is Chocolate Day in honor of Milton Hershey's birthday, so let's indulge. Start this spell when you have a day or a few hours to yourself. Place upon your altar things that represent comfort for you: bath salts, special scents, foods that you enjoy, even a favorite movie. Change into something soft and flowing. Call upon the directions and say:

> I have worked hard now to relax
> to honor myself, this spell I cast.
>
> I shall not worry or fret about
> the problems I can live without.
>
> I take this time to honor me,
> indulge my soul, so mote it be!

Spend the next few hours doing exactly what you want to do. Eat chocolate, have a bubble bath, and honor the goddess or god within yourself.

Nancy Bennett

Notes:

rebirth. This is a spell of transformation and should be started now, as we enter the dark season. Before frost touches the ground, fill a small flowerpot with rich topsoil or potting mix. Charge the soil with life force by leaving it in the Sun for a day. Bring it indoors or leave in a potting shed over winter. Place a goddess symbol, such as a corn dollie, beside the pot. Touch the soil occasionally as you think of what it is you wish to change in your life. When the time feels right early next spring, start your favorite herb or flower seeds in the pot, then transplant into the garden. As the plants grow, your wish will be fulfilled.

James Kambos

Notes:

September 14
Monday

4th ♋
☽ → ♌ 6:39 pm

Color of the day: Silver
Incense of the day: Rosemary

An Earth Goddess Spell

For centuries, agricultural goddesses were honored at this time of year. They controlled the changing seasons and the cycles of death and

September 15
Tuesday

4th ♌

Color of the day: Gray
Incense of the day: Cedar

Leaf Magic

Today is Tuesday and we are in a waning Moon phase. Since Tuesdays are associated with Mars and passion and protection and we are just a week or so away from the equinox, let's look around and see what we can find for a bit of natural magic. Gather a few red-orange leaves or a few red chrysanthemum flowers and hold them in the palms of your hands. Charge these natural items with courage and protection. Repeat the verse:

> Autumn's natural bounty
> will help me today,
>
> Turn back any obstacles that
> are in my way.
>
> Red is a Mercury color, so
> warm and bright,
>
> Grant me courage and protection, both day and night.

Keep the natural items with you for a few days. When they fade, return them to nature.

Ellen Dugan

Notes:

H oliday Lore: Keirou no Hi, or "Respect for the Aged Day," has been a national holiday in Japan since 1966. On this day, the Japanese show respect to elderly citizens, celebrate their longevity, and pray for their health. Although there are no traditional customs specifically associated with this day, cultural programs are usually held in various communities. Schoolchildren draw pictures or make handicraft gifts for their grandparents and elderly family friends or neighbors. Some groups visit retirement or nursing homes to present gifts to residents.

September 16
Wednesday

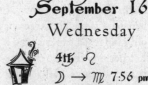

Color of the day: Topaz
Incense of the day: Bay laurel

Doorway Blessing
I n a large bottle, combine 5 cups of vinegar, a few handfuls of salt, 10 drops of High John the Conqueror oil, 1/4 cup poppy seeds (for invisibility), and 1/8 cup each of chili powder and thistle. Stew on low heat for 1 hour. Once the potion has cooled, wash the outside of all your doors and windows with the potion. Take your time doing this and create accompanying chants and rituals if you'd like. Reapply this potion any time you feel the need for added protection.

Estha McNevin

Notes:

September 17
Thursday

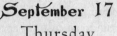 4th ♏

Color of the day: White

Incense of the day: Balsam

Spell for Late Bloomers

The feast day of Hildegard of Bingen is celebrated today. "The Sybil of the Rhine" composed music and wrote seventy poems and nine books in the twelfth century. In a time when 30 was the life expectancy, 42-year-old Hildegard experienced visions that became the source for her music and writings. What greater inspiration for those of us considering a career change late in life? As you play a recording of her chants, arrange an altar with a cloth of rainbow colors and candles of various hues. In the center of the altar, secure a yellow candle in your cauldron and surround it with quartz crystals. Light the candle and say:

> Hildegard, help me
> find inspiration.
>
> Help me realize that it's never
> too late to become the person
> I've always dreamed of.
>
> In the coming months, help me
> to hold true to my higher self.

Lily Gardner

Notes:

September 18
Friday

 4th ♏

New Moon 2:44 pm

☽ → ♎ 9:26 pm

Color of the day: Pink

Incense of the day: Violet

Spell for Drive and Focus

Today the Moon is new and we are in the astrological sign of Virgo. Virgo is an Earth mother and is typically pictured holding a sheaf of wheat. The element associated with Virgo is earth, and the colors are earthy tones, such as brown and blue. Virgos are a practical, perfectionist lot, so let's use this opportunity to call for a little practicality and drive to begin new projects and to stay focused on completing our existing ones. Light a brown, spicy-scented candle and repeat three times:

> An Autumn New Moon that
> falls under Virgo's domain,
>
> Has the power to make my
> goals succeed and sustain.
>
> Practicality is a gift of a
> Virgo New Moon,
>
> I will stay focused and
> determined, obtaining
> success soon.
>
> This autumn candle spell is
> spun from the heart

*Worked for the good of all
with a Witch's art.*

Allow the candle to burn out in a safe place. Good luck on your new projects and goals!

Ellen Dugan

Notes:

from a car you wrecked, etc. You can also load your pockets with bread to charge with all the old energy to be discarded. Another custom is to eat apples dipped in honey or bread with honey on it. The traditional Jewish bread challah is especially splendid with honey or honey butter! This represents the sweetness of the new year.

Elizabeth Barrette

Notes:

September 19
Saturday
Rosh hashanah

 1st ♎

Color of the day: Blue
Incense of the day: Pine

Rosh hashanah Casting Off
Today is the Jewish New Year. The term *Rosh Hashanah* literally means "head of the year." It is a time for looking back at the mistakes and accomplishments of the past year and for making plans regarding the year to come. One magical custom of Rosh Hashanah is *tashlikh* or "casting off." Go to a river this afternoon and throw the contents of your pockets into the water, symbolically discarding negative influences from the old year. You may toss photos associated with a bad breakup, a key

September 20
Sunday

1st ♎

Color of the day: Yellow
Incense of the day: Hyacinth

Car Protection Charms
It is always a positive thing to add extra protection to our vehicles. These are some simple methods of creating protection charms for your car. Obtain a small silver pentacle. Cleanse it with a good smudging, and bless it to the protection of your car. With a fine black ribbon, bind it up close around the mounting post of your rearview mirror so that it's not

dangling in the way but is able to be charged daily by the light of Sun and Moon through the windshield. You may also charge a crystal for the specific purpose of protecting your car. Place the crystal in a secure location in the vehicle where it will not end up sliding all over the car. In the case of either charm, if your car has mechanical issues or a close call with an accident, take the charm out of the car, cleanse it, and recharge it to its original intent.

Winter Wren

Notes:

September 21
Monday
Ramadan ends

1st ♎

☽ → ♏ 12:52 am

Color of the day: Lavender
Incense of the day: Hyssop

To Promote happiness

Use this spell to promote a sense of happiness. You'll need: a quiet space outside, a soft cloth to sit on, a small bowl, and one tablespoon each of lavender and marjoram. As

the Sun is setting, go outside with your cloth and find a comfortable sitting position. Next, place the bowl in front of you. Visualize yourself being happy and smiling. Smell the lavender and then place it in the bowl. Repeat this visualization with the marjoram. Combine the herbs together with your fingertips and say this incantation:

> Oh ancient ones, hear my words, hear my plea.
>
> I call upon your divine energy to bring about magic right,
>
> Grant me the blessing of happiness tonight.

When you are ready, stand up and sprinkle the mixture clockwise around your blanket. Finally, take a few moments to meditate on your desire for more happiness.

Gwinevere Rain

Notes:

September 22
Tuesday
Mabon – Fall Equinox

 1st ♏

☉ → ♎ 5:18 pm

Color of the day: Scarlet
Incense of the day: Basil

Balance

Today is the autumnal equinox
in the Northern Hemisphere
(Spring Equinox in the Southern
Hemisphere), a time when day and
night are equal in length. Today,
focus on finding balance in your
life in whatever areas you need it.
Decorate your altar or other area,
such as a mantle or shelf, with seasonal decorations and as you do so,
concentrate on balancing the items
equally on each side. Both sides don't
have to be identical, but they should
feel balanced. Perform the following
ritual: cut an apple in half across the
middle as evenly as possible. Take a
bite from each half and put one on
each side of the altar with your decorations. Recite the following chant:

Balance in the Earth and me
Balance to keep harmony.
Equal measure, day and night
Balance of the dark and light.

Take a few more bites from each apple
half if you desire (equally), then put
them outside for wildlife to enjoy.

Ember

Notes:

September 23
Wednesday

1st ♏

☽ → ♐ 7:43 am

Color of the day: White
Incense of the day: Lilac

Nuclear Family Day

The days after a sabbat usually
include a holiday hangover,
residual energy from the celebration
hanging around, unfettered and in
the way, even if proper grounding
was performed. What better time
to pull in and have fun with your
nearest and dearest? Come straight
home from work, cancel extracur-
ricular activities, meetings, outings,
sports, etc. Convene at home as early
in the evening as possible. Decorate
the kitchen or the dining room in
seasonal colors or with artwork by
the kids. Exchange small, homemade
gifts, or write a poem, story, or song
for each other. Prepare the evening
meal together. Eat together, catching
up on the latest news. Clean up
together. Spend the evening together

playing games, taking a walk, or performing some other activity that does not involve electronic devices. Celebrate and remind yourselves how much fun you have together.

Cerridwen Iris Shea

Notes:

abundance are oak leaves, acorns, gold finches, stars, and rosettes. Paint the disk all white; when it dries, lightly sketch your design. Fill in the designs with paint. When the paint dries, outline each design with the paint pen. Before hanging your hex sign, enchant it:

> Upon this harvest feast day,
> This hex sign do I charge
> Prosperity and abundance
> Bring blessings small and large.

Hang the sign high in your home.

Mickie Mueller

Notes:

September 24
Thursday

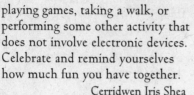 1st ♐

Color of the day: Green
Incense of the day: Myrrh

Abundance hex Sign

Today is Schwenkenfelder Thanksgiving, celebrated in the Pennsylvania Dutch areas of the United States. Although these people were mostly Christian, they practiced their own methods of magic, the best known of which are Pennsylvania Dutch hex signs. Today's an auspicious day to create your own hex sign for prosperity and abundance. You'll need a wooden disk (available at any craft store); some white, green, red, and yellow acrylic paints; and a black paint pen. Research hex designs on the Internet. Traditional symbols for

September 25
Friday

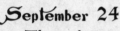 1st ♐
☽ → ♑ 6:19 pm

Color of the day: Purple
Incense of the day: Rose

Saint James Day Apple Magic

> Never pick apples before
> Saint James Day
> When they get their
> final blessing.

The apple is the centerpiece for spells concerning health and romance. The following charms date back many hundreds of years. Peel an apple in one continuous ribbon. If thrown over the left shoulder, the ribbon will resemble the initial letter of your future lover's name. Or place the ribbon behind your front door to summon your lover. The Danes believe if the apple presented to you by your lover withers, the giver is unfaithful. To reveal a future spouse's identity, name two apple seeds (known as pips) and place them on your cheek. The pip that sticks to your cheek is your future mate. Gamblers count the number of the pips in an apple to choose a lucky number. An apple a day keeps the doctor away. If you rub a birthmark with a piece of apple, the birthmark will then fade.

Lily Gardner

Notes:

September 26
Saturday

1st ♑

2nd Quarter 12:50 am

Color of the day: Black
Incense of the day: Magnolia

Enderi

The Middle Days, *Enderi*, are three days in the middle of the *Loa*, the Elven year. As the fifth of the seven Elven feasts, these days were set aside for rest and travel before the Cold Season of Hrivë arrives. In *Tië eldaliéva*, Enderi aligns with Oromë, Lord of the Forests, the handsome, hound-loving hunter and warrior who blows his piercing horn, Valaróma, and rides Nahar, a white horse that shines silver at night. As Vána's husband, he loves Arda, the Earth, and the Elves most of all and would travel to them, inspiring them to make the journey to the Blessed Realm. To meet Oromë, light any autumn-colored candle and imagine yourself anywhere in nature, especially the woods. You hear the distinct sound of his horn. He then arrives on horseback, beckoning you to join him. You mount Nahar and ride. He travels everywhere and you watch him slay many monsters to keep all of us safe. You thank Oromë for his strong, ever-present protection, and return to the here and now.

Calantirniel

Notes:

may they flee and may they
vanish. So mote it be.

Raven Digitalis

Notes:

September 27
Sunday

 2nd ♑

Color of the day: Gold
Incense of the day: Frankincense

Bring Out Your Dead . . . Bugs!
Today the Moon in Capricorn,
which is ruled by Saturn. One
of the things that Saturn is attuned
to is death energy. This can be har-
nessed in a number of ways, but for
the sake of this short spell, let's use it
simply for banishing. If you find the
corpse of a bug, keep it. I like to keep
a little "bag o' bones" in my hidden
ritual supplies and use the insect
bodies in banishing magic. Use the
following in a spell to banish harmful
influences. Surround a black candle
with banishing herbs (like nettles,
poplar, and wormwood). Place the
insect corpse at its base, light the
candle, and say:

> As I light this candle of
> night, may it enhance my
> psychic sight. From my life,
> harmful influences banish,

September 28
Monday
Yom Kippur

 2nd ♑
☽ → ♒ 7:06 am

Color of the day: White
Incense of the day: Clary sage

Spell for Understanding
The balance of the year is moving toward the last harvest
and internal focus. To seek inner
wisdom and understanding, hold a
malachite stone in your hand and sit
before your altar. Sit quietly for several
minutes and move your awareness
inside you. Find a candle there and
observe the flame, the wick, and
the candle color and size. All these
details give you understanding of
who you are. Observe and don't
judge. If you are unhappy with any
aspect of the candle, use your awareness to encourage the candle to
change. Using your breath, breathe

into the candle the qualities that you wish to explore during the coming season of introspection. See the color become clear and the flame brighten as you continue to breathe your wisdom. When you are finished, contemplate your inner light for a few minutes. Then, move your awareness outside your body, back into the here and now. Move your awareness to the stone so the wisdom gained invigorates it. When you're done, you can carry the stone with you during this season as a reminder of your inner light.

Gail Wood

Notes:

September 29
Tuesday

2nd ≈

Color of the day: Red
Incense of the day: Ginger

An Apple Love Spell

Apples are said to be the fruit of love. While they are in season, show someone special how much you care about them by performing this spell. Follow the instructions in the following verse. Save the seeds for a future spell.

> When the wild geese begin
> to fly,
> And the autumn wind begins
> to sigh,
> After the grasses in the field
> begin to brown,
> Go to an orchard where apples
> may still be found.
> Pick an apple which is fiery red.
> This you'll serve to the one
> who turns your head.
> Breathe upon it, and hold it
> to your heart,
> Whisper, "You and I shall
> never part."
> On a night when the Moon
> rides high and the wind
> is still,
> Place your enchanted fruit
> upon a windowsill.
> On the following eve, slice
> it and serve it to your
> special one,
> And tell them, "You are my
> Star, you are my Moon,
> you are my Sun."

James Kambos

Notes:

September 30
Wednesday

2nd ♒

☽ → ♓ 7:26 pm

Color of the day: Brown
Incense of the day: Lavender

Maternal Connection

On a long piece of white cloth, write out the known names of your female ancestry. Begin with the oldest members that you know. After each name, tie a knot in the cloth as you speak to your ancestor as if she were present. Tell her what you know of her life; if you know nothing, appeal to her spirit to guide you toward a greater understanding of your own heritage. Once all of the known names are positioned, tie two final knots on either end to seal the cloth. Wrap this around your waist until the ends meet, and comfortably tie them together and trim off any excess. Belts like this offer a great link with lost loved ones. The amount of memory and energy we put into our ancestors greatly determines how much comfort and support they can offer us in times of need. Embroidering and quilting are both crafts that help us to document ancestry, and self-decorated belts can serve us in the same way. Because they wrap around our midsection, belts have clear connotations with matrilineal ideals. Use the following chant to seal the energies into your ancestral belt:

> Blood and bone,
> Life and home,
> Family is all fortune.

Estha McNevin

Notes:

October is the tenth month of the year. Its name is derived from the Latin word meaning "eight," as it was the eighth month of the Roman calendar. Its astrological sign is Libra, the scales (September 22–October 23), a cardinal air sign ruled by Venus. The color comes quietly. Scarlet. Orange. Gold. Suddenly, every hill, neighborhood, and roadside is ablaze with color. Every color in the rainbow spills across the October landscape. It is pure magic. October skies are the bluest of the year, and in the distance the haunting cry of wild geese can be heard as they fly in V-formation, following an instinct as old as time. Every doorstep is decorated with signs of the season—pumpkins, mums, and friendly ghosts can be found in most neighborhoods. Soon the pumpkins are carved with fanciful faces and turned into jack-o'-lanterns. And we're reminded the Wiccan observance of Samhain, or Halloween, is at hand. Samhain is the last harvest festival of the year and a time to remember the spirits of the dead. Seasonal magic can include simply lighting a jack-o'-lantern to guide the way for visiting spirits. October's Full Moon, the Blood Moon, bathes the harvested fields with an amber light. The Blood Moon encourages us to honor our ancestors. It illuminates the gateway between the physical and spiritual worlds.

October 1
Thursday

2nd ♓

Color of the day: Green
Incense of the day: Nutmeg

Wisdom and Prosperity

Prosperity is more than monetary wealth—it also means to thrive and blossom, to flourish and to be in a state of growth and expansion. Success can be measured in many ways. In what ways are you prosperous? In what ways would you like to be? Focus on those qualities and visualize them as you light one green candle and one purple candle. Remember that wisdom should be developed in sync with prosperity, for it takes wisdom to recognize true prosperity and to keep it. As the candles burn, meditate on the following:

> Grant me wisdom, help
>   me know,
> As I learn, the more I grow.
> Let life's lessons grant to me,
> Wisdom and prosperity.

Ember

Notes:

Holiday lore: According to Shinto belief, during the month of October the gods gather to hold their annual convention. All of the *kami* converge on the great temple of Isumo in western Honshu, and there they relax, compare notes on crucial god business, and make decisions about humankind. At the end of this month, all over Japan, people make visits to their local Shinto shrines to welcome the regular resident gods back home. But until then, all through the month, the gods are missing—as a Japanese poet once wrote:

> The god is absent;
> the dead leaves are
>   piling up,
> and all is deserted.

October 2
Friday

2nd ♓

Color of the day: Pink
Incense of the day: Mint

Mental Clarity Spell

Sometimes in the midst of a situation, our emotions take over and we cannot make good decisions. To rediscover your mental clarity, gather together cinnamon incense for good luck, clarity, and communication; a bowl of water; a white candle; and a small black candle. Light the cinnamon incense and breathe in its spicy smell. Hold the bowl of water and pour all of your emotions into it. Let your feelings flow. Light the black candle so the light is reflected into the bowl and say, "Banish the bad, the ugly, and the distracting," three times. Then light the white candle on the opposite side of the bowl and say, "In this light all good remain," three times. Breathe deeply until all the negativity flows into the black candle. Let it burn completely away. Pour the water out into Mother Earth and bury the remains of the black candle there. Keep the white candle and burn it when you need clear thinking. When the white candle is nearly gone, transfer the good feelings into another candle.

Gail Wood

Notes:

October 3
Saturday
Sukkot begins

 2nd ♓
☽ → ♈ 5:20 am

Color of the day: Brown
Incense of the day: Sage

Meditrinalia

Meditrina was a Roman goddess of healing. Libations in her name were made by drinking both old and new wines and stating that one was healed. The actual date of her festival, Meditrinalia, hinged on the harvest; it could occur anywhere from early to mid-October. Some scholars believe it was celebrated for the duration of that time, and that the goddess was created after the reason for the libation. A modern twist on this festival is to see how to mix and match the old and new in your life. What needs harvesting? What needs healing? What can be joined together, and what needs to be separated out? What needs to move in a new direction? Pour a libation of your favorite beverage in honor of Meditrina, celebrate your accomplishments, and declare yourself healed.

Cerridwen Iris Shea

Notes:

October 4
Sunday

 2nd ♈
Full Moon 2:10 am

Color of the day: Gold
Incense of the day: Heliotrope

Full Moon Ritual for Self Discovery

Go outside in the evening when the Moon is full and spread a silver cloth on the ground. Place upon it a small mirror, a picture of yourself, a knife, a silver cord, and your journal. Call the directions and, facing the Moon, say:

> Oh vision of mystery, vision of light,
>
> Shining orb in the ebony of the night.
>
> I shall hold you in my memory unbinded
>
> Drink deep of the vision you have provided.

Place the mirror facing the picture of yourself and bind them with a silver cord. Cut a lock of your hair and place it inside the journal. Place the mirror and picture on a table near your bed and the journal within arm's reach. Every night before you go to sleep, write your thoughts in the journal. At the next New Moon ritual, spend time contemplating those words.

Nancy Bennett

Notes:

October 5
Monday

3rd ♈
☽ → ♉ 12:33 pm

Color of the day: Gray
Incense of the day: Clary sage

Silent Sophia

In Greek tradition, this is the Day of the Holy Spirit. Sophia is the spirit of female wisdom, a hidden aspect of the Goddess. She often disguises herself as a white dove. The Gnostics call her Hagia Sophia, the Great Mother, and they say she was born from silence. The four steps to mastering magic are: to know, to will, to dare, and to keep silent. Sophia rules over the last step. She is the patron goddess of understanding when to keep your mouth shut, and she reminds us that wisdom is best achieved with "ears open, lips closed." As much as possible, spend this day in silence. Listen instead of speaking. Because Sophia is a hidden goddess, consider placing a shawl or veil over your head while you meditate. At the end of the day, especially, think back over what you have learned.

Elizabeth Barrette

Notes:

October 6
Tuesday

3rd ♉

Color of the day: Black
Incense of the day: Ylang-ylang

Enchanted Halloween Decorations

Ah October, the season of the Witch is here! Haul out your Samhain/Halloween decorations, but before you put them up, let's enchant them for protection on this day that is sacred to Mars. The Samhain seasonal colors of orange and black are perfect for this spell. After all, black, red, and orange are Mars colors, too. Use this charm to put some real magic in your decorations this year! Set your decorations out and hold your hands over them while repeating the charm:

> *I enchant these decorations
> on this Mars day.*
>
> *May courage and protection
> surround us always.*

Bats and pumpkins, Witches
and ghosts, black cats
and ghouls,

Now in my hands, they will
become protective tools.

This fun October spell is
spun from the heart,

Worked for the good of all
with a Witch's art.

Now, have fun decorating for Samhain and enjoy the season of the Witch.

Ellen Dugan

Notes:

October 7
Wednesday

3rd ♉
☽ → ♊ 5:46 pm

Color of the day: Brown
Incense of the day: Lilac

Broom Magic

One way to clear your house of negative influences and "bad luck" is with some good old-fashioned broom magic. Obtain a good corn or straw broom. Give the broom a smudging to clear it of any previous influences. Once it is ready, prepare yourself for a good sweeping session. Start at the front of your house and work toward the back, ritually sweeping all the rooms. Carpet can be difficult, but sweep over it anyway. As you are sweeping, focus on negativity, bad vibes, and unwanted energies being swept away right along with the dust bunnies. Sweep all the debris, physical and ethereal, toward the back door. When it is all collected there, sweep it out the door and into a dust pan, which is then emptied into the trash can to be carried away from your home for good.

Winter Wren

Notes:

for their floral springtime beauty, it's the clusters of berries ripened to a brilliant red in the fall that contain the most magical power. In fact, the berries, leaves, and bark of the dogwood have a reputation for granting wishes and protection. They have long been used in folk magic spells and amulets. To make a wish come true, collect three red dogwood berries, a dogwood leaf that has also turned red, and a few pieces of bark. Place all of these items on a piece of white fabric or in a pouch, and tie it up with red yarn. Speak words of power affirming your wish over this magic bundle. Pass the bundle above the flame of a red candle. Extinguish the candle and hide your magic bundle until you receive your wish.

James Kambos

Notes:

October 8
Thursday

 3rd ♊

Color of the day: Turquoise
Incense of the day: Apricot

A Dogwood Tree Spell For Fall

Each spring, the lovely dogwood trees dot the Appalachian hills where I live with their white flowers. Although the dogwoods are known

October 9
Friday
Sukkot ends

 3rd ♊
D → ♋ 9:48 pm

Color of the day: Rose
Incense of the day: Thyme

Day of Felicitas
We celebrate the feast day of Felicitas, the Roman goddess of good fortune. While Fortuna ruled the fates of nations, Felicitas oversaw the personal happiness of her citizens. Make your own wheel of fortune this year using a small wreath of dried grapevine with as many spokes as you have wishes. Decorate the altar with flowers and small cakes or gifts of fruit as an offering to Felicitas. Light a stick of sandalwood incense. On small squares of colored paper, write your wishes: red for love, green for money and health, pink for friendship, yellow for creativity, brown for home, blue for spirituality, and white for miscellaneous wishes. Be sure to make your wishes specific. Fold the papers and attach to the spokes of the wheel. Place the wreath in a box and keep it hidden away. It's important at this point to forget your wishes. Leave your offerings to Felicitas at the base of a tree. Set a time in the future when you will open the box and check off the wishes that have come true.

Lily Gardner

Notes:

October 10
Saturday

 3rd ♋

Color of the day: Gray
Incense of the day: Pine

Herbal Witch Ball
It's not even Samhain yet, but the winter holiday merchandise is already out, especially in the arts and craft stores. Pick up the biggest clear glass ornament you can find. Remove the metal top and hanger. Place inside it protective herbs and flowers; I suggest a dash of sea salt, rue, heather, rosemary, yarrow flowers, or any protective herbs and flowers you like to use. Fill the ball about halfway full. Hold it in your hands and fill it with your energy:

I enchant this Witch ball
Of herbs and blossoms fair
Shielding this Witch's home
By earth, fire, water, and air.

Hang your herbal Witch ball in the window or near the front door. Keep it free of dust. You may wish to replace the herbs every six months

or so; it's best to do so on a Saturday during the waning Moon.

Mickie Mueller

Notes:

recite "Goddess, bless and keep _____ _____ far away from me!" Fling the leaf into the water. Turn around and walk away without looking back.

Magenta Griffith

Notes:

October 11
Sunday

3rd ♋
4th Quarter 4:56 am

Color of the day: Amber
Incense of the day: Eucalyptus

Banish the Bothersome

This is an ethical way to get rid of people in your life whom you need to have gone, such as a schoolmate who teases you all the time or an annoying co-worker. Find a dead leaf, one that is perfect, without any part missing or torn. Write the person's name on the leaf with a permanent pen or marker. Go to a stream or river that flows fast. Stand on a bridge, if possible; a place on the bank can work if the water flows fast and deep at that spot. Focus your energy and imagine the person going away from you, transferring to another school or job, moving to another town. With the leaf in your left hand,

October 12
Monday
Columbus Day (observed)

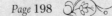

4th ♋
☽ → ♌ 1:02 am

Color of the day: Lavender
Incense of the day: Rosemary

To Summon True Love

Kiss a pale pink candle 64 times to invoke within it the energy of Venus. Imagine the candle to be your greatest lover, your perfect match. Truly invite the energy of pure love into your lips so that each kiss is delivered with devotion and sincerity. When you are done, light the wick while slowly vibrating the word LOVE; this should be done similarly to an OM vibration. As the candle burns, kiss the air around you and around the flame. Again, put all of your desire for love and your genuine desire to cultivate honest affection before any sexual ideas or feelings of embarrassment. See this as a stolen moment of energy with your manifested lover. Let go of insecurities and feel with each kiss that you are meeting true lips. For the rest of the day, greet everyone you meet with a kiss.

Estha McNevin

Notes:

fold it three times. When the water has boiled, drop in the cloves of garlic. Say this incantation:

By this Witch's brew,
bubbling, stinky stew,
problem: you are banished,
your task: to vanish,
be gone!

Finally, drop in the parchment and visualize your problem vanishing. Turn off the stove. When the mixture cools, strain the water but bury the garlic and parchment.

Gwinevere Rain

Notes:

October 13
Tuesday

 4th ♌

Color of the day: Gray
Incense of the day: Geranium

To Banish a Problem

If you are encountering an obstacle in your life that you'd like to overcome, perform this kitchen Witch spell. You'll need: an old pot, stovetop burner, 3 cloves of garlic, a piece of yellow parchment paper, and a pen. To begin, gather your items by the stove. Fill the pot halfway with water and set to boil. Now, write on the parchment the problem or obstacle you are facing. Afterward,

October 14
Wednesday

 4th ♌
☽ → ♍ 3:45 am

Color of the day: Yellow
Incense of the day: Honeysuckle

Overcome Writer's Block Spell

As the season begins to chill, many authors use this indoor time to write, but the chill can also slow down our thinking and creativity! Light a yellow or orange candle sprinkled with rosemary, sage,

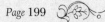

peppermint or lobelia, and use an Eight of Swords, Wheel of Fortune, and Empress tarot images. Flip the Eight of Swords card over, thereby releasing the blockage, and place the Wheel of Fortune over it to represent time moving forward. Finally, focus on the natural creative ability of the Empress. Actually see these inspired ideas flowing into you as you easily allow your fingers to dance on your keyboard. Keep the Empress image near your work area and make some time every day to write. Know that your heart and your head are already clearing the writing path for you!

Calantirniel

Notes:

to receive spiritual messages from our immediate reality. You can even do this right now, with this book, if you wish! Either think about something that you want to gain insight about or approach the divination ready to receive whatever message the universe wants to deliver. Have on hand a sharp needle or pin. After meditating, hold the pin up high, open the book at random, and stab the pin into the pages. Afterward, write down the words (on both the front and back of each page) that the needle stabbed through. This will form a random string of words that can be interpreted by the divinator. Look for the messages being delivered; they're not always easy to see but are profound once they are recognized!

Raven Digitalis

Notes:

October 15
Thursday

 4th ♏

Color of the day: Crimson
Incense of the day: Mulberry

Bibliomancy for Daily Insight
Bibliomancy can be defined as "divination by means of a book." This type of divinatory magic can be performed anytime, and it's a fun way

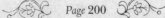

October 16
Friday

4th ♏

☽ → ♎ 6:29 am

Color of the day: Purple
Incense of the day: Vanilla

Table Blessing

Today is World Food Day, so why not bless your table? Gather with friends and family around a kitchen table laden with food. In the center, place several ears of corn and a jug of water. With hands clasped and spirits high, say:

Ha Haii Wuhti, she who brings the corn.

Ha Haii Wuhti, nourisher reborn.

Bless this table with this water.

Bless this table with this corn.

Ha Haii Wuhti, we raise our voice with thee!

Blessings to this bounty, Ha Haii Wuhti!

Share the water and break bread. At the end of the meal, give each guest an ear of corn to make a corn doll to carry the blessings back to their home. Ha Haii Wuhti is the mother of the Hopis who brings water and food to all beings. Ha Haii Wuhti likes to be loud, so be sure to speak this spell strongly!

Nancy Bennett

Notes:

October 17
Saturday

4th ♎

Color of the day: Blue
Incense of the day: Sandalwood

Chronos, God of Time

There's Kronos, the murdering Titan. And there's Chronos, the God of Time. While stresses brought on by time constraints tempt us to invoke the former, take some time today to honor the latter. What does time mean to you? We talk about it in active, often aggressive terms: We kill it, we waste it, we take it, we make it, we give it, we lose it. What is positive about time? What can we learn from its unyielding persistence? How can we find ways to work with it, rather than fight it? Time spent within a circle is considered "time out of time." Step into that zone today. Experiment with stretching it to meet your needs and compressing it to make unpleasant tasks go by faster. Instead of viewing it as a battle, view it as a game. Can you find ways to outwit it? And still respect it?

Cerridwen Iris Shea

Notes:

October 18
Sunday

 4th ♎
New Moon 1:33 am
☽ → ♏ 10:22 am

Color of the day: Orange
Incense of the day: Hyacinth

Red Magic For the New Moon

Red, the color of the life force, is an appropriate color to utilize for an October New Moon ritual. Since October's Moon is also known as the Blood Moon, red takes on a special significance for magic performed this month. For this spell, you'll need a sheet of clean white paper and a red ink pen. Also have on hand a red-colored seasonal object of nature. This could be a leaf (maple would be perfect), berries, or some flower petals from a red mum. Draw the shape of a new crescent Moon in red at the top of the paper. Beneath the Moon symbol, write out one or two goals you want to begin working toward or any positive wish you may have. When finished, trace an invisible pentagram shape with your finger over the paper. Fold the paper like a letter and insert into an envelope, along with the plant material you've selected. Seal the envelope. Hide your written spell for one lunar month. If needed, repeat all or part of your wish again at the next New Moon. When your goal is achieved, burn the envelope and contents in a ritual fire as a gesture of thanks.

James Kambos

Notes:

October 19
Monday

 1st ♏

Color of the day: Silver
Incense of the day: Narcissus

Tarot Deck Blessing

When you purchase a new tarot deck, use this spell to empower it for successful readings.

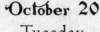

You will need: the deck, a piece of moonstone, a vibrant purple cloth, and 3 teaspoons of mugwort. To begin, lay the purple cloth on your altar with the deck in the center. Sprinkle the mugwort around the deck in a clockwise circle. Next, hold the moonstone between your palms. Whisper into your cupped hands, "Awaken with light, moonstone sacred and bright." Place the moonstone on top of the deck. Fold the fabric in to cover the deck, trying not to let the herbs or moonstone fall out. Say this incantation:

> By magical herb and stone,
> I empower thee, new tarot.
> Assist me in my divination,
> Provide me with clear and
>   focused readings.
> So mote it be!

Leave the wrapped deck on your altar for the night.

Gwinevere Rain

Notes:

October 20
Tuesday

1st ♏
☽ → ♐ 4:49 pm

Color of the day: Maroon
Incense of the day: Cinnamon

Freeze Negativity

Sometimes it is necessary to block negative influences or people from our lives. Ice magic is a very effective way to "put the freeze" on things that will not otherwise take no for an answer. Find an object that represents the influence or person you need to restrain from your life. If it is indeed a person, a picture or letter from that individual is best. Place the object in the center of a sheet of foil. Close up the foil with at least seven folds in such a way as to form a packet. Light a black candle and drip wax from it along the closure of the packet while chanting, "No longer can you enter my life, no longer can you cause me strife, on ice you go, on ice you stay, go you now away this day." Place the packet in the back of your freezer and leave it there.

Winter Wren

Notes:

October 21
Wednesday

1st ♐

Color of the day: Topaz
Incense of the day: Marjoram

Enchant a Ring

This spell is for a silver ring set with a stone, but you can easily adapt it for a different piece of jewelry. Allow the ring to be exposed to a full day of sunlight and a full night of moonlight, perhaps near a window. Visualize sunlight and moonlight infusing the ring with energy for whatever purpose you choose. Enchant the ring with this charm:

> Simple silver circlet round,
> In thee magic to be bound.
> Sun and Moon enchant
>   this ring,
> More than just a pretty thing.
> Lend your energy to me,
> For good of all, so mote it be.

Ember

Notes:

October 22
Thursday

1st ♐

Color of the day: Green
Incense of the day: Balsam

Mr. Splitfoot's Red-Thread Charm

This is a charm from Old Craft tradition. To make a special request, tie a red thread around your left wrist. (Or right wrist, if you're left-handed.) Someone else can do the tying, but don't explain the string to them. Do this in the Horned One's name (the red thread is one of His symbols). Simply call on Him, as Old Hornie or Mr. Splitfoot, and state your request. Be as specific as possible. Wear the thread until it falls off. Several times a day, you should focus on the thread, call to the Horned One, and repeat your request. Don't tell anyone else what the thread is for, even if they ask. When the thread breaks, your request will soon come to pass. If it doesn't, Mr. Splitfoot has denied your request. Sometimes, sadly, the answer is "no."

Magenta Griffith

Notes:

October 23
Friday

1st ♐

☽ → ♑ 2:40 am

☉ → ♏ 2:43 am

Color of the day: Coral
Incense of the day: Alder

Secret-Keeping Spell

Gossip is powerful energy, and it's hard to resist spreading a good story. To keep your counsel and the secrets of those who trust you, make a sachet of lavender, rose, and juniper. Take the sachet to your altar and present it to the elements and the Spirit.

> By the power of air, protect
> the knowledge I keep;
>
> By the power of fire, give me
> the will to resist disclosure;
>
> By the power of water, wash
> away exposure;
>
> By the power of earth, give
> me the power to keep silent.
>
> By the spirit of all I hold
> dear, as I will it, please make
> it so.

Place the sachet in a pouch and tuck it wherever you might need its support. Breathe the scent whenever you need to reinvigorate your promises.

Gail Wood

Notes:

October 24
Saturday

1st ♑

Color of the day: Indigo
Incense of the day: Patchouli

Global Warming Spell

By now, most people understand the threat of global warming. Part of this problem comes down to one thing: it breaks the buffering effect. For example, forests absorb rain, releasing water slowly back into the sky; this buffers the tendency for flood and drought cycles. Clear-cutting forests destroys that buffer. Worldwide, we are watching the weather get more extreme: bigger storms, longer droughts, fiercer heat waves, etc. Here's a spell to help buffer the weather. You'll need a small bowl of hot water, a small bowl of cold water, a large bowl, and a besom (or a bundle of twigs). Pour the hot and cold water into the large bowl. Dip the besom in the tepid water and flick it in a circle around you, saying:

> Not too hot,
> Not too cold:
> Just right.
> Not too wet,
> Not too dry:
> Just right.
> As above,
> So below:
> Just right!

Elizabeth Barrette

Notes:

your favorite clowns or comedians, for example, Groucho Marx, Lucille Ball, or the Three Stooges. Tell jokes, dance a silly dance, or read a funny book. End the circle by eating at least one of the candies.

Magenta Griffith

Notes:

October 25
Sunday

1st ♑

☽ → ♒ 3:08 pm

2nd Quarter 8:42 pm

Color of the day: Yellow
Incense of the day: Juniper

Silliness Spell

Sometimes, you just need to cast a silliness spell when you, or someone you know, needs a dose of humor. Here's my favorite silly magic. Get a package of multicolored chocolate candies. At Halloween and other holidays, you can buy packages that are only certain colors, like orange and black or red and green. You can also order bags online that are just the colors you want. Use your favorite color or colors to make a circle around you. (Lay down strips of paper or foil to put them on, unless your floor is clean enough to eat off of!) Pick your favorite number between about 50 and 100, and use that number of candies. Invoke the elements or quarters by calling on

October 26
Monday

2nd ♒

Color of the day: Ivory
Incense of the day: Neroli

Day of Solitude

In the modern world, it seems to be one long, hectic, stressful holiday season from Samhain to Twelfth Night. It's difficult to put yourself first, but every once in a while, you have to draw firm boundaries for your own well-being. Today is a day of solitude. Take a day off from work and your family responsibilities. Go to a museum or take a walk or a yoga class or spend the day meditating. But do it on your own. It's very important to stay away from the television and the computer and to keep your cell phone and other phones turned OFF. You can't be successful at being with others if you aren't any good at being alone and taking on all aspects of your own personality. Use today to face parts of yourself, both good and bad, that you've avoided. Truly listen to yourself.

Cerridwen Iris Shea

Notes:

feline has served to protect our households from vermin and snakes. Renowned for their agility and prowess, cats guard us and help dispel our fears. To alleviate anxiety or sorrow, as well as to cultivate self-love, pet a black cat 82 times, a number aligned with Anael, the angel of Venus. With each stroke, purr.

Estha McNevin

Notes:

October 27
Tuesday

2nd ♒

Color of the day: Red
Incense of the day: Bayberry

A Cat Petting Meditation

In ancient Egypt, petting cats was akin to prayer. The feline persuasion was perceived to have empathic qualities not found in other animals. Indeed, the ancient Egyptians believed that cats were highly telepathic, spiritually aware, and advanced beyond our basic psychic levels. Bast (or Bastet), the Egyptian cat deity, was believed to be the mother of all life. Throughout history, our domestication of the

October 28
Wednesday

2nd ♒
☽ → ♓ 3:45 am

Color of the day: Brown
Incense of the day: Bay laurel

Spell for Psychic Skills

Today is a Wednesday, a Mercury day, and we are in a waxing Moon phase. With Samhain around the corner, this is a good time to try to increase your psychic communication skills. Arrange an orange and a purple candle in their holders. Any size or style of candle is fine. The orange candle is for the Samhain season, and the purple candle is for psychic power. (Both of these colors are associated with Mercury.) Light the candles and repeat the following charm:

> By the powers of Mercury,
> increase my psychic skills,
>
> Intuitive knowledge now
> flows smoothly, that is my will.
>
> This communication spell is
> spun from the heart,
>
> Worked for the good of all,
> with a Witch's true art.

Let the candles burn out in a safe place.

Ellen Dugan

Notes:

October 29
Thursday

 2nd ♓

Color of the day: Turquoise
Incense of the day: Jasmine

Norse Winternights Begins

The Norse people remember their ancestors during the Winternights—between October 29 and November 2—which mark the beginning of winter in the Norse lands. This is also the beginning of the Norse Wild Hunt, and divination is traditional. If you read runes, or other oracles, Winternights is an excellent time for consulting the fates about the upcoming year. For this spell, gather and light three candles: white, red, and black. Holding your hands above your runes or other oracle, speak:

> Winds of the north do I
> now feel
> As I call to the sister fates
> Urdh the spindle, Verdandi
> the wheel
> Skuld cuts the fine thread
> —or waits
> Sisters of Wyrd, the
> Ladies three,
> 'Twas never a wiser band
> Casting the runes you
> inspire me
> I implore you to guide
> my hand

Read your runes or other oracle to discover the path of your upcoming year. Leave an offering of red food and drink for the fates.

Mickie Mueller

Notes:

Holiday lore: Many villages in the English countryside share the tradition of "lost-in-the-dark bells." Legend tells of a person lost in the dark or fog, heading for disaster, who at the last moment was guided to safety by the sound of church bells. The lucky and grateful survivor always leaves money in his or her will for the preservation of the bells. This day commemorates one particular such case, a man named Pecket in the village of Kidderminster, in Worcestershire, who was saved from plummeting over a ravine by the bells of the local church of St. Mary's. In honor of this event, the bells still ring every October 29.

October 30
Friday

2nd ♓

☽ → ♈ 1:56 pm

Color of the day: Purple
Incense of the day: Yarrow

Be True to Thyself

What would we be if we truly believed in ourselves, immune from fear? This poppet magic will reinforce our journey of self-discovery. Mix together 5 drops of ylang-ylang oil, 3 drops of lavender oil, and 5 drops of geranium oil. Rub this mixture on an orange candle. Melt three white candles in a glass pan. When the wax becomes pliant, light your orange candle. Rub your hands with your prepared oil and fashion a little doll from the wax. Trace the symbols of your Sun sign, your Moon sign, and your initials. Press two small crystals that are most meaningful to you into the doll, one in the third eye and one in the heart chakra. This doll represents the courageous, creative, intelligent, loving you, the self you are capable of being. When you're finished with your poppet, wrap it in an orange cloth and keep it hidden so that only you know where it lives. Tell your poppet your hopes and your secrets. Use it whenever you find yourself losing your center. Remember above all to love and believe in yourself.

Lily Gardner

Notes:

October 31
Saturday

halloween – Samhain

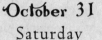 2nd ♈

Color of the day: Blue
Incense of the day: Magnolia

honoring Your Dearly Departed

Hail be Halloween! As they say, the "veil between the worlds" is now at its thinnest. This is the ideal time to communicate with and pay homage to those who have crossed the veil and left this world. Indeed, countless celebrations of death take place on or near this day each year around the world. This is the Celtic (and Wiccan) New Year and is most definitely the witchiest holiday of them all! During your Samhain celebration, allow yourself time to enter a meditative state. Think about family, friends, and pets that have died. Bring to mind the fondest memories of them all and speak aloud any messages you wish for them to hear—they will in fact hear what you have to say. Leave for them offerings of food, drink, and incense, and allow your energy to merge with theirs enough to say "hello" and "blessed be." Tonight, spend as much time with them as you'd like.

Raven Digitalis

Notes:

November is the eleventh month of the year. Its name is derived from the Latin word for "nine," as it was the ninth month of the Roman calendar. Its astrological sign is Scorpio, the scorpion (October 23–November 21), a fixed water sign ruled by Pluto. November is a month of quiet beauty. The colors of autumn have faded and fallen leaves crunch underfoot. The wild grasses have been bleached a tawny color and rustle in the breeze. But beneath the bareness there is promise: if you look closely at the bare branches, they are covered with next year's buds. November teaches us there is a tomorrow. The season's first fires glow on the hearth and firewood is stacked by the door. A good magical activity for a November night is to write a request on a piece of paper using soot from a previous fire, then burn it. As the paper burns, meditate on your wish. At Thanksgiving we gather family and friends and celebrate what we have to be grateful for. To appreciate the magic of a November night, one should walk beneath November's Full Moon, the Frost Moon. The sky, no longer obscured by a canopy of leaves, is open. Stars glitter. These are the same stars our most ancient ancestors gazed at in wonder. November nights are a time to contemplate the great mysteries—the Earth, stars, wind, and our place in the cosmos.

November 1
Sunday
Day of the Dead – All Saints' Day –
Daylight Saving Time ends 2 am

2nd ♈
☽ → ♉ 7:44 pm

Color of the day: Orange
Incense of the day: Frankincense

Día de los Muertos

Today is the Mexican *Día de los Muertos* (The Day of the Dead) which is a raucous festival when the people remember their loved ones who have crossed over. Huge parades are held with flamboyant skeleton costumes, graves are brightly decorated, and altars are set up in homes with offerings for the dead when they come to visit. There are even beautiful sugar skull treats. In Mexico, death is not feared but embraced on this day. On your altar, place marigolds, white candles, happy photos of your dearly departed, and their favorite foods. Play their favorite music softly. Add Mexican skeleton toys or sugar skulls if you wish. Concentrate on happy memories and stories of them.

> I loved you in life, as I love
> you in death,
>
> Thoughts of you always
> bring joy to me.
>
> Until the day that I will see
> you again,

> You will *dance in my*
> *warm memories.*

Come to peace with your memory of your loved one, grateful for having known them. When you are done, you may leave the food outside under the Full Moon as an offering to feed your loved one's spirit as they continue on their travels.

Mickie Mueller

Notes:

Holiday lore: The time between sundown on Samhain to sundown today, the Day of the Dead, was considered a transition time, or "thin place," in Celtic lore. It was a time between the worlds when deep insights could pass more easily to those open to them. Through the portals could also pass beings of wisdom, of play, and of fun. And while in time these beings took on a feeling of otherness and evil, as our modern relationship between the realms has been muddled, today can be a day to tap into the magic and wonder of other worlds.

November 2
Monday

2nd ♉
Full Moon 2:14 pm

Color of the day: Lavender
Incense of the day: Neroli

A General Blessing

It is always good to have a blessing spell handy. It can come in useful at most any time. A simple blessing can be accomplished with no additional "tools" whatsoever, simply the intent of the words used in the blessings.

> *Lady and Lord, I call forth*
> *your blessings*
> *Lend your energy and*
> *protections to _____*
> *Let your strength fulfill the*
> *tasks at hand*
> *By all the power there is*
> *in me*
> *I cast this charm, so mote*
> *it be.*

Focus a gathering of your energies into the palms of your hands and then, holding some part of whatever is being blessed, focus those energies onto or into that subject.

Winter Wren

Notes:

November 3
Tuesday
Election Day

3rd ♉
☽ → ♊ 11:53 pm

Color of the day: Maroon
Incense of the day: Ylang-ylang

Clean the Closets

Today is not a good day for most ritual work, but it would be productive for cleaning and getting rid of things you no longer need, both on the material level and the psychic level. When is the last time you evaluated your path, your activities? What things do you have for a ritual that you never performed, a hobby you no longer engage in, a sport you no longer play? Now is the time to move those things out of your life to make room for your future self. You could make this into a ritual by casting a circle around your whole house or living area. Meditate on who you are now and who you wish to become. Then, go through the areas you want to tidy and choose items that no longer belong. Put them in garbage bags or boxes for later disposal: garage sale, donation, recycling, trash.

Magenta Griffith

Notes:

November 4
Wednesday

 3rd ♊

Color of the day: Brown
Incense of the day: Lavender

Divination Spell

To enhance your divination ability, spread out a cloth or scarf in your favorite color. Place your divination tools on the cloth and sprinkle with cinnamon and lavender. Sit before this spread and light a white candle for connection to spirit and pure insight. Light frankincense incense. Wave your divination tool through the incense and the candle, inviting the wisdom of the universe to come through. Wrap the tools with the herbs. Place your receiving hand on top of your tools and wave the candle around your head and your heart. Next, wave the incense while asking the wisdom of the tool and the universe to speak compassionately through you.

Gail Wood

Notes:

November 5
Thursday

3rd ♊

Color of the day: White
Incense of the day: Clove

A Celtic Bonfire Spell

Traditionally, this is Bonfire Night in England, which observes the failed Gunpowder Plot of Guy Fawkes. Many English Witches, however, believe the ritual bonfires burnt on this night date back to Celtic times. To the Celts, this day marked the end of the Samhain observance. The Celts believed this was the beginning of the dark half of the year. The bonfires were a way to pay tribute to the life-giving Sun before entering the dark season. Spells on this holy night should focus on burning away all problems and fears. This could be done in several ways. You could simply write down your problems and burn the paper in a ritual fire. Another way is to select small twigs from trees you feel are appropriate to your need. Then snap them in half before feeding them to the blaze. If you wish, poppets symbolizing your need may also be burnt in a fire. After your fires, save the ashes, for they are considered to be sacred. In late winter or early spring, they should be spread over a field or garden to ensure fertility.

James Kambos

Notes:

Allow the candle to burn out on its own. When it's finished, roll up any leftover wax and the original spell together. Dispose of it in a public garbage can well away from your property.

Ellen Dugan

Notes:

November 6
Friday

3rd ♊

☽ → ♋ 2:42 am

Color of the day: Purple
Incense of the day: Orchid

Removing a Love Spell

If you foolishly cast a love spell that backfired on you, a Friday in the current waning Moon phase is the time to remove it. You'll need a gray candle for neutralizing qualities and a copy of the original spell you used. Paint a big white X over the spell. Place the candle in a holder, centering it on the original spell. Light the candle and visualize the problems caused by the original spell. To harmlessly dissipate them, say:

> *Love created through magic*
> *is a false love, and now I cast*
> *it away,*

> *I neutralize the effects my*
> *spell has caused and bring*
> *healing instead today.*

November 7
Saturday

3rd ♋

Color of the day: Indigo
Incense of the day: Ivy

Invocation to the Crone

As the year wanes, life dwindles and withdraws. Flowers die and go to seed. Trees lose their leaves. Birds fly south. Animals hibernate in their snug dens. The world grows old. This is the time of the Crone goddess. Her withered limbs have carried her a long way; now she is tired and ready to rest. Ancient wisdom twinkles in her eyes. Call on her and she will share it with you.

> *Crone Goddess, Hag Goddess,*
> *Grandmother Moon –*

Hear me, I'm calling you!
Let me bring you a blanket
To warm your old bones.
Let me sit at your feet
And listen to your stories.
Crone Goddess, I'm calling you!
Come to me now!

Elizabeth Barrette

Notes:

behind us. These are often passing spirits, astral entities, or energetic imprints left from past events. The next time you happen upon a spot of questionable energy, use the following spell. Whether the energy you sense is actual or just "in your head" (though the case is usually the former), this will help the situation. With the pointer finger of your projecting hand (the hand you write with), trace a large banishing pentagram. See it glowing in blue flame between you and the adverse energy, and say, "Harm not me, this energy I see. As I will, so mote it be."

Raven Digitalis

Notes:

November 8
Sunday

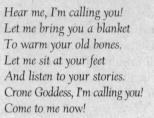

3rd ♋

☽ → ♌ 5:23 am

Color of the day: Yellow
Incense of the day: Almond

Protection from Strange Energy

At this time of year, the veil between our world and that of the ancestors and spirits is mighty thin. With the Moon in Cancer, it's a good time to learn a simple energetic protection exercise. We all have moments where we encounter adverse energy from a certain location. At times, our psychic senses can feel this energy coming from an even more specific area, like in front of or

November 9
Monday

3rd ♌
4th Quarter 10:56 am

Color of the day: Gray
Incense of the day: Narcissus

Fitness Pact

Fitness allows us to have a better quality of life. Millions of people start every January with resolutions pertaining to fitness. By February, the majority abandon them. Our New Year begins with Samhain. Why not come up with a sacred fitness program we can keep? Take time to reflect on the types of exercise you need to achieve the level of fitness you desire. Make a list of the types of workouts you enjoy. See how much of these two lists overlap. Start slowly. Make your fitness time ritualistic: start with a fitness prayer or a moment or two in Tadasana, or Mountain, pose. Don't leap from zero fitness to full fitness right away. You'll grow exhausted, injured, frustrated, and might give up. Build your practice, as you've built your spiritual practice. Ask the goddess Nike for her blessing—you don't have to wear clothes bearing her name in order to receive her support!

Cerridwen Iris Shea

Notes:

November 10
Tuesday

4th ♌
☽ → ♍ 8:30 am

Color of the day: Black
Incense of the day: Geranium

Long Lost Friend Spell

If you've ever lost touch with an old friend, try this spell to help bring them back into communication with you again. If you can, find a picture of them; if not, just write their name. You'll need a plain magnet, which you can usually pick up in a craft store. Paint the magnet yellow with a purple planetary Mercury symbol in the middle. Sign your name on the other side. Now stick the photo or name to your fridge with your Mercury magnet.

> My dear old friend, we have
> lost track,
>
> If you also wish our
> friendship back,
>
> This magnet will draw thee
> to me,
>
> As we both will, so mote it be.

Wait, you're not done yet! Magic often takes the path of least resistance, so start searching phone books and the Internet. You may just find that your long lost friend is looking for you, too.

Mickie Mueller

Notes:

life you lead. Tell the warriors of old how grateful you are that their sacrifices helped make possible the benefits you enjoy today.

Elizabeth Barrette

Notes:

November 11
Wednesday
Veterans Day

 4th ♏

Color of the day: White
Incense of the day: Honeysuckle

honoring Veterans

Today is Veterans Day. This holiday was founded to honor all those who have fought for peace and freedom. Many Pagan traditions, particularly the historic tribal ones, have a particular reverence for warriors. Some Native American tribes have special societies for warriors. According to the Asatru, warriors who fall in battle are carried by Valkyries to Valhalla. Are there any veterans in your family tree? If so, honor them today; if not, you may choose a family friend or just honor all veterans in general. Speak their names, if you know them. Drink a toast in their memory, preferably mead or ale, but fruit juice will suffice if you avoid alcohol. Brag about the fine land you live in and the happy

Historical lore: Veterans Day commemorates the armistice that ended the Great War in 1918. Oddly, this war ended on this day, November 11, at 11 am (the 11th hour of the 11th day of the 11th month). Though Congress changed Veterans Day to another date in October at one point during this century, in 1968 they returned the holiday to November 11, where it stands today. The number 11 is significant. In numerology, it is one of the master numbers that cannot be reduced. The number 11 life path has the connotation of illumination and is associated with spiritual awareness and idealism—particularly regarding humanity. It makes sense then that this collection of 11s commemorates the end of an event that was hoped to be the War to End All Wars. Unfortunately, it wasn't the last such great war, but we can at least set aside this day to ruminate on notions of peace to humankind.

November 12
Thursday

 4th ♍
》 → ♎ 12:22 pm

Color of the day: Green
Incense of the day: Apricot

Let Go/Manage Change Spell

With the Sun in the death sign of Scorpio and the Moon growing dark in the analyzing sign of Virgo, this is a perfect time to let go and release all that is not needed anymore. Light a black or red candle sprinkled with black pepper, comfrey, or lobelia, and use the Death and Judgment (Rebirth) tarot images. When looking at the Death card, willfully funnel everything into the candle that you wish, or need, to release. If you cannot recognize what you need to release, see yourself doing so regardless (you will know what is holding you back soon enough). You may feel like crying, and that is a wonderful sign—cry! See this energy going to the Spirit to be transformed. Now, visualize with the Judgment, or Rebirth, card. Fill this void with love and light, and see your wishes now having room to manifest—you are in fact "reborn." Rejoice in knowing that you were able to bravely faced this dark time. Go forward and accept your new-found vitality!

Calantirniel

Notes:

November 13
Friday

4th ♎

Color of the day: Rose
Incense of the day: Alder

Venus Spell

Whether you consider today a lucky day or not, it's a good day for magic. Feminine energy is high; Venus rules over pleasure and emotions. Do something for yourself today that makes you happy, either alone or with friends. Invoke the blessings of Venus by lighting one pink candle and one green candle and decorating your personal space or altar with a bouquet of flowers.

> *Goddess of beauty and love,*
> *your gentle gifts govern this day;*
>
> *Bring harmony into my life,*
> *let love lead the way.*

Ember

Notes:

November 14
Saturday

 4th ♎
☽ → ♏ 5:24 pm

Color of the day: Black
Incense of the day: Rue

A Children's Spell

Children flood temples in India today to receive blessings from the Goddess. Celebrate this festival with your children by taking them to the park or to a hillside. Have your child make a wish and blow bubbles. Watch the bubbles float up into the sky carrying your child's wish up to the Goddess. It's important not to speak of the wish, in order for it to come true. Have the child make as many wishes as they like and join in if you have a mind to do so. Leave an offering of fruit or flowers for the Goddess at the base of a tree. To protect your child from illness and negativity, hang a string of little bells from the ceiling over your child's bed. Coral has been used as protection for children for thousands of years. If you're lucky enough to find a piece of broken coral washed up on the beach, by all means, put it on the windowsill of your child's room for extra protection.

Lily Gardner

Notes:

November 15
Sunday

4th ♏
Color of the day: Gold
Incense of the day: Heliotrope

Cut-Away Spell

If you need to separate yourself from a person, this would be an excellent time to do a "cut-away" spell to sever your psychic connection. This could be a former boyfriend or girlfriend, an ex-spouse, someone you used to work with, or even someone you used to consider a friend. You need an athame or other ritual knife for this spell. If you don't have one, the largest kitchen knife you have would work, especially if you have had it for a long time. Do not cast a circle, because you want to interact with the energies outside of you. Stand facing north and point the knife away from you. Chant "_____, I cut you out of my life" over and over while turning in a circle, pointing the knife away from you until you reach the position you started in. Then point your knife down, and touch the tip to the ground.

Magenta Griffith

Notes:

November 16
Monday

 4th ♏
New Moon 2:14 pm

Color of the day: Silver
Incense of the day: Lily

Compassionate New Moon Spell

Perform this spell if you'd like to stimulate balance in your life and become a kinder, more compassionate person. It is best to cast a circle. You'll need a flowing white outfit, a small hand mirror, rose incense, one black candle, and one white candle. In your flowing white outfit, light the incense and set the items on your altar. Place the two candles a hand's space apart, with the black one on your left and the white one on your right. Light the wicks of the two candles and hold the mirror up to your face. Say this incantation to your reflection: "I seek to be compassionate and loving, balanced and harmonious." Put the mirror down between the two candles and stand. Hold your arms up high with palms facing the sky and say:

> Oh ancient ones
> I take within me your
>   many blessings.
> Guide me on this path
> Help me achieve my
>   perfect balance!

To finish the spell, hold the black candle and walk counterclockwise within your circle. When you return to your altar, pick up the white candle and walk clockwise within sacred space. Now, meditate or write in your Book of Shadows.

Gwinevere Rain

Notes:

November 17
Tuesday

1st ♏
☽ → ♐ 12:22 am

Color of the day: White
Incense of the day: Ginger

Home Blessing Spell

Today is Homemade Bread Day. Bread is a potent symbol of the hearth as the heart of the home. To bless your home, pack a basket with a loaf of bread, salt, spice, and wine and cover with a cloth. Identify the heart of your home and set up a small altar that includes your chalice and athame, rose quartz for affection, and a green candle. Place the basket on the altar. Create sacred space, calling in the gods. Unpack the basket and arrange the items on the altar. Present each item to the elements and the gods. For the bread say, "May this home always have nourishment." Eat some bread. For the salt say, "May this home always have flavor." Put some salt in your chalice. For the spice say, "May this home always have spice to keep things lively." Put some spice in the chalice. For the wine say, "May this home always have something to celebrate." Present your chalice and athame to the elements and the gods. Slowly lower the blade into the chalice and say, "As the blade is to the God, so the chalice is to the Goddess, together they are one. Meld these blessings to hearth and home. So mote it be!" Close your circle and enjoy the bounty of your hearth.

Gail Wood

Notes:

November 18
Wednesday

1st ♐

Color of the day: Yellow
Incense of the day: Marjoram

Psychic Enhancement Tea

Sometimes the psychic senses can seem blocked or stymied. A small bit of meditation over a cup of the following tea can be a great help at such times. Blend the following ingredients finely in a mortar and pestle: 1 tablespoon dried mugwort; 1 teaspoon each dried lemon balm, dried yarrow, and dried peppermint leaves; and 1/4 teaspoon ground cinnamon. Place in tea ball or tea bag. Brew in boiling water about 10 minutes. Add a bit of sugar or honey to taste. As you sip the tea, inhale the fragrant steam. Visualize your third eye becoming more open and its vision becoming clearer. Continue this visualization until your finish your tea and then proceed with your psychic work.

Winter Wren

Notes:

November 19
Thursday

1st ♐

☽ → ♑ 10:00 am

Color of the day: Turquoise
Incense of the day: Mulberry

Pantry Purge

Hestia and Rosemerta are my patrons of home, hearth, and cupboard. A well-stocked larder is a tribute to them and a way to feel secure and abundant. Unfortunately, we often leave things in our pantries that are stale and out-of-date. This encourages the accumulation of stagnant energy, which ripples out to affect other areas of our lives. Light a flowery or citrusy candle or incense. Play energizing music. Open your cupboards. Take everything out. Wipe the shelves down with baking soda and vinegar and dry thoroughly. Change the shelf paper. As you return items to the shelves, make sure you only put back things that are still fresh and things you will use. Items that are still edible but no longer part of your lifestyle can be donated to a local food bank. Items that are outdated should be thrown out. You'll be amazed at how many obstacles in your life disappear with the cupboard rubble!

Cerridwen Iris Shea

Notes:

November 20
Friday

1st ♑

Color of the day: Coral
Incense of the day: Cypress

Black Candle to Channel Sorrow

Today's Moon is in Capricorn, which is ruled by Saturn. Saturnine energy is attuned to darker emotional energies, sorrow in particular. If you feel yourself overwhelmed with sorrow, take some time to calm down, reflect on the situation, and ground and center your energy. Bring to mind the things that influenced you to become overwrought with sadness, and meditate on ways that the situation(s) can be alleviated. When you have successfully separated, to some degree, from the darker emotions you are experiencing—which may take a long time to do, depending on the situation—light a black candle. Cupping your hands around the flame, feel your sadness entering the candle and transforming through the alchemical fire. Continue this visualization for some time. When done, stash the candle in aluminum foil for future use, or let it burn down to the end. This spell is one way to align and balance your energy when you are feeling overwhelmed with heavy, dark emotions.

Raven Digitalis

Notes:

Think of the person and say:

> Though the time has gone
>   by fast
> Think of me, while this I cast
> No matter how far you
>   have roamed
> Find a way back to my home.

Now seal the envelope with red wax. On the back of the letter write the person's name and yours. Draw a red circle around it in a clockwise manner. Now mail it to yourself and wait to hear from them.

Nancy Bennett

Notes:

November 21
Saturday

1st ♑

☽ → ♒ 10:11 pm
☉ → ♐ 11:22 pm

Color of the day: Blue
Incense of the day: Sage

A Spell for Regaining Contact

Hello! Today is World Hello Day. World Hello Day was begun as a result of the conflict between Egypt and Israel in 1973. The object of today is to say hello to ten people in the promotion of peace. Has it been too long since your last hello with someone? Place their name in an envelope (include a photo if you have it), and put it on your altar.

November 22
Sunday

1st ♒

Color of the day: Yellow
Incense of the day: Marigold

To Invite Good Luck

Use this spell if you'd like more luck to enter your life! You'll need: a blank sheet of white paper, envelope, green crayon, and gold sparkles. Start the spell by using your crayon to draw a four-leaf clover onto the blank sheet of paper. Place your palms above the image and visualize yourself surrounded by lucky energy. Next, sprinkle the gold sparkles on top of the clover and chant the following:

> *Luck come my way, sparkle*
> *like gold, be here to stay.*

When you're ready, fold the paper carefully, trying to keep all the sparkles inside. Then tuck the paper invitation into the envelope. Seal it and address the envelope to Luck from you. Finally, draw a pentacle on the flipside and keep the charm in a safe place (such as a box on your altar or a drawer).

Gwinevere Rain

Notes:

time for spellwork that inspires peace between all beings on Earth. You'll need a white, pink, purple, green, or blue candle and the Ace of Cups and World tarot images. Light the candle and tie a piece of yarn with twenty-four evenly spaced knots (to represent all the world's longitudes). Then tie this knotted yarn into a bow around the two tarot images, facing each other. Visualize peace, love, beauty, spirituality, light and—most of all—natural balance for all who inhabit this wondrous planet! Know that your magic will be very effective as you do your part, like a small pebble causing a tidal wave.

Calantirniel

Notes:

November 23
Monday

 1st ♒

Color of the day: Ivory
Incense of the day: Rosemary

Peace on Earth Spell

With the Sun in exploring, philosophical Sagittarius and the waxing Moon in friendly, humanitarian Aquarius, this is a wonderful

November 24
Tuesday

1st ≈

☽ → ♓ 11:07 am

2nd Quarter 4:39 pm

Color of the day: Red

Incense of the day: Cedar

A Banishing Spell

To whip up an effective potion for banishing adverse vibrations, soak 2 cups Mimosa plant in 6 cups of vinegar. Add in 1/3 cup sea salt, and a Solomon's seal root. Shake or stir the mixture while shouting: "BANISH, BANISH, BANISH!" Let this mixture stew on a shelf for 4–10 weeks until the herbs are swollen and the liquid has darkened considerably. This is a great brew to toss in the laundry with ritual clothes and can be diluted for daily use as a room or linen spritz.

Estha McNevin

Notes:

November 25
Wednesday

2nd ♓

Color of the day: Topaz

Incense of the day: Lilac

Saint Catherine's Love Magic

The feast of Saint Catherine is rich with old custom, a day when unmarried women (called Catterns) are honored. The friends of the unmarried Catterns often make for them outrageous hats, traditionally of yellow and green color, which they are supposed to wear for the entire day. For those unhappy with their single status, Saint Catherine has a longer track record than Internet dating for finding mates. You can make a Cattern cake today by adding 4 tablespoons of butter, 2 tablespoons of caraway seeds, and 2 tablespoons of sugar to a batch of bread dough. Knead the special dough and separate into two loaves. Cover the loaves and let them rise until they reach the top of their tins. Bake for 20–25 minutes in a 400-degree oven. Light a yellow and a green candle and speak the following English prayer:

> A husband, Saint Catherine,
> A handsome one, Saint Catherine,
> A rich one, Saint Catherine,
> A nice one, Saint Catherine,
> And soon, Saint Catherine.

When you've completed your spell, jump a burning candle and make a wish. It will come true on Saint Catherine's Day.

> *Kit be nimble, Kit be quick*
> *Kit jump o'er the candlestick.*

> Lily Gardner

Notes:

November 26
Thursday
Thanksgiving

 2nd ♓

☽ → ♈ 10:10 pm

Color of the day: Green
Incense of the day: Myrrh

Thanksgiving

Today is Thanksgiving Day in the United States. To celebrate, use this part spell/part ritual to give thanks and spread the abundance to others. Ask your dinner guests to bring something to donate. If you're alone, set aside items to donate to an upcoming food pantry collection. Make this a part of your tradition each year and bless the items with a

spell for abundance. If you're comfortable doing so, make this ritual part of your family's gathering today. If not, perform this ritual in private to further enhance the festivities of the day. Gather the donated items together in a basket or box. Light a white candle as you bestow blessings on the items:

> *With thankful hearts we*
> *give this food,*

> *In love and hope and*
> *gratitude.*

Touch the items and visualize them helping those in need.

> Ember

Notes:

November 27
Friday

2nd ♈

Color of the day: Purple
Incense of the day: Vanilla

A Transformation Spell

November is a time of change and transformation. We are moving from autumn into winter.

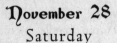

Sometimes, what we want doesn't come quickly enough and we get discouraged. Perhaps this spell can get things moving for you. Perform this spell on a windy night when you can feel the season turning. Upon your altar, place one black and one green candle. Between them place a photo of what it is you want—a new car, a house, whatever. Light the candles. On black paper write with silver ink:

> The world is dark, but the
> Spirit lives.

> The world is dark, but the
> Spirit burns.

Visualize the transformation taking place. See your life changing. Let the candles burn out and leave the written charm on your altar overnight.

James Kambos

Notes:

November 28
Saturday

2nd ♈

Color of the day: Indigo
Incense of the day: Sandalwood

Spell to Warm the Hearth

In the flurry of the season before Yule, it is a good time to do a welcoming spell for your hearth and home. Begin by cleaning a room you wish to use to entertain in the near future. Once done, sweep round it thrice in a clockwise fashion while chanting:

> In this room where friends
> will meet, happy thoughts
> each heart complete.

When finished, sprinkle salt water in every corner, proceeding clockwise while chanting:

> In this room let peaceful
> chords strike the tone of
> every word.

Bring in a small candle. Light the wick and carry the candle around in a clockwise direction, saying:

> With this flame I warm the
> hearth, where friendship
> reigns while peace imparts.

Blow out the candle but keep it in the room. Whenever you have guests over to your home, you can relight it to rekindle the flame of fellowship.

Nancy Bennett

Notes:

What may seem at first to be chaos will carefully construct an order for itself! Have a magical journal or pen and paper on hand to record any words or phrases that stand out to you. Above all else, try to remain open. The exercise is more powerful if you select artists that have personal meaning for you. Practicing active listening will help you open your mind to the wisdom that can be found in chaos.

Estha McNevin

Notes:

November 29
Sunday

2nd ♈

☽ → ♉ 5:34 am

Color of the day: Amber
Incense of the day: Juniper

Receiving Messages in Chaos

Oftentimes, the chaos and noise of life carry subtle messages that we overlook if we're not carefully engaged in the experience. Sound is received much faster by the body than it is processed by the brain. When we open ourselves to other frequencies of energy, we alter the general stream of our consciousness and awaken to new ideas. To summon increased sensitivity to the message within the chaos, try selecting four diverse albums and listening to them all at the same time while meditating. It is best if the albums are from four unrelated musical genres. Four is the number associated with competition and death, and it therefore bears similar alignments as does the number zero.

November 30
Monday

2nd ♉

Color of the day: Lavender
Incense of the day: Hyssop

Psychic Cleansing

Today is a Moon's day, and we have a waning Moon phase—a great time to do psychic cleansing. If you do lots of tarot readings or healing work for friends, you may be accidentally carrying around psychic garbage. So here's a way to get rid of it using lunar magic. You will need a silver candle in a holder set on a flat work surface and some silver glitter. With the glitter, draw a counterclockwise spiral around the candleholder. Light the candle and repeat the charm:

I release and banish all
psychic pollution today,

As the candle burns,
negativity will fade away.

Trapped in glitter and then
burned away by fire,

I am now clear and free, that
is my desire.

Allow the candle to burn out in a safe place, then clean up any wax and the glitter. Carefully and neatly dispose of it away from your home and property.

Ellen Dugan

December is the twelfth month of the year. Its name is derived from the Latin for "ten," as it was the tenth month of the Roman calendar. Its astrological sign is Sagittarius, the archer (November 21–December 21), a mutable fire sign ruled by Jupiter. Just as the fox has glided silently through the frozen December woodland, winter has crept quietly across the land. The silence comes and snow frosts the pines. The nights are long, but there is still reason to rejoice. In December, at Yule (the Winter Solstice), the return of the Sun God is celebrated, and the Yule log is burned to represent the strengthening Sun. Hanukkah, Kwanzaa, and Christmas are celebrated around the world, and each has its own special message. The month is known for the preparation of special foods and pastries; kitchens everywhere are filled with the scents of spices and herbs. Holiday lights twinkle and seasonal decorations, rich with Pagan magical symbolism, adorn many homes. Pine and the Yule tree represent eternity. Holly and mistletoe are used to draw love and protection. Nuts symbolize fertility. Candles and stars are symbols of divinity. December's Full Moon is the Cold Moon. It is a moon of ice and frost, distant but beautiful. New Year's Eve brings us to the threshold of another year. One year ends, one begins. And the enduring pattern of the seasons continues.

December 1
Tuesday

2nd ♉
☽ → ♊ 9:23 am

Color of the day: Red
Incense of the day: Cinnamon

Release Your Inner Passion

Warning: This spell is hot! Only cast it if you want your eyes to sparkle with fiery passion. You will need: musk incense, ritual broom, red ribbon, and an edible strawberry on a dish. Light the incense, taking in the rich scent. Then hold the red ribbon in your hands. Visualize yourself surrounded by lustful, passionate energy; infuse it into the ribbon. Next, tie the piece of ribbon around the base of the broom (right above the bristles). Stand up and sweep your circle moving clockwise as you say this chant, "Bristle, stalk weaving wonders." Afterward, return to your ritual workspace and pick up the strawberry. Look at the beautiful red color. Touch it to your lips, tracing them slowly with the fruit. Say, "May the fruits of my desires be as succulent as this berry" Take a bite and then finish the berry.

Gwinevere Rain

Notes:

December 2
Wednesday

2nd ♊
Full Moon 2:30 am

Color of the day: Yellow
Incense of the day: Lavender

Making My List

Sometimes it's hard to get into a season of giving, light, and excitement when we feel we have a lot to accomplish in a short amount of time. You will need a sheet of paper, pen, dragon's blood powder, a fireproof bowl, and a red candle. Light the candle and make a list of all the things you have to do in the next month. Be as detailed as you like. When you are finished, take a strong look at the list. Spread dragon's blood power over it for energy and invigoration. Roll the paper and the powder into a tube and light it with the candle, saying, "To the spirits I send my list, not one thing will be missed." Say this over and over until everything is burnt to ashes. Bury the ashes in the ground and go about your business, confident you will get it all done.

Gail Wood

Notes:

December 3
Thursday

 3rd ♊

☽ → ♋ 11:00 am

Color of the day: Green
Incense of the day: Nutmeg

A Spell of Redemption for Women

Bona Dea (the Good Goddess) was a Roman goddess mostly worshipped in a temple on the Aventine Hill. Only women held her rites, even drawings of men and male animals were forbidden. Sorry, guys, this one is for the ladies. She was associated with women's mysteries, healing, and freedom from slavery and violence. This is a spell for any women who are trying to escape violent or oppressive situations, or even the slavery of their own fear, and it should be followed up by appropriate legal support and/or counseling. Light a purple candle. Make a list of what oppresses you and draw a snake over those words.

> Bona Dea, Good Goddess,
> protect me,
>
> Deliver me from abuse
> and slavery
>
> Help to me stand strong
> and free
>
> Healing my wounds,
> I honor thee.

Burn the paper and send the ashes to the wind.

Mickie Mueller

Notes:

December 4
Friday

3rd ♋

Color of the day: Rose
Incense of the day: Violet

Car Safety Blessing

This is a good spell to perform before you travel on snowy days. Find or make a talisman to hang from your car mirror. Some good forms to use are a horseshoe shape, a miniature shield, or a loved one's picture. Hold it in your hand and walk around your car, brushing the talisman against it. Call the directions and then start to walk in a clockwise circle around your vehicle. Call upon the goddess Soteria:

> Great Goddess Soteria, she
> who keeps the traveler safe
>
> Preserver of life, please bless
> this charm.

> Keep this vessel and all who travel within
>
> Free from harm, free from harm, free from harm.

End by climbing into the car and hanging the talisman from the mirror. These talismans can be made for others and make a great Yule gift for those who love to travel.

Nancy Bennett

Notes:

December 5
Saturday

3rd ♋
☽ → ♌ 12:07 pm

Color of the day: Blue
Incense of the day: Pine

Balancing the Self

Carve two lines down the entire length of a gray candle. They should run in a loop from wick to wick. In the center on the left side carve a minus (–) symbol, and assign the right side a plus (+) symbol. Fill in the space by carving symbols and words to express your objectively perceived faults on the negative side and your objectively perceived assets on the positive side. Try to use up every bit of space on the surface of the candle. When done, anoint with patchouli oil for grounding and balancing these polarities within you. Burn your balancing candle over the course of seven days for immediate relief or gradually over time for a more consistent effect. As the wax melts and dissipates, envision any imbalances being weighted or evened out. Let the flame serve as a reminder that perfection is contained only in an instant and can no more be elongated than any other momentary force. We all have faults. The very nature of perfection is stamped out by the progressive force of life. We are each bound to the tides of change. To truly navigate life, we must know the innovation of self-disciplined balance.

Estha McNevin

Notes:

December 6
Sunday

 3rd ♌

Color of the day: Gold
Incense of the day: Eucalyptus

Blessing the Day

Each day brings a whole new host of opportunities. Both for personal growth and magical development, it helps to acknowledge these possibilities with a daily blessing. Here is a spell to bless your day that you can customize for your own needs.

I bless this day as it comes to me, full of promise and potential.

I give thanks for the things I have, for they fulfill my desires:

Now list three things you already have and enjoy.

I give thanks for the things I have not, for everyone needs goals:

List three things you would like to have but do not yet.

I give thanks for the good things that may happen, because gratitude increases positive energy.

I give thanks for the bad things that may happen,

because challenge increases growth.

May my divine patrons guide and guard me:

Now you may name the specific gods and goddesses you worship.

In all these ways, with all my heart, I bless this day.

Elizabeth Barrette

Notes:

December 7
Monday

 3rd ♌
☽ → ♍ **2:05 pm**

Color of the day: Gray
Incense of the day: Clary sage

Glamour Spell

Today is a Moon's day and we are in a waning Moon phase. Here is your big chance to work a little glamoury type of magic to blend in and go unnoticed. This type of magic comes in handy when the boss is on the warpath—or if you need to go about your magical business without curious neighbors spying on you. Use your common sense and be careful how often you use this spell; nobody wants to be unnoticed for too long. Stand under the light of the Moon and repeat this verse:

By the light of the Goddess' waxing Moon,

May I be unseen, now hear this Witch's tune.

A glamour is cast, I will just quietly blend in,

The magic will last for one day, and then it's time to end.

The spell will hold for 24 hours.

Ellen Dugan

Notes:

Holiday lore: Cultures around the world have shared a penchant for the ritual burning of scapegoats, enemies, and devils. There's something primal about the roar of a large bonfire and its ability to bring purging light to a community. Today is such a day in the highland towns of Guatemala. Men dress in devil costumes during the season leading up to Christmas, and children chase the men through the streets. On December 7, people light bonfires in front of their homes, and into the fires they toss garbage and other debris to purify their lives. At night, fireworks fill the air.

December 8
Tuesday

3rd ♍
4th Quarter 7:13 pm

Color of the day: White
Incense of the day: Basil

A Fireside Meditation

Have you ever stopped to think how magical a fire is? Think about the wood. It came from a tree that was rooted in Mother Earth and reached for Father Sun, so it contains both female and male energies. And then there's the flame—fire is almost alive. In it we see the Sun and the raw primal energy of life itself. Think about the hearth. The very word conjures images of warmth and security. The first hearth was the cave floor and it was there that the human race tamed fire. Our early ancestors learned fire would cook food and provide comfort. And around the hearth, homes were built. The ancients also learned they could scry by gazing at the flames. So, when the raw December wind roars and rattles the shutters, join me by the fire. Please, come and sit a spell.

James Kambos

Notes:

recipe for everyone. Lists of specialty vendors are also welcome. You can dedicate the party to any goddess of the hearth or harmony, or you can use Barbara Ardinger's wonderful book *Finding New Goddesses* to create your own for the occasion. Start and finish the party with a circle cast hand to hand. Feed each other. Most importantly, laugh and enjoy each other's company!

Cerridwen Iris Shea

Notes:

December 9
Wednesday

 4th ♏
☽ → ♎ 5:47 pm

Color of the day: Brown
Incense of the day: Honeysuckle

Cookie Party Day

One of the best ways to celebrate with friends before the holiday madness takes hold is to have a good, old-fashioned cookie party. It takes a bit of planning. You need to decide if the cookies will be made at the party or if each person will bring previously baked cookies. It takes some coordination so you don't wind up with thirteen variations on the chocolate chip cookie (although maybe that could warrant its own party). Whichever way you decide to organize the gathering, participants should bring enough copies of their

December 10
Thursday

4th ♎

Color of the day: Turquoise
Incense of the day: Balsam

Cauldron Divination

On this dark December night, gaze into the fire of your cauldron to see the ghosts of the past and divine your future in the New Year. Gather pinecones, dried bay leaves, and sprigs of dried lavender. Make sure your cauldron is deep and situated on a heatproof surface in a quiet candlelit room. Light the pinecones with a black candle and let them burn down until they're red embers. Toss the lavender and a few bay leaves on the embers. Gaze with unfocused eyes into the smoke that rises from your fire. You will see shapes that have meaning only to you. Perhaps while gazing into the fire, thoughts will occur to you. Allow yourself to stay in this quiet and daydream. When your fire dies out, thank the spirits of fire and write your visions in your magical book.

Lily Gardner

Notes:

New Moon (tonight), stand a birthday candle in the sand and say, "Lady Moon, by three times three, as I will, so mote it be." Then light the candle. While it burns, visualize what it is that you would like to bring into being. The next night, do the same thing, but light 2 candles, with 3 on the third night, 4 on the fourth, and so on. Do this for 9 nights in all: 3 for the Wane, 3 for the Dark, and 3 for the New. You'll need exactly 45 birthday candles to do this spell $(4 + 5 = 9)$, so be sure to buy enough before you start.

Magenta Griffith

Notes:

December 11
Friday

 4th ♎
☽ → ♏ 11:31 pm

Color of the day: Pink
Incense of the day: Thyme

Nine-Day Candle Spell
Nine is the Moon's number (the other is 3: 3 × 3 = 9), so when you have a favor to ask of Lady Moon, here's what you do. Cover a plate or shallow bowl with sand. After nightfall four nights before the

December 12
Saturday
hanukkah begins

4th ♏
Color of the day: Indigo
Incense of the day: Sage

honoring the Lady of Guadalupe
As Hanukkah begins for some parts of the world, in Latin America (particularly Mexico), today is the 478th anniversary

of the discovery of the Lady of Guadalupe, which literally brought an end to an ongoing bloody religious war. Her discovery in the year 1531 was by none other than a child, who claims she visited him at sunrise on this cold day. He brought back red roses (which were out of season) along with a cape that had her image inside. To this day, no one can figure out how the image appeared in this fabric! Although the Lady of Guadalupe has a very Catholicized "Mother Mary" energy, her original form is that of the Aztec Moon goddess Tonanzin, who brings love, peace, abundance, and fertility. Visit the Catholic seven-day candles section of your grocery or dollar store and obtain a Lady of Guadalupe Candle. Sprinkle it with rose petals and light the candle at sunrise. Rather than reading the Catholic prayer, say something from your heart—similar to this:

> Lady of Guadalupe, who is also known as the Aztec Mother Moon goddess Tonanzin, please show me your great powers of mothering love, nurturing, and abundance, and remove the patriarchal fear that resides in us. Allow me to be a conduit of your comforting energy to all who encounter me. It is done.

Let the candle burn to the bottom, snuffing it before leaving it unattended. Look forward to amazing synchronicities, unexpected gifts, and grateful, elated feelings for the coming year!

Calantirniel

Notes:

December 13
Sunday

 4℞ ♏

Color of the day: Yellow
Incense of the day: Hyacinth

Enchant Your Morning Coffee/Tea

Wake up! Sometimes it is difficult to get out of bed without that morning cuppa coffee or tea. Hey, there's nothing wrong with that! Why not add a little magical boost to your drink when you make it? This can help focus your energy for the day and is especially beneficial because water itself has been scientifically proven to change its molecular structure based on thought and intention directed to it. Check out the studies of Dr. Masaru Emoto for more on this! Cup your hands to the prepared cup of coffee or tea. Visualize it glowing with the colors of the rainbow; first with red, followed by orange, yellow, green, blue, indigo, violet, and finally white. Put your nose to the cup and inhale deeply, bringing to mind the fields in which the steeped plant was grown, knowing that this is part of the sacred harvest of Earth. Say:

> May this libation fill my body, my mind, and my spirit. May I be awake, aware, and blessed this day and all others. So mote it be!

Raven Digitalis

Notes:

December 14
Monday

 4th ♏
          ☽ → ♐ 7:25 am

Color of the day: Lavender
Incense of the day: Hyssop

Making Amends

We've all at times spoken too soon, too loudly, or in haste and wished we could take it back.

Use this spell on yourself to try to prevent saying the wrong thing if you are in a risky situation. Or, use the spell to help clear the air after you've done it. Find a clear quartz crystal or quartz cluster. Direct the flow of energy through the crystal(s) and visualize it flowing out toward your intended recipient(s). Light an incense of your choice and imagine it carrying your message.

> May these words ring true and clear,
>
> Let it be known my intent sincere;
>
> Help ease the pain my words have caused,
>
> Next time before I speak, I'll pause.

If possible, follow up your spell with a direct apology.

Ember

Notes:

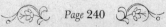

December 15
Tuesday

 4th ♐

Color of the day: Maroon
Incense of the day: Bayberry

Spell to Banish Negative People

Sometimes it feels like you continuously encounter toxic people, those who lie and gossip. Perform this spell to banish whatever is drawing this type of person to you. You'll need a 6 × 9-inch piece of cardboard, scissors, a black marker, and half a yard of black fabric. To begin, sketch an outline of a human figure on the cardboard (imagine tracing a large gingerbread cookie). Next, cut it out and turn it to its side. Across as much of the figure as possible, working head to toe, write "negative people" with the marker. Then wrap the fabric around the cardboard image as you say this incantation:

> In this ritual hour I take
> back my power.
>
> I sever the ties between myself
> and those who are negative
> and lie.

Keep the figure wrapped up in the black fabric in the bottom of a drawer.

Gwinevere Rain

Notes:

December 16
Wednesday

4th ♐
New Moon 7:02 am
☽ → ♑ 5:32 pm

Color of the day: White
Incense of the day: Bay laurel

Festival of Sapienta

Today is sacred to Sapienta. Sapienta is the Latinized version of "Sophia," the goddess of wisdom. Wisdom mixes common sense with experience and compassion. Today, do not let anything be a reflexive response (unless you need it to be for safety's sake). Take time to consider your responses and respond out of wisdom rather than the knee-jerk emotion of the moment. In the morning, light a candle. Meditate. Spend a few moments inviting Sapienta to be an active participant in your day. Notice what a difference a bit of consideration makes in your actions and reactions throughout the day. In the evening, light a white candle in honor of Sapienta. Thank her for her participation in your day and ask for her continued influence in your life.

Cerridwen Iris Shea

Notes:

December 17
Thursday

1st ♐ ♑

Color of the day: Purple
Incense of the day: Myrrh

Saturnalia

Today is the first day of the weeklong festival of Saturn, the Roman god of agriculture and harvest. This Roman festival featured the giving of small gifts (saturnalia et sigillaricia). During this festival, slaves and masters switched roles. It was a time of banquets, merriment, and fine clothing. Take the time today to dress festively. Embrace the beauty of you as you go out to undertake your routine. Today is a good time to remember the people in your life whom you might not ordinarily gift. Consider practicing some random acts of kindness for people who are more integral in your life than you might think. These acts need not be material in nature, just sincere expressions of thoughtfulness. Do this for the simple joy it brings. Enjoy the day to its fullest.

Winter Wren

Notes:

Holiday lore: Saturnalia was the Roman midwinter celebration of the solstice, and the greatest of the Roman festivals. It was traditional to decorate halls with laurels, green trees, lamps, and candles. These symbols of life and light were intended to dispel the darkness of the season of cold. The festival began with the cry of "Io Saturnalia!" Young pigs were sacrificed at the temple of Saturn and then were served the next day. Masters gave slaves the day off and waited on them for dinner. Merrymaking followed as wine flowed and horseplay commenced. Dice were used to select one diner as the honorary "Saturnalian King." Merrymakers obeyed absurd commands to dance, sing, and perform ridiculous feats. It was also a tradition to carry gifts of clay dolls and symbolic candles on one's person to give to friends met on the streets.

December 18
Friday

Islamic New Year

1st ♑

Color of the day: White
Incense of the day: Mint

Living with higher Intentions

Everything we do in life has purpose, and every action has a consequence. This is a good day to contemplate the path your life has taken and what, if anything, you wish to change. Today, think of ways to bring more purpose to your life. Is it by embracing a new challenge? Is it by giving more to your community? Is it by being a better friend? Write down your challenges and place them in a wooden box. When you are done, break bread with friends or family and give thanks for the many blessings life has given you. Let this box sit upon your altar and recheck it once every New Moon to see how you have progressed on your goals. This is a great family spell for the entire house to share.

Nancy Bennett

Notes:

December 19
Saturday
hanukkah ends

1st ♑
☽ → ♒ 5:38 am

Color of the day: Gray
Incense of the day: Sandalwood

holly Magic

Decorating homes with holly and evergreens this time of year dates back to the Roman Saturnalia. On December 19 the Romans celebrated Ops, the goddess of abundance, with holly and evergreen boughs. They gave their friends sprigs of holly for good luck. Pinch off a holly leaf and carry it in your pocket for good luck. Men carry the prickly (male) leaves; women, the smooth (female) leaves. Gather holly branches and decorate your home for good luck. The evil spirits of winter will snag in their jagged leaves. In silence, pluck nine holly leaves and wrap them in a white cloth. Tie the cloth in nine knots and place under your pillow tonight and your dreams will come true. Folk wisdom states that all holly and Yule greenery must be cleared out of your home by Twelfth Night, January 6. For every pine needle left in the home, one goblin can enter. It's also considered bad luck to burn holly leaves.

Lily Gardner

Notes:

usually be.) Finally, make a blot or offering to the gods; those associated with runes prefer mead or ale.

Elizabeth Barrette

Notes:

December 20
Sunday

1st ≈

Color of the day: Orange
Incense of the day: Almond

Fire Rune Spell

In winter, hearth fires give light, heat, and cheer. Offerings are often tossed into hearth fires. Traditionally, rune spells involved carving the relevant runes on wood and burning it. So, winter is a good time for rune spells. First, choose three runes representing your desire, such as Gebo (luck), Wunyo (success), and Jera (growth) for a household blessing. Next, split a stick lengthwise and carve the runes into the flat face of the wood. Use red paint or ink to color each rune. While concentrating on its particular power, name each rune aloud. Then throw the stick into the fire. (If you don't have a fireplace or woodstove, you can make a small fire in a heatproof cauldron or other container in the kitchen or living room where a hearth would

December 21
Monday
Yule – Winter Solstice

1st ≈
☉ → ♑ 12:47 pm
☽ → ♓ 6:42 pm

Color of the day: White
Incense of the day: Lily

Seal the Sun

Using six orange, six yellow, and six white candles, invoke solar energy into the wax by carving varying symbols for the Sun. Carefully anoint each candle with frankincense essential oil. Roll the candles in powdered myrrh when done to symbolize the innate solar energy. Set the candles to burn in a circle. As they illuminate the space, use the following prayer to draw the last power of the Sun for the long, dark days of winter:

Our Father Sun
Who art in the heavens,
Hallowed be all your names
Thy kingdom come
That my will be done
On Earth as it is in heaven.
Give me this day
My daily bread
And deliver me from selfishness
That it may not consume me
Fill me now Lord of Light
With all your golden essence that
Winter may not claim me
For I am a child of the SUN.

Do not extinguish the candles, letting them burn down slowly instead. Place solar objects and yellow clothing near the candles to absorb the light. Should winter depression find you, merely seek out these objects and meditate clearly on this spell.

               Estha McNevin

Notes:

December 22
Tuesday

1st ♓

Color of the day: Black
Incense of the day: Ylang-ylang

Protection from Peeping Toms

The symbol of the eye has been used in nearly every human cultural tradition. More often than not, the symbol of the eye holds protective value and has long been associated with having "extra eyes," or enhanced vision. Throughout history, this desire for awareness has presented itself through the symbolism of the eye. A clear symbol of knowledge and perception, the eye is also linked with invisible forces, the unknown, and unexplainable events in life. The all-piercing eye is a common theme in spiritualist and psychic studies. To the unconscious mind, the eyes represent our entryway to the Earth plane: the gateway to our soul. Drawing eyes on doorframes, windows, and mirrors is a common tradition in eastern Mediterranean cultures. Because these entryways are portals of unpredictable energy brought in by residents and visitors, they have long been perceived as energy vortexes. Using the eye to mark these vortexes stabilizes energy and promotes harmony.

               Estha McNevin

Notes:

Holiday lore: The Yule season is a festival of lights and a solar festival, and it is celebrated by fire in the form of the Yule log—a log decorated with fir needles, yew needles, birch branches, holly sprigs, and trailing vines of ivy. Back porches are stacked with firewood for burning, and the air is scented with pine and wood smoke. When the Yule log has burned out, save a piece for use as a powerful amulet of protection through the new year. Now is a good time to light your oven for baking bread and confections to serve around a decorated table; sweets have an ancient history. They are made and eaten to ensure that one would have "sweetness" in the coming year. Along these lines, mistletoe hangs over doorways to ensure a year of love. Kissing under the mistletoe is a tradition that comes down from the Druids, who considered the plant sacred. They gathered mistletoe from the high branches of sacred oak with golden sickles. It is no coincidence that Christians chose this month to celebrate the birth of their savior Jesus. Now is the time when the waxing Sun overcomes the

waning Sun, and days finally begin to grow longer again. In some Pagan traditions, this struggle is symbolized by the Oak King overcoming the Holly King—that is, rebirth once again triumphing over death. And so the holly tree has come to be seen as a symbol of the season. It is used in many Yuletide decorations. For instance, wreaths are made of holly, the circle of which symbolized the wheel of the year—and the completed cycle. (*Yule* means "wheel" in old Anglo-Saxon.)

December 23
Wednesday

 1st ♓

Color of the day: Topaz
Incense of the day: Lilac

Betwixt and Between

Today is Nameless Day, the day on the Celtic Lunar calendar that is not assigned to a month. It is the perfect time to travel to what the Celts call, "betwixt and between." Create sacred space in your usual way. Light sandalwood incense for inspiration and magic and go into a meditative state. Find yourself standing on the shoreline of a vast body of water. It is twilight, between day and night. The rhythm of the wave lulls you deeper. You see creatures of the water frolic in the deep waves. You are mesmerized by the waves rushing along the shore, creating that special place between the wave and the shore. You watch for a long time and then your spirit guides you into that between place. You explore the wonders of betwixt and between until your spirit guides you back to the shore. You thank the spirits of that place and take a deep breath to return to the here and now.

Gail Wood

Notes:

December 24

Thursday

Christmas Eve

1st ♓

☽ → ♈ 6:39 am

2nd Quarter 12:36 pm

Color of the day: Crimson
Incense of the day: Nutmeg

Winter Faeries

Tradition states that the winter faeries are out in force on this night. While you are decking the

halls, why not invite the winter faeries inside for a little break from the cold? They are sure to bring prosperity and good luck to your home during the darkest days—as long as you set some ground rules. You will need a sprig of fresh holly and ivy arranged around a green candle. Both of these plants are well loved by the faeries. Light the candle and repeat this holiday charm:

The holly brings magical protection and the ivy fidelity,

May the faeries of winter find a haven of warmth and love, here with me.

Now protect well my home, ring in cheer, and holiday fun,

As I will it so shall it be, and faeries, bring harm to none!

Allow the candle to burn out in a safe place.

Ellen Dugan

Notes:

December 25
Friday
Christmas Day

2nd ♈

Color of the day: Purple
Incense of the day: Rose

Pine Tree Magic

Pine trees are the noble ancient ones of the tree kingdom. At this time of year, both Pagans and Christians pay tribute to the pine as a symbol of everlasting life. There are even songs dedicated to the trees as holiday decorations! Our early ancestors gathered their branches at the Winter Solstice to remind them that even in the bleakness of winter, life endures. Take a moment during your holiday festivities and look at your Yule tree, or any evergreen growing outdoors. Connect with its energy. We should be in awe of their simplicity and strength. These graceful evergreens we call pines were ancient before there was a human race. When the great mountains of our planet rose and the lakes and rivers were formed, they were here. They have withstood advancing sheets of ice, hostile armies, and countless seasons. They teach us that winter—whether it's the winter season or the winter we sometimes feel in our hearts—does not last forever.

James Kambos

Notes:

December 26
Saturday
Kwanzaa begins

2nd ♈

☽ → ♉ 3:26 pm

Color of the day: Blue
Incense of the day: Pine

A Spell of Gratitude

Gratitude is one of the most profound emotions we can feel. To be grateful is to feel content and to acknowledge the things in your life that you truly and fully appreciate. So often, we go through life forgetting to say "thanks" to life itself. We often focus on the negative and forget to count our blessings. Gratitude is essential on any spiritual path—including the path of life itself! Today is the day after Christmas (which is, for Witches, a holiday about family, friends, and love, rather than a celebration of Christian mythology), and is shortly after Yule, the Winter Solstice, which celebrates the rebirth of the Sun rather than the "birth of the son" (same mythos, different skin). Because this time of year represents rebirth, renewal, gift-giving, and love, it's a perfect day to give thanks to the universe. Take a walk in nature by yourself, smelling the natural smells, feeling the Earth and the trees, and seriously paying attention to the profundity of the natural world. Give an offering of food or incense, and say your own prayer of gratitude to the spirits and the gods.

Raven Digitalis

Notes:

in the center of the map and objects similar to the one you wish to find at the four corners. For example, if you can't find a piece of jewelry, put other pieces of jewelry at the corners. Using a pendulum (if you don't have one, you can contrive one by tying a heavy thread to a ring), focus your mind on the lost object, letting the pendulum swing freely. Move it over the map until it swings more actively; this will indicate in some manner where the object can be found.

Magenta Griffith

Notes:

December 27
Sunday

 2nd ♉

Color of the day: Amber
Incense of the day: Heliotrope

Spell to Find Lost Objects

Draw a rough map of where you lost the object; a floor plan of your house if you think you lost it at home, for example, or a city map if you don't know where you lost the object. On a small table with nothing else on it, spread out the map of your area with north on the map at the north end of the table. Put a compass

December 28
Monday

 2nd ♉
☽ → ♊ 8:13 pm

Color of the day: Silver
Incense of the day: Rosemary

Prosperity Feng Shui Spell

Nothing like getting a "jump" on bringing abundance for 2010! If you have a nearby store that carries Feng Shui items, obtain a frog with a coin in his mouth and a mobile with images of at least two fish (six

and eight fish would also work well).
Light a red candle in a bowl of water
(symbolizing prosperity) and bless
the frog and fish mobile in any way
that feels right to you. When you're
finished, point the frog at your front
door (his job is to bring opportunities
for money into the house), and
then hang the fish mobile in the
left rear corner of the house. This
is the "wealth" section, and the fish
will keep money in the house so it
doesn't leave just as soon as it comes
in. During the year, remember every
night to face the frog back into the
house (just turn him around), and to
turn the frog toward the door every
morning. You may purchase a "double
frog" so you don't have to do this.
Keep the frog and the fish mobile,
as well as these areas of your house,
clean. Now get ready for money to
roll in and stay!

Calantirniel

Notes:

December 29
Tuesday

2nd ♊

Color of the day: White
Incense of the day: Ginger

Battle for the Sales Spell

All's fair in love, war, and clearance sales! Use today's Mars
energy to brave the post-holiday
sales. Come on, you know those
deals are out there. Holiday greeting
and Yule cards to use next year,
decorations, and candles . . . they're
practically giving them away! Be
sharp and on your guard to get the
really good deals that are left on the
shelves! For this good luck shopping spell, you will need a 4-inch
square of red fabric, a small magnet,
bloodstone, holly, a pinch of ginger,
cinnamon, allspice, and a gold-
colored ribbon. Bundle all the items
in the fabric and tie the bundle
closed with the ribbon. Ring a bell
in every room of your house and
then charge your bag by saying:

> 'Tis Tuesday now, and at
> an early time,
>
> Bargain hunting I go
> forth undaunted.
>
> Braving the battle for
> low-priced finds,
>
> By my wits shall I find
> what I wanted.

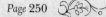

Pocket the charm bag as you brave the sales and see what your good luck brings you!

Mickie Mueller

Notes:

Notes:

December 30
Wednesday

 2nd ♊
☽ → ♋ 9:45 pm

Color of the day: Yellow
Incense of the day: Marjoram

Memories

Today is a good day to reflect on memories from the previous year. Allow the energy of Mercury the messenger to help you remember events, good times, and even sorrow, so that you may learn from all your experiences of the past. Light an orange or yellow candle and try to replay the year in your mind.

> Memories return to me
> To discover what I need
> To learn, to grow and
> help to see
> My way in what the
> future brings.

Ember

December 31
Thursday
New Year's Eve

 2nd ♋
Full Moon 2:13 pm

Color of the day: Green
Incense of the day: Clove

Full Moon Reflection

This last night of the year closes with a Full Moon. It is a wonderful time for reflection before embracing the revelry of the night. Light a white candle and take time to say thank you for all that you have experienced in the year past. Release the energy of the passing year into the night as you set forth on your enjoyment of the evening. As you go out, seek the Lady in all Her glory in the night sky. Salute Her and pay homage to Her as She lights your way into the night.

Lady Mother, light so bright
Shine your way across
my night
Your presence I do hold
so dear
As I say farewell to this
fine year.
So mote it be.

Winter Wren

Notes:

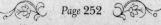

A Guide to Witches' Spell–A–Day Icons

 New Moon Spells

 Full Moon Spells

 New Year's Eve, Day

 Mabon

 Imbolc

 Samhain, Halloween

 Valentine's Day

 Thanksgiving

 Ostara, Easter

 Yule, Christmas

 April Fool's Day

 Health Spells

 Earth Day, Earth Spells

 Home and Garden Spells

 Beltane

 Protection Spells

 Mother's Day

 Travel and Communication Spells

 Father's Day

 Money and Success Spells

 Litha

 Love and Relationship Spells

 Lammas

 Grab Bag of Spells

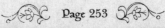

Daily Magical Influences

Each day is ruled by a planet that possesses specific magical influences:

Monday (Moon): peace, healing, caring, psychic awareness, and purification.

Tuesday (Mars): passion, sex, courage, aggression, and protection.

Wednesday (Mercury): conscious mind, study, travel, divination, and wisdom.

Thursday (Jupiter): expansion, money, prosperity, and generosity.

Friday (Venus): love, friendship, reconciliation, and beauty.

Saturday (Saturn): longevity, exorcism, endings, homes, and houses.

Sunday (Sun): healing, spirituality, success, strength, and protection.

Lunar Phases

The lunar phase is important in determining best times for magic.

The waxing Moon (from the New Moon to the Full Moon) is the ideal time for magic to draw things toward you.

The Full Moon is the time of greatest power.

The waning Moon (from the Full Moon to the New Moon) is a time for study, meditation, and little magical work (except magic designed to banish harmful energies).

Astrological Symbols

The Sun	☉	Aries	♈
The Moon	☽	Taurus	♉
Mercury	☿	Gemini	♊
Venus	♀	Cancer	♋
Mars	♂	Leo	♌
Jupiter	♃	Virgo	♍
Saturn	♄	Libra	♎
Uranus	♅	Scorpio	♏
Neptune	♆	Sagittarius	♐
Pluto	♇	Capricorn	♑
		Aquarius	♒
		Pisces	♓

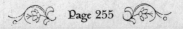

The Moon's Sign

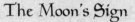

The Moon's sign is a traditional consideration for astrologers. The Moon continuously moves through each sign in the zodiac, from Aries to Pisces. The Moon influences the sign it inhabits, creating different energies that affect our daily lives.

Aries: Good for starting things, but lacks staying power. Things occur rapidly, but quickly pass. People tend to be argumentative and assertive.

Taurus: Things begun now do last, tend to increase in value, and become hard to alter. Brings out an appreciation for beauty and sensory experience.

Gemini: Things begun now are easily changed by outside influence. Time for shortcuts, communications, games, and fun.

Cancer: Stimulates emotional rapport between people. Pinpoints need, supports growth and nurturance. Tend to domestic concerns.

Leo: Draws emphasis to the self, to central ideas or institutions, away from connections with others and emotional needs. People tend to be melodramatic.

Virgo: Favors accomplishment of details and commands from higher up. Focus on health, hygiene, and daily schedules.

Libra: Favors cooperation, compromise, social activities, beautification of surroundings, balance, and partnership.

Scorpio: Increases awareness of psychic power. Precipitates psychic crises and ends connections thoroughly. People tend to brood and become secretive under this Moon sign.

Sagittarius: Encourages flights of imagination and confidence. This Moon sign is adventurous, philosophical, and athletic. Favors expansion and growth.

Capricorn: Develops strong structure. Focus on traditions, responsibilities, and obligations. A good time to set boundaries and rules.

Aquarius: Rebellious energy. Time to break habits and make abrupt change. Personal freedom and individuality is the focus.

Pisces: The focus is on dreaming, nostalgia, intuition, and psychic impressions. A good time for spiritual or philanthropic activities.

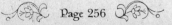

Glossary of Magical Terms

Altar: a low table that holds magical tools as a focus for spell workings.

Athame: a ritual knife used to direct personal power during workings or to symbolically draw diagrams in a spell. It is rarely, if ever, used for actual physical cutting.

Aura: an invisible energy field surrounding a person. The aura can change color depending upon the state of the individual.

Balefire: a fire lit for magical purposes, usually outdoors.

Casting a circle: the process of drawing a circle around oneself to seal out unfriendly influences and raise magical power. It is the first step in a spell.

Censer: an incense burner. Traditionally, a censer is a metal container, filled with incense, that is swung on the end of a chain.

Censing: the process of burning incense to spiritually cleanse an object.

Centering yourself: to prepare for a magical rite by calming and centering all of your personal energy.

Chakra: one of the seven centers of spiritual energy in the human body, according to the philosophy of yoga.

Charging: to infuse an object with magical power.

Circle of protection: a circle cast to protect oneself from unfriendly influences.

Crystals: quartz or other stones that store cleansing or protective energies.

Deosil: clockwise movement, symbolic of life and positive energies.

Deva: a divine being according to Hindu beliefs; a devil or evil spirit according to Zoroastrianism.

Direct/Retrograde: refers to the motions of the planets when seen from the Earth. A planet is "direct" when it appears to be moving forward from the point of view of a person on the Earth. It is "retrograde" when it appears to be moving backward.

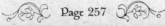

Dowsing: to use a divining rod to search for a thing, usually water or minerals.

Dowsing pendulum: a long cord with a coin or gem at one end. The pattern of its swing is used to predict the future.

Dryad: a tree spirit or forest guardian.

Fey: an archaic term for a magical spirit or a fairylike being.

Gris-gris: a small bag containing charms, herbs, stones, and other items to draw energy, luck, love, or prosperity to the wearer.

Mantra: a sacred chant used in Hindu tradition to embody the divinity invoked; it is said to possess deep magical power.

Needfire: a ceremonial fire kindled at dawn on major Wiccan holidays. It was traditionally used to light all other household fires.

Pentagram: a symbolically protective five-pointed star with one point upward.

Power hand: the dominant hand, the hand used most often.

Scry: to predict the future by gazing at or into an object such as a crystal ball or pool of water.

Second sight: the psychic power or ability to foresee the future.

Sigil: a personal seal or symbol.

Smudge/Smudge stick: to spiritually cleanse an object by waving incense over and around it. A smudge stick is a bundle of several incense sticks.

Wand: a stick or rod used for casting circles and as a focus for magical power.

Widdershins: counterclockwise movement, symbolic of negative magical purposes, sometimes used to disperse negative energies.

Spell Notes: